# Human Rights, Human Wrongs

# Human Rights, Human Wrongs

## The Oxford Amnesty Lectures 2001

Edited by

**Nicholas Owen**

OXFORD
UNIVERSITY PRESS

*This book has been printed digitally and produced in a standard specification in order to ensure its continuing availability*

# OXFORD
UNIVERSITY PRESS

Great Clarendon Street, Oxford OX2 6DP

Oxford University Press is a department of the University of Oxford.
It furthers the University's objective of excellence in research, scholarship,
and education by publishing worldwide in

Oxford New York

Auckland Cape Town Dar es Salaam Hong Kong Karachi
Kuala Lumpur Madrid Melbourne Mexico City Nairobi
New Delhi Shanghai Taipei Toronto
With offices in
Argentina Austria Brazil Chile Czech Republic France Greece
Guatemala Hungary Italy Japan South Korea Poland Portugal
Singapore Switzerland Thailand Turkey Ukraine Vietnam

Oxford is a registered trade mark of Oxford University Press
in the UK and in certain other countries

Published in the United States
by Oxford University Press Inc., New York

ISBN 978-0-19-280219-4

# Contents

*Contributors*                                                    vii

*Acknowledgements*                                                 x

Introduction                                                       I
NICHOLAS OWEN

**1.** Right to Intervene or Duty to Assist?                      26
TZVETAN TODOROV
*(Introduced by Niall Ferguson)*

**2.** Human Rights, Sovereignty and Intervention               49
MICHAEL IGNATIEFF
*(Introduced by Timothy Garton Ash)*

**3.** How Can We Prevent Crimes Against
Humanity?                                                         89
PETER SINGER
*(Introduced by John Broome)*

**4.** Bringing International Criminals to Justice               138
GEOFFREY BINDMAN
*(Introduced by John Gardner)*

**5.** Righting Wrongs                                           164
GAYATRI CHAKRAVORTY SPIVAK
*(Introduced by Robert J. C. Young)*

**6.** Racism Within                                             228
GITTA SERENY
*(Introduced by Jonathan Glover)*

# CONTENTS

**7.** War and Photography                     251
SUSAN SONTAG
(*Introduced by Hermione Lee*)

**8.** The Balm of Recognition: Rectifying Wrongs
through the Generations                         274
EVA HOFFMAN
(*Introduced by Roy Foster*)

*Endnotes*                                      304
*Index*                                         349

# Contributors

GEOFFREY BINDMAN is Visiting Professor of Law at University College, London, and senior partner of Bindman & Partners. He acted for Amnesty International and other human rights organizations in the attempt to extradite the Chilean dictator Augusto Pinochet.

JOHN BROOME is White's Professor of Moral Philosophy at the University of Oxford and author of *Weighing Goods: Equality, Uncertainty and Time* (1991) and *Ethics out of Economics* (1999).

NIALL FERGUSON is Professor of Political and Financial History at the University of Oxford, and author of *The World's Banker: the History of the House of Rothschild* (1998) and *The Pity of War* (1998).

ROY FOSTER is Carroll Professor of Irish History at the University of Oxford and a Fellow of Hertford College.

JOHN GARDNER is Professor of Jurisprudence at the University of Oxford and a Fellow of University College.

TIMOTHY GARTON ASH is Kurt A. Körber Senior Research Fellow in Contemporary European History at St Antony's College, Oxford and author of *We the People: The Revolution of '89 Witnessed in Warsaw, Budapest, Berlin and Prague* (1990) and *History of the Present: Essays, Sketches and Despatches from Europe in the 1990s* (1999).

JONATHAN GLOVER is Director of the Centre for Medical Law

and Ethics, King's College, London. He is the author of *Causing Death and Saving Lives* (1977) and *Humanity: A Moral History of the Twentieth Century* (1999).

EVA HOFFMAN is a writer. Her books include *Lost in Translation: A Life in a New Language* (1989), *Exit into History: a Journey through the New Eastern Europe* (1993) and *Shtetl: The Life and Death of a Small Town and the World of Polish Jews* (1997).

MICHAEL IGNATIEFF is Carr Professor and Director of the Carr Center for Human Rights Policy, John F. Kennedy School of Government, Harvard University, and the author of *Blood and Belonging: Journeys into the New Nationalism* (1993), *The Warrior's Honour: Ethnic War and the Modern Conscience* (1998) and *Virtual War: Kosovo and Beyond* (2000).

HERMIONE LEE is Goldsmiths' Professor of English Literature, University of Oxford. Her books include *Virginia Woolf* (1996).

NICHOLAS OWEN is University Lecturer in Politics and Fellow of Queen's College, Oxford.

GITTA SERENY is a journalist and historian of Nazi Germany. Her books include *Into That Darkness: from Mercy Killing to Mass Murder* (1974), *Albert Speer: His Struggle with Truth* (1985) and *The German Trauma* (2000).

PETER SINGER is DeCamp Professor of Bioethics at the Center for Human Values, Princeton University. His books include *Animal Liberation* (1975), *Practical Ethics* (1979), *Writings on an Ethical Life* (2002), and most recently, *One World: Ethics and Globalization* (2002).

SUSAN SONTAG is a novelist and essayist. Her books include *The Benefactor* (1963), *Against Interpretation* (1966), *Styles of Radical Will* (1969), *On Photography* (1977), *The Volcano Lover* (1992) and *In America* (1999). Her latest collection of essays is entitled *Where the Stress Falls* (2001).

GAYATRI CHAKRAVORTY SPIVAK is Avalon Foundation Professor of humanities at Columbia University and the author of 'Can the Subaltern Speak?' (1988), *In Other Worlds: Essays in Cultural Politics* (1987), *The Post-Colonial Critic: Interviews, Strategies, Dialogues* (1989), *Outside in the Teaching Machine* (1993) and *A Critique of Postcolonial Reason: Toward a History of the Vanishing Present* (1999).

TZVETAN TODOROV is Directeur de Recherches at the Centre National de Recherches Scientifiques in Paris and author of, among others, *The Conquest of America* (1982), *On Human Diversity* (1989), *Facing the Extreme* (1991), *Imperfect Garden, The Legacy of Humanism* (1998).

ROBERT YOUNG is Professor of English and Critical Theory, Wadham College, Oxford and author of *White Mythologies: Writing History and the West* (1990), *Colonial Desire: Hybridity in Culture, Theory and Race* (1995), and *Postcolonialism: An Historical Introduction* (2001).

# Acknowledgements

These lectures were originally given in Oxford in February and March 2001. The lecturers were given the opportunity to develop and revise their texts in the light of the points and questions made by the audience after the lectures, and of each other's contributions. I would like to thank all eight of them for coming to speak in Oxford, and for allowing us to publish their lectures in aid of Amnesty International. I am also very grateful to those members of the academic staff of the University of Oxford, past and present, who introduced the speakers or wrote the introductions to each lecture. They are Malcolm Bowie, John Broome, Niall Ferguson, Roy Foster, John Gardner, Timothy Garton Ash, Jonathan Glover, Hermione Lee, Laurence Whitehead and Robert Young. Without the hard work of the other members of the Oxford Amnesty Lectures committee, there would be no lectures and no book. They are Nicholas Bamforth, Justine Burley, John Gardner, Chris Miller, Fabienne Pagnier, Deana Rankin, Richard Scholar, Stephen Shute, Kate Tunstall and Wes Williams. For special assistance with the editing of the book, I would like to thank Randall Hansen, Andrew Hurrell, John Hyman, Antje Pedain and Adam Roberts.

Nicholas Owen

# Introduction

**Nicholas Owen**

Estimates of progress in the field of human rights over the last few decades vary greatly. Some point to the positive developments: the widening acceptance of human rights claims by governments that had hitherto ignored them, and the emergence of advocacy groups, including Amnesty International itself, dedicated to monitoring and publicizing human rights abuses, and lobbying for action to end them. We might note too the growth of a network of human rights conventions and instruments, of international systems for scrutinizing the extent to which they are observed, and of the increasing use of human rights conditions in trade negotiations, aid programmes and arms sales, where they formerly had no place. Others point out how far there still is to go. The seeming international consensus about human rights is largely a product of Western hegemony, not of genuinely secured agreement. Indeed, there is considerable dispute over the extent and status of human rights, seen most clearly in the argument that social duties, such as respect for community standards, may sometimes take precedence over individual rights, such as the right to free expression. Monitoring of human rights abuse remains very patchy, redress very partial, while prevention hardly happens at all.

Intriguingly, this divergence of view does not seem to be based on different interpretations of what has actually happened, but on different expectations and assumptions about what is possible. It is against these highly varied backgrounds that the record of recent years is being judged. Partly with this thought in mind, the 2001 Oxford Amnesty Lectures examined a set of contemporary dilemmas for advocates of human rights. These include the questions of how we learn about wrongdoing that takes place elsewhere; whether and how we should understand the motives of those who commit abuse; and how they and those they have hurt can come to terms in its aftermath. The lectures also consider the question of what kinds of institutions—international organizations, international courts, investigatory commissions—are appropriate for achieving these ends. Finally, they also take apart some of the assumptions of contemporary human rights discourse, notably the identities of, and relations between, the 'we' who take it upon ourselves to right wrongs and the 'they' whose wrongs are to be righted.

As Michael Ignatieff argues in his lecture, the character of human rights abuse has changed considerably since the end of the Second World War. As long as most human rights abuses were carried out by states against dissidents within their borders, the favoured technique for human rights activists was to press for 'soft interventions': forms of public denunciation or shaming, diplomatic pressure such as trade embargoes, the withdrawal of co-operation, etc. States were seen as the likely violators of human rights, yet capable of improvement if subjected to sufficient pressure of the right type. However, it is now becoming clear that while such abuses have hardly ceased, many of the modern problems of human rights arise not where the state is too strong, but where weak and internally divided states cease to be able to guarantee social order. In the most extreme form, the so-called 'failed state', 'soft interventions' are ineffective. Failed states simply lack the capacity to protect human rights. Activists therefore have had to face the choice between a principled refusal to intervene, tempered perhaps by humanitarian aid where it can be supplied, and endorsing a more active involvement, ranging from mediation and the good offices of third parties, through harder forms of intervention, such as the deployment of peacekeepers, the arming of proxies, and perhaps even coercive military occupation.

This choice forms the subject matter of the first two lectures. Tzvetan Todorov argues against a presumed 'right of intervention' and in favour of a 'duty to assist'. He reminds us that the claim of a right to intervene in defence of universal rights and values has an uncomfortable ancestry. The medieval Crusaders, the European 'civilizing missions' of the nineteenth century, and the Soviet Union in the twentieth all made similarly lofty claims for their own depredations. These histories show, in Todorov's view, that it is temptingly easy to mistake for universal human values what are merely our own interests and desires. Like their historical forbears, the militant apostles of human rights risk assuming that moral rightness is embodied in them alone, and that it is their right and duty to perfect mankind. Their insistence on a single, simple set of universal values, and their own historically given part in enforcing them on others, smacks of arrogance and threatens to foreclose still necessary debates about what human rights we have.

Todorov also draws attention to the ways in which the goals of 'humanitarian intervention' are compromised by its methods. For one thing, military intervention often destroys such authority as remained in the 'failed state', thereby making it harder for it to protect its citizens from human rights abuses. This is somewhat counterproductive when it is precisely the state's lack of authority which has led it to condone human rights abuses in the first place. Armed intervention may also risk widening a local conflict, drawing in hitherto uninvolved states, and thereby prolonging conflict. Worst of all, it is compromised by the interests of those states that alone are able to supply the necessary military force. It is, of course, a good thing, Todorov suggests, that people want to see certain universal rights protected and observed. But in their haste to make rapid progress, they are making common cause with those who have quite different interests. Universal values must eventually imply the demand for universal policing and a universal state structure. But even where belief in human rights is widely shared across cultures, there is still great value in pluralism as regards systems of government.

The rights that we should be most concerned with are, according to Todorov, those belonging to the objects, not the subjects, of intervention. These create a duty to assist. This entails at least a duty of *assistance*—in both the French and English senses of the word: the duty of being present and bearing witness when wrongs are committed, and also of providing more active forms of aid and support where it is possible to do so. Perhaps the crucial difference is that assistance is offered, not imposed. It is open to the recipients of assistance to refuse it, a choice that is not given to the objects of 'humanitarian intervention'.

The neutral humanitarianism and assistance recommended by Tzvetan Todorov are, however, regarded by Michael Ignatieff as an insufficient response to modern ethnic wars. Neutrality in such conflicts may not be practical or possible, and is effectively to side with the stronger power. It is a 'hedged bet'; a way of satisfying the consciences of the West, while ducking the necessarily painful choices of how to prevent or end conflict. The responsible choice is, Ignatieff suggests, 'not to provide humanitarian aid to all parties, but to decide who should win'.

Despite these differences, Ignatieff shares many of Todorov's concerns about the intractability of using military force from outside to resolve deep-seated conflicts and protect human rights. The effort to define a set of rules to govern intervention has generated perverse and contradictory effects as the actors on each side exploit their inconsistencies. Setting thresholds for intervention, for example, may not discourage abuse, but merely define the limits within which it is deemed acceptable. Low-intensity abuse over many years may go unnoticed simply because it never quite crosses the threshold that would justify intervention. If intervention can only be justified by genocide, it may arrive too late to help. Insisting on a ceasefire may, at least temporarily, make the fighting worse as each side struggles to push the battlefront a few miles further in its own favour. Forced negotiations under international auspices may legitimize the gains of the invader, thereby creating a new set of grievances. Even well-intentioned humanitarian aid may, misdirected to the perpetrators of violence as well as to its victims, make matters worse by prolonging the conflict. Perhaps most perversely of all, desperate victims may calculate that provoking greater repression is worthwhile if their sufferings will attract support, and perhaps trigger intervention, from outside.

Further difficulties arise when we consider how such interventions are to be brought to an end. The act of intervention itself, at least initially, thoroughly undermines the authority of local institutions, and it may take a very long time for them to recover sufficient legitimacy to rebuild structures capable of protecting human rights. At the same time, once the immediate conflict is ended, there is pressure for the early withdrawal of peacekeepers, both from the countries that originally sent them, and from those best placed to inherit their powers. Semi-permanent military occupation by outsiders, even humanitarian ones, soon comes to resemble imperialism. But if a fragile peace is to survive, it may be important for peacekeepers to stay, rather than pull out under the cover of supposedly free elections. Caught between these conflicting demands—keeping the peace, reaching a just settlement, encouraging 'local capacities'—the humanitarian occupiers can easily find themselves hopelessly compromised.

Judgements about the rights and wrongs of 'humanitarian intervention' imply judgements about the institutions and procedures through which decisions are made. It has often been argued that the existing machinery is profoundly unsatisfactory. The interpretation and application of the rules are subject to the interests of the existing great powers; indeed, largely those of one great power in particular. They are carried out by such powers selectively and inconsistently, often with a view to extending their own influence rather than redressing injustice or protecting human rights. Interventions occur only in weak states, and only when it suits the interests of the most powerful states. These interests may be, as Todorov suggests, the old-style imperial gains of regional influence, access to markets and strategic advantage. But such powers also have a strong interest in making these gains while endangering as few of their own combatants as possible. This may generate its own perverse effects. Interventions that employ a cautious strategy of 'high-tech, low-risk' warfare— missile bombardment, rather than the use of ground troops, for example—may be simply less effective at ending conflict.

They may even expose the local population to greater risk, particularly if the responding power is less concerned about civilian casualties than is its opponent.

The inconsistent application of the new ethics of 'humanitarian intervention' is simply an illustration of the general problem that human rights have to be established and enforced in an international system that is still made up of largely sovereign states, and structured by great differences of power. In such a system, the weaker states are often unable to exert any significant influence, and the most powerful states are usually able to evade serious criticism of their own human rights records. For this reason, it has often been suggested that it is only by negotiating enforceable international agreements and strengthening multilateral institutions that progress can be made. These need not necessarily be at the global level. Regional human rights systems, though uneven in their coverage, may achieve consensus and practical advances more readily than global initiatives. But it is to the higher level of the United Nations that it is most common for human rights activists to look. At first sight it is not obvious why this should be so. The UN is hardly less dominated by the most powerful states than the international system within which it operates. Its rules do not easily allow it to address human rights abuses unless it can plausibly be argued that they represent a threat to international peace. Its bureaucratic procedures seem to paralyse it at times of crisis. Yet it possesses the great advantage of universal membership, and as such remains the one truly global forum to which states feel they must pay regard, if only because there are so many other things that they can best achieve through membership.

In his lecture, Peter Singer suggests some ways in which the United Nations might be strengthened to prevent acts of genocide. His prescriptions include a stronger General Assembly, reorganized to take account of its members' differences in population size, and reform of the Security Council, with the removal of its members' power of veto. He also calls for sterner measures to be taken against member states that consistently fail to respect democracy and human rights. Membership of international organizations such as the World Bank and the World Trade Organization could be made conditional upon meeting minimum standards of democracy and human rights. States that fail to meet these conditions would become outcasts, unable to trade with the rest of the world. More controversially, they would be more vulnerable than other states to intervention in the event of widespread human rights abuses. In Singer's view, state sovereignty can only properly be derived from popular sovereignty; that is, from the will of the people, freely expressed. If this definition were to be generally applied, states that failed to satisfy a minimal test of democracy would thereby lose their rights to sovereignty, and would become legitimate targets of intervention by the United Nations if their governments committed or sanctioned crimes against humanity. This is importantly, however, a right and not a justification. Whether or not the United Nations should exercise its right to intervene in such cases would be determined by a further, consequentialist test, similar to that of 'reasonable hope' in the Just War tradition discussed by Michael Ignatieff. Where intervention risked making matters worse in the ways described by Ignatieff and Tzvetan Todorov, perhaps through widening a local conflict to a region, or endangering civilian populations, it would not be attempted, though we should not think of this as removing the right to intervene, but only the justification we have to exercise the right.

As Singer recognizes, the last of these would be a very radical step for the United Nations to take, and is almost inconceivable given its present composition and structure. Such a new role could only be developed gradually and cautiously, without risking the withdrawal of some member states and the loss of such authority and effectiveness as the United Nations currently commands. The expulsion and ostracism of states that are not minimally democratic and that commit crimes against humanity would have to be a last resort, for it might in some cases be less effective than critical but constructive engagement with them. Bank loans, trade and aid have their own contribution to make to human rights. Outlawing such states might actually discourage reform, by demoralizing internal opposition, and making it easier for the regime to repress dissent. Using membership of international organizations as a lever works best where, as in the European Union, joining has clear benefits, and existing commitments to human rights are strong. Nevertheless, Singer's recommendations seek to build on some of the most encouraging developments of recent years, notably the growing importance of democracy as a criterion of sovereignty, and of the capacity of international organizations to 'enmesh' even governments that do not care much about human rights by making progress a condition of access to things they do care about.

A further institutional development has been the long battle to set up an International Criminal Court (ICC), raised in Peter Singer's lecture and discussed in more detail by Geoffrey Bindman. The ICC, when it finally begins work in 2003, will be able to try crimes of genocide, crimes against humanity and war crimes committed after that date. But, as Geoffrey

Bindman suggests, it would be unwise to expect too much of it. Some states, including China, India and Pakistan, have not signed the statute establishing the Court at all, and others, such as Russia, the United States and Israel, have not ratified it. The Court's jurisdiction is intended to complement, not replace or override, that of national courts, and it is unlikely to act when crimes against humanity are being investigated by the states themselves, even if those investigations are proceeding slowly or ineffectively. Its jurisdiction will not be retrospective, nor is it likely to investigate crimes itself unless instructed to do so by the UN Security Council. In practice, as has already been the experience of the International Criminal Tribunals for the former Yugoslavia, it will be very hard for the Court to try crimes committed in non-signatory states, or even in signatory states where the authorities are uncooperative, unless there is an international force in place to gather evidence and detain suspects.

These limitations follow in large part from the unease of some states about the prosecution of their military officers, and as such, might seem irksome to those who care about the protection of human rights. Geoffrey Bindman argues that the ICC should be able to claim jurisdiction even in cases where a local decision not to prosecute has been taken in the interests of national reconciliation. He also suggests that even if it is not possible to strengthen the ICC itself, UK law might be changed to make it easier to prosecute war criminals and the perpetrators of crimes against humanity. The UK could, for example, close the loopholes through which General Pinochet struggled to escape, by permitting prosecutions not just of UK citizens and residents, but also of those visiting the UK, and by weakening the claims of state and diplomatic immunity which formed an important part of the Pinochet defence. Of course, as John Gardner points out in his intro-duction to Geoffrey Bindman's lecture, human rights activists need to think carefully about the implications of moves of this kind. In their desire to get 'known abusers' into court, they may be tempted to bend rules—such as those that provide for the right to be tried in a national court—which on other occasions they would want to insist upon. Moreover, it may be that the weaknesses of the Court itself are sadly necessary ones. The experience of the Yugoslav and Rwandan tribunals suggests that, unfortunately, it is often politically necessary to promise amnesties and immunities to military leaders to per-suade them to participate in peace talks. War crimes trials and the pursuit of suspects, though demanded by justice, may even prolong conflict and rights abuses, making it harder for recon-ciliation to be achieved. In such situations, the best course for the prosecutor of an International Criminal Court might well be to stay out. However, none of this is to suggest that the development of the ICC is unwelcome, but only that it marks quite a small first step on the road to international justice.

A further argument made by Tzvetan Todorov against 'humanitarian interventions' in the name of human rights is that they tend to produce a colonial mindset. Intervention is ostensibly justified in terms of universal rights, shared and accepted by both the intervening party and the object of its intervention. Yet, at the same time, through the act of intervention a distinction is made between those whose task it is to define and enforce the rights, and those whose task it is to accept and observe them. The divide between those who 'right wrongs' and those whose 'wrongs are righted' is the subject of Gayatri Spivak's lecture. Human rights, she argues, are not just about having or claiming a right, but about who is and who is not the dispenser of rights. Objections of this type are often phrased in terms of the eurocentrism of human rights discourse, and, in particular, its historical and current practice of excluding—despite its pretensions to universality—disadvantaged groups. But Spivak draws the line in a different place. The work of righting wrongs is not claimed by Europeans and Americans alone, but is shared, albeit unevenly and inconsistently, with social elites in the colonized world and diasporic intellectuals in the universities of Europe and America. Human rights discourse positions these 'righters of wrongs' against the 'perennially wronged' impoverished and ill-educated rural poor of the global South. Human rights work, like some of the other products of the colonialism from which it has emerged, constitutes for Spivak an 'enabling violation'—an outcome which, though positive in some ways, cannot be used to justify what caused it. What is needed is not to empower the 'righters of wrongs' to intervene more readily, or indeed, to encourage them to settle in for a lengthy period of humanitarian nation-building. The task instead is to provide an education that will subvert the assumption that the work of human rights is the inalienable prerogative of the 'righters of wrongs', and that the role of the 'perennially wronged' is no more than passively to receive these rights from above.

Spivak's own educational strategy is described in detail in her lecture. It is designed to operate on both sides of the divide. At what must now be seen as the spiritual home of the 'righter of wrongs'—the humanities faculty of the North American university—Spivak tries to develop in her students the capacity to 'learn to learn from below', and to destabilize the conviction that the task of righting wrongs belongs only to those called by history to dispense bounty to the less fortunate. Among the growing numbers of hastily trained human rights workers in the global South, Spivak argues for a different type of educational supplementation. Too often such activists, the descendants of the anti-colonial resistance movements, are impatient to take charge of the victims of oppression, to try to 'raise their consciousnesses' and to exhort them to claim rights which must—sometimes quite literally—be dictated to them. In these circumstances, the quick and vicarious battles won by the 'righters of wrongs' on behalf of oppressed and ill-educated villagers are inauthentic and short-lived.

In their place, Spivak argues for the fashioning of a different type of education: one that stitches together the re-activated cultural axioms, methods of conflict resolution, and ethical imperatives of the subaltern groups with the habits and principles of democratic politics. She reminds us that in the global South, many children learn to read, but for the children of the middle classes, the purpose of reading is understanding, while for those of the rural poor it is simply to learn to spell and memorize. Here too it is a reconfigured humanities, likewise prepared to 'learn to learn from below', which offers a means to recover and reclaim dormant ways of thinking. Without surmounting the pedagogical failures and unimaginative rote-learning characteristic of education in the global South, there is little chance of the rural poor becoming the subject of human rights, rather than the object of benevolence from above.

For Peter Singer, education, though clearly desirable, will not be enough to prevent human rights abuses. At the start of his lecture, Singer gives a striking exposition of accounts of genocide given in the Bible and other ancient texts. All that has really changed, as the history of the last century shows so clearly, is our technical capacity to kill, not (in any significant sense) our disposition to do so. Genocidal impulses, Singer suggests, are implied by the basic biological desire to maximize the number of one's own genetic descendants. Of course, circumstances usually encourage us to seek this advantage through the building of co-operative relationships rather than the violent destruction of our rivals. Genocidal war, unless wholly one-sided, would presumably reduce one's likelihood of having descendants. Nevertheless, the disposition to commit crimes against humanity is clearly not confined to a small, identifiable group. Ignorance, poverty, injustice and exploitation may make people more likely to resort to it, but are not necessary conditions. If this is so, it presents the depressing prospect that improving education, and addressing economic inequalities and political injustice, may help but not be sufficient. Singer's own proposals thus do not aim so much to reduce the propensities to violence, as to restrain them in a strengthened framework of international law. This leaves the problem that international law must itself be administered by human individuals who themselves possess the impulses they seek to restrain.

Singer's troubling account of the origins of genocide directs us to a further theme of the 2001 Amnesty Lectures. Human rights activists have often been discouraged from probing too deeply into the question of why human rights abuses occur. For one thing, it is sufficient work to deal with their consequences. For another, the demands of campaigning often tempt activists to construct simple stories of heroes and villains which will provide a strong, emotional prompt to action. To understand too much about the motives of the abusers may make it harder to condemn them. The victims of abuse, caught up in traumatic events, may naturally think in these terms too. To stand in solidarity with them requires the activist to understand, even to adopt, their perspective. However, from other perspectives, such black-and-white thinking is often inadequate both as a description of how and why rights abuse actually occurs, and as a means of enabling societies and individuals to come to terms with its legacy. If the activist is serious about wanting to understand the full complexity of the causes of human rights abuse, then he or she may be required to maintain at times a certain critical distance from the perspective of the abused. Harder still, it may require the activist to understand the motivations of the abuser. Yet the holding of such critical distance can induce moral equivocation, and the appreciation of the complexity of the situation can collapse into a kind of paralysed detachment. The dilemma, for those who care about human rights, is how to hold both of these perspectives at once, neither forcing difficult and complex political situations into a single simple mould, nor disengaging from the struggle to understand and assist.

The author and journalist Gitta Sereny has explored these questions in her many books and articles, and also in the Amnesty lecture printed here. She has done so especially through the close questioning of those who committed or countenanced genocidal killing, especially during the German Third Reich. 'I am interested above all', she writes, 'in how individual human beings succumb to, or resist evil.' Sereny's work does not exculpate those responsible for abuses, but it does attempt to understand them as human beings, rather than simply condemn them as monsters. What has been striking in her interviews is that the perpetrators of genocide seem neither pathologically disposed, nor even especially ideologically driven. She found Albert Speer, the subject of perhaps her most famous book, 'not immoral, not amoral, but somehow infinitely worse, morally extinguished'. Franz Stangl, the Commandant of Treblinka, emerges from her account as little more than an unimaginative, careerist police officer manipulated by the Nazis. Of course, it should be borne in mind that it is no easy matter to recover the motivations of the perpetrator at such a distance from events. What may begin as a shared search for truth is inevitably compromised, however great the forensic skills of the questioner, by the desire of the questioned not so much to recover the past as to reach an accommodation in the present.

On hearing or reading Gitta Sereny's accounts, people often ask themselves whether they, under similar conditions, might not act in similar ways. Of course, to think that we teeter on the verge of atrocity, only held from the abyss by the weak bonds of conscience and fortunate circumstance, is no less facile than to suppose that it is only the innately evil few who are capable of terrible acts. Thick and specific—yet not unique—sets of circumstances, not appearing immediately but slowly developing over long periods, seem to provide the preconditions for genocide, perhaps most importantly the widespread perception of other ethnic groups as radically different, and the projection upon them of the characteristics of inferiority. But much of this is experienced by very large numbers of people in broadly similar ways, only a few of whom commit atrocities, many more of whom stand by while atrocities are committed, and some of whom refuse to co-operate or even oppose them. Explaining this variety of responses is far from simple, yet essential if we are to understand why genocide occurs. What seems distinctive about the perpetrators of mass killing studied by Gitta Sereny is not their racist views alone—Stangl, she tells us, was probably no more anti-Semitic than other Austrian provincials of his time—but a certain dislocation of normal human feelings, massively exaggerated by repeated exposure to violence. The roots of this moral cauterization are enormously complex. Something, Sereny suggests, surely correctly, must be owed to the experience of neglect and abuse in childhood, and the brutalization of young men by war. Yet, significant as this must have been to individual psychologies, it seems insufficient to account for the varied responses of participation, tolerance and dissent we find even among those who have had unhappy childhoods or experienced the horrors of the battlefield, when pressed to commit or condone horrific acts.

Just as hard to explain as the action of the perpetrator, but just as necessary to a full understanding of genocide, is the inaction of bystanders. Gitta Sereny's interviewees offer explanations which have become very familiar: ignorance, of course, and when this is implausible, the impracticality of resistance. Between the lines of their replies, one can see more humdrum motives too: the blind eye turned to please a superior, the avoidance of social awkwardness, the seemingly minor moral compromise to gain a promotion. One has the strong sense that in many cases it was only later that such men and women realized the implications of the choices they had made. In her lecture, Sereny challenges us with a striking contemporary parallel: the policies of West European governments towards immigrants and asylum seekers. Here, she suggests, some of the same forces are at work: the assertion of differences between 'us' and 'them'; the failure to accord 'them' the moral respect we would expect for ourselves; and the subtle denigration of those seeking asylum or citizenship by the press and even the agencies of the state itself. Moreover, it is an injustice that makes us practically all bystanders, employing many of the familiar habits and justifications: ignorance of the problem and the supposed futility of opposing the existing policies. As we read Sereny's powerful accounts of how civic-minded, educated individuals became, often reluctantly and gradually, morally compromised and conditioned to tolerance of abuse, it is a comparison worth bearing in mind. We know the impact that bystanders can make when they choose to speak up; and we know that they are more likely to do so when they are directly asked or personally confronted.

Especially significant in the asylum debate, in Gitta Sereny's view, is the persistence of 'inner racism'—the sense of difference created by our troubled histories and the willed separateness of our social lives—which dulls our sense of common humanity and allows intolerance to spread. Few could disagree with her plea for child-rearing strategies designed to promote tolerance, and for public policies to contest 'inner racism' rather than surrender to it. Yet the lesson of her studies of the atrocities of the Third Reich suggests a wider conclusion too. Arguably, it was not simply the widespread existence of racism in Germany which led to genocide. The crucial part was played by the Nazis themselves in creating the conditions—through coercion, social pressure and propaganda—in which these prejudices could express themselves as mass murder. What this might suggest is the great power of the specific social conditioning of individuals; not simply the broad experiences and attitudes shared with co-nationals, but those specific to the organizations and groups within which our social selves are created and moulded. Particularly significant is the power of certain types of organization to condition the behaviour of their members, especially in habituating them to obedience to authority. Through the establishment of routine and complex procedures, such organizations can discourage the individual from perceiving, and hence questioning, the larger moral situation in which they are playing a part. Through the licence that command affords to leaders, inhibitions can be smothered, and cruelty and violence unleashed. Quite extraordinary degrees of conformity can be induced in small, authoritarian groups, which wholly consume the separate identities of their members, and which deploy ideological indoctrination, peer pressure and appeals to careerism to induce cohesive behaviour. In such settings, the social norms and rules which usually justify or encourage questioning and dissent may no longer work. If that is right, then the task for human rights activists may be not just to unearth their own, and others', privately held sentiments of 'inner racism'. It will also be necessary to consider the precise social and political conditions that may allow these prejudices to gain unexpectedly powerful public expression as widespread, systematic abuses of human rights.

Few of us, especially few of us among the 'righters of wrongs', witness atrocity directly. We experience it mediated through images, most importantly, in the modern age, the photograph. In her ground-breaking study *On Photography* (1977), Susan Sontag famously argued that without a supporting political consciousness, photographs of atrocity can do little to stimulate our moral responses. They can depict, but not explain, events. Images of suffering at first make distant events more real, but later, as they became over-familiar, anaesthetize feelings of pity, indignation and anger. Moreover, socially concerned photographers trying to convey the truth of terrible events find that their images also stand in an aesthetic relationship with their subject-matter, beautifying distress, composing the harsh irregularities of human suffering into a pleasing spectacle.

In her Amnesty lecture, Susan Sontag takes up these themes again to consider how far the problems identified in *On Photography* have been confirmed by the photographic coverage of recent conflicts. The evidence suggests a mixed verdict. Despite its limitations, photography has proved to be the lever by which Western societies are moved to action, whether humanitarian or military. From the Biafran famine to the Bosnian War, photojournalism has been one of the chief reasons for the rise in public attention to human rights issues. Our mind's ability to absorb and respond seems to have survived near-saturation by daily images of distress. It has also survived the efforts of some postmodern thinkers to depict war as little more than constructed spectacle.

Susan Sontag's presence during the siege of Sarajevo in the years 1993–1996—itself a fine demonstration of what it means to accept Todorov's duty of *assistance*—gave her a new sense of the mobilizing power of images. The limitations of the medium are still apparent, however, and are made wonderfully clear in Sontag's account of the ambivalent relationship between the Western photojournalists in Sarajevo and the local population, to whom they were both intrusive, scoop-hungry 'angels of death', and at the same time committed supporters of the Bosnian cause and a lifeline to the outside world. Old worries remain: the mixed motives that draw photojournalists to troublespots; the mixed responses that gruesome, painful images of distress evoke in us; and, above all, the inability of photographs to explain what they depict. Even the most powerful images of the Bosnian War, such as the photograph by Ron Haviv which has been reproduced as the cover of this book, tell us only, like Goya's etchings, that 'this is how it happened', but not *why* it happened. Photographs of suffering may make us aware of the capacity of human beings to inflict hurt on each other. But, as Susan Sontag puts it, 'they cannot do the intellectual or moral work for us'.

Photographs also play an important part in the construction of memory. The final lecture in the series, by the writer Eva Hoffman, considers how, after wrongdoing, acts of recognition and remembering can enable victims and perpetrators to come to terms with what has happened. Neither forgiveness nor retribution can be sufficient responses. It is unreasonable to expect the former, and the latter merely prepares the ground for renewed conflict. Instead, Eva Hoffman proposes that the first stage must be the recognition of wrongs done, both of the victims' experience and of the perpetrators' responsibility for them.

The characteristic mechanism for recognition is, of course, the Truth Commission. Truth Commissions have sometimes been regarded as an unsatisfactory method of achieving reconciliation. They usually take place amid efforts to achieve and deepen democracy, and as such, their revelations, whatever their cathartic power to heal the wounds of the victims, must also be judged for their wider effects on democratic transition. From this perspective, the immediate aftermath of the toppling of tyranny may be the worst time to try and establish the truth, while the old regime stands ready to return to power in the event of crisis, or retains significant support among judges, soldiers or law enforcers. What worked in South Africa does not necessarily work elsewhere, often simply because the balance of power between the victim and perpetrator has not really changed, and both sides know it. For this reason, Truth Commissions have often been accompanied by amnesties, which prevent cases being brought to trial and the victims from receiving not merely the truth but justice as well. The perpetrators too, though often cannily taking the opportunity that a Truth Commission affords to evade conviction or dismissal, do not usually regard it as an impartial tribunal, but as the stage for a morality play in which they are cast as repentant sinners. The weight of political expectation pressing down on a Commission may discourage it from exploring the ambiguities and subtleties of collaboration, collusion and resistance, in favour of a simple demarcation of guilty and innocent. Given the huge differences of perception between the two sides, it may be hard to agree on the facts of what happened, and near-impossible ever to come to a mutual understanding of why it happened. For the victims, therefore, the proceedings can often seem peculiarly unsatisfying, and the perpetrators, even when they take the process seriously, may find the Commission unwilling or unable to understand the impulses that led them to wrongdoing. The value of Truth Commissions seems to lie more in the opportunity they afford for the uninvolved and outsiders to discover the truth, than in their ability to foster reconciliation.

In her lecture, Eva Hoffman offers an important reconceptualization of the processes of recognition, truth and reconciliation. First of all, she insists that whatever the difficulties, it matters to name wrongs as wrongs. It matters not just that the victims' stories are told, but that their truth is acknowledged by the perpetrators, as a partial reversal of the imbalance of power in the initial situation. She does not underestimate the difficulties of truth-telling. It may sometimes feel too early to remember. Certainly, it is tempting for a still-divided, fragile society to try and bury its past. Yet the repressing of memories,

Eva Hoffman suggests, may be profoundly unhealthy, and is likely to create unbearable burdens for those most directly traumatized. It will also allow dangerous myths to grow up, for it is out of the distorted half-memories of terrible events that later generations construct new justifications for violence. By contrast, truth and the recognition of truth help to create and sustain an agreed history. The effect of this is to reduce the likelihood of the recurrence of human rights abuses. She also identifies a crucial set of actors in the process of reconciliation and the addressing of trauma: the 'post-generation'; that is, the children of perpetrators and victims. The 'post-generation' is still in touch with the living, painful memories of suffering. But it is also the generation that has to decide how these memories will be expressed in historical understanding and communal remembrance in the future. Its task—even its obligation—is to try to ensure that these memories do not harden into communal myths and convictions that lead to cycles of revenge, but that, fully evoked and recognized, they allow future generations to bridge their antagonisms. To realize this, she suggests, means the children of victims and the children of perpetrators have to come, or be brought, together in the project of constructing a common history. What may make this task a little easier is that the psychological damage, so unequally distributed in the first generation, is more equally so in the 'post-generation'. The children of perpetrators, like the children of victims, have memories that also need to be disinterred and recognized, with the additional difficulty that their feelings of love for their parents pull hard against the need to condemn their actions.

'Oxford', as Susan Sontag observes at the start of her lecture, 'is far from the killing fields and the refugee camps. We are not the unjustly jailed.' If it is possible to extract a single, concluding theme from this series of lectures, then it is 'the problem of distance'. In places like Oxford, it is easy for human rights to become little more than a worthy cause, with which all progressively minded people should—and many do—identify, but which makes no further demands on them. The 2001 Lectures, however, suggest some conclusions that are a little less comfortable. From a distance, relying on powerful but simplifying images of suffering, it is temptingly easy for us to over simplify the situations in which human rights abuse occurs. Yet these are rarely simple and amenable to a quick fix. Rather they are complex and multi-layered problems, in which humanitarian relief, the securing of a political settlement, and the achievement of justice are potentially conflicting goals. Human rights, to be meaningful, must be indivisible and universal; yet they may clash with other desirable, progressive aims, such as democracy, local accountability, pluralism and respect for diversity.

Activists need to think harder about these issues, and also the question of what methods it is legitimate to use in protecting human rights. This requires taking the state seriously, and in particular its potential for helping to solve, as well as create, the problems of human rights. We should continue to support and strengthen international organizations that seek to protect human rights. We might look forward to an emboldened transnational, civil society that would supplement, or even supplant, the state and state-dominated agencies. But the wait will be a long one, and it is important not to put too much stress on the fragile structures that have already been built. For the present, states will continue to monopolize most of the effective means by which rights can be made real. If so, then those sympathetic to human rights will have to overcome some of their traditional suspicions of the state and its power, and think about how to engage with it more positively.

Another aspect of the 'problem of distance' is that it creates a culture of rights in which the roles—abusers, victims, activists—are largely fixed in advance. In such a culture, the redress of human rights abuses becomes a means by which concerned metropolitan activists can appropriate the concerns of the oppressed, speaking for them and interceding on their behalf, seeking to empower the 'victim' against the 'abuser', without ever quite disturbing the unequal relationship of power between 'victim' and 'activist'. More troubling still is the possibility that the institutionalization and professionalization of human rights work—the research institutes, the conferences, and even the lecture series—serve to harden the distinction between the 'righters of wrongs' and 'those whose wrongs are righted'. This creates a very real dilemma. Many of the most effective human rights advocacy groups claim to speak for the world, yet draw their strength from that small part of it with the wealth and resources to undertake this kind of work. Their difficult task is to continue to be effective, but in ways that do not reinforce existing hierarchies of power and status. Most obviously, this means that they need to consider not only rights abuse that happens elsewhere, at a distance, but that which occurs in their own societies. But it also means that they need to engage in dialogue about human rights with those they aim to help, and thereby to earn the authority which they too often assume.

# Introduction to Tzvetan Todorov

*Niall Ferguson*

Professor Tzvetan Todorov is Director of Research at the *Centre National de Recherches Scientifiques* in Paris, where he has lived since 1963. Besides his many books—I counted 63 entries in the Bodleian Library's electronic catalogue—he has accumulated an impressive haul of academic honours: among them the Charles Lévêque Prize of the *Académie des Sciences Morales et Politiques* and the first Maugean Prize of the *Académie Française.* He also is an Officer of the *Ordre des Arts et des Lettres.*

Born in Bulgaria in 1939, Professor Todorov was recently described by *L'Express* as 'l'apôtre de l'humanisme'—the apostle of humanism. His reputation was long ago established as one of the leading exponents of structuralism in the study of literature—among his pioneering works in this field was *The Poetics of Prose* (1971). But he came to my attention as a historian relatively recently, with his remarkable book *Face à l'extrême* (1991), which appeared in English as *Facing the Extreme: Moral Life in the Concentration Camps* (1999). This is a brave and often moving attempt to find, amid the horrors of the mid-twentieth century's most abominable prisons, what Todorov calls 'ordinary virtues' (as opposed to 'heroic' ones).

One of the great strengths of this book, it seemed to me, was Todorov's readiness to draw comparisons—which are still regarded in some quarters as taboo—between Nazi concentration camps and the Soviet gulag. He cites the tragic and telling case of Margarete Buber-Neumann, who had the misfortune to be imprisoned by Stalin in the 1930s and then deported to Germany after the Nazi–Soviet pact and imprisoned in Ravensbrück. She saw the SS man and the NKVD man salute each other when she was handed over. 'I ask myself', she wrote, 'which is really worse: the lice-infested corncob-walled cabins in Birma [Kazakhstan] or the nightmare-order of Ravensbrück . . . It is hard to decide which is the least humane—to gas people in five minutes or to strangle them slowly, over the course of three months, by hunger?'

Over time, it might be said, Todorov has shifted his focus away from semantics and towards the study of ethics. And his subject in this lecture is an ethical one that goes to the very heart of recent debates about human rights and international law. Professor Todorov addresses a question of his own devising: 'Right to Intervene or Duty to Assist?' He argues, in essence, that there can be no *absolute* right of foreign intervention in the internal affairs of a state, even if crimes against humanity are being committed. However, he suggests there may be a limited and pragmatic rationale for such interventions, particularly if they are carried out by neighbouring states, presumably out of self-interest as much as altruism.

It was an argument of considerable interest when he made it in his Oxford lecture, at a time when many in his audience were still pondering the significance of the 1999 Kosovo War. Since 11 September 2001, however, it has gained in importance, most obviously because of the intervention of the United States-led coalition in Afghanistan. It is an argument that will not convince everyone (and I admit to some scepticism on my own part). But like everything that Todorov writes, it is a powerful and original intellectual challenge that cannot easily be ignored.

# 1

# Right to Intervene or Duty to Assist?

## Tzvetan Todorov

The recent military intervention in Kosovo has often been presented as arising from a new doctrine, summarized in the phrase 'the right to intervene' (*le droit d'ingérance*). This is taken to mean that a group of states, such as those behind NATO, has the right to undertake armed intervention anywhere in the world where massive and systematic human rights violations are taking place. The principle has been defended by the Secretary-General of the UN, Kofi Annan,[1] by the former President of the United States, Bill Clinton ('If anyone seeks to commit mass crimes against an innocent civil population, they should know that we shall, insofar as we are able, prevent them')[2] and by other public figures, who have acted as spokesmen for the doctrine. Thus Vaclav Havel on Kosovo:

There is one thing no reasonable person can deny: this is probably the first war that has not been waged in the name of 'national interests', but rather in the name of principles and values. If one can say of any war that it is an ethical war, or that it is being waged for ethical purposes, then it is true of this war.[3]

One might dispute the application of the principle of intervention to the case of Yugoslavia without rejecting the principle itself. Less controversial examples could be cited in justification of the right to intervene. Would it not have been better to intervene against Hitler in 1938? Or in Cambodia in

1976 to prevent the genocide? Or in Rwanda immediately after the massacre of Tutsis began in 1994?

The right to intervene had no sooner been formulated as a doctrine than objections were raised. These objections rely on various arguments. One of the most common has been to point out that it requires us to abandon the principle of national sovereignty; this principle has hitherto underpinned international relations, and its abandonment would bring more dangers than benefits. How strong are these arguments?

First and foremost, we should put aside the case of countries that form part of a larger entity, federation or confederation, and which have *de facto* given up a part of their sovereignty. Such is notably the case with the member states of the European Union. It therefore comes as no surprise that, in the year 2000, certain of these countries condemned Austria for allowing an extreme-right party to take a share of executive power. The European Union aspires not only to the status of a common economic and financial market, but to that of a community whose members share certain political values, such as the stigmatization of racism and xenophobia. The Austrian extreme right has the legitimacy of the ballot-box; but if Austria wishes to continue to enjoy membership of the European Union, it should be ready to accept this infringement of its sovereignty. It could, of course, refuse any such infringement; but in that case, it should leave the Union and give up the advantages that EU membership implies. This is, after all, a contract whose terms were defined in advance.

We must distinguish such cases from those in which a country has not bound itself to a particular form of conduct. Resistance to the right to intervene has been particularly lively in countries belonging to neither Western Europe nor North America: countries from the southern hemisphere, from Africa and Asia. Contrary to what Havel appears to believe, the theory of the right to intervene is not a new one. On at least two occasions in history, European states have justified their actions outside their borders by reference to 'values and principles' rather than national interest. On both occasions, the European states began with the conviction that right was on their side, and that other countries in other continents were allowing wrong to triumph. European armies therefore marched out to impose right on others by force.

The first wave of intervention was conducted in the name of the superiority of the Christian religion; all the peoples of the world were to be given access to the true God, and Christians living among infidels were to be liberated. Those who launched the Crusades of the eleventh to the thirteenth centuries were no less convinced of the justice of their cause than we are of our own. Like us, they were motivated by a universalist (a 'humanitarian') impulse, that of allowing everyone to enjoy an indisputable benefit: they therefore sought to replace Islam with Christianity. Similarly, in the fifteenth and sixteenth centuries, the conquest of America was justified on the grounds that it would allow the Christian faith to expand. Moreover, Columbus went in search of a 'Western passage' to Asia, seeking in this way to provide the funds required for a further crusade, which was to liberate Jerusalem for ever.[4]

The second great wave of intervention occurred in the nineteenth and twentieth centuries, and was this time conducted in the name not of Christian values but of profane European civilization: progress, industry, hygiene and sometimes, even at that stage, human rights. Great Britain and France, then the two most advanced democracies in Europe, led this new wave of colonization. It is said that, after the outstandingly sanguinary conquest of Indochina, the 'first concern' of Paul Bert, former member of the French republican government and new Governor of Vietnam, was to 'have the Rights of Man posted up in Hanoi'.[5] The reality was somewhat remote from the posters. In a later but comparable example in 1947, the French authorities that pride themselves on belonging to the 'Fatherland of Human Rights', decided in Madagascar to set fire to railway wagons into which they had locked Malagasy rebels. They also tested the resilience of other Malagasy rebels by throwing them out of airborne military aircraft, a technique we next encounter in Argentina.

It might further be observed that the imperialist policy of Soviet Russia always paraded the noblest intentions. Thus, when the Red Army invaded Poland in 1920, a tract was distributed, signed by the field commandant of the Soviet forces, General Tukhachevski. It read: 'We bring peace and happiness to the working classes on the points of our bayonets!'[6] Twenty years later, in September 1939, when the Red Army occupied eastern Poland under the terms of the Stalin–Hitler Pact, Molotov, then Soviet Prime Minister, rehearsed these terms: 'The army of liberty . . . which carries on its banners the sublime words "Fraternity of Nations, Socialism and Peace", has begun the most just campaign ever waged by mankind.'[7] We see, then, that conquests made in the name of communist ideology were also presented as the triumph of right.

It might be objected that, today, human rights values are accepted in theory almost everywhere in the world, even in those countries where they are daily trampled underfoot. Such was not the case with values of Christianity or Western civilization. That human rights enjoy such prestige is a matter for rejoicing, but it is somewhat beside the point. The universal love preached by Christianity and the reign of reason asserted by the European powers of the nineteenth century were universal values also worth defending. But there could be no guarantee that they would triumph by way of military actions undertaken in order to impose them. Jerusalem under the Crusaders was not the incarnation of universal love, and the ruins of Hanoi following the French occupation did not exemplify human rights. Even supposing the instigators of these actions to have been sincere, the means they employed ran a not inconsiderable risk of compromising their goals.

The suspicion current in non-European countries is, then, understandable. They have not forgotten previous interventions made 'for their own good'. Declared good intentions offer no guarantees, and are often mere camouflage. Moreover, imposing right by force is never an unmixed benefit. If one is forced to conquer a country in order to return it to the straight and narrow, its inhabitants are unlikely to be grateful. 'People are being killed in the name of humanitarian principles', as the Japanese daily *Asahi Shimbun* noted relative to Kosovo.[8]

Finally, before we inflict our universal values on others, it might be proper to ask their opinion: if we acknowledge that they are no less human than we are, their opinions weigh no less in the balance than ours. However much their governments incur our censure, should we, where the will of an electorate has been freely expressed, simply discount it? In the past, we have frequently mistaken for universal values what was merely the reflection of our own traditions and desires. A little modesty or circumspection would be in order here. In this perspective, it is easy to understand why *Asahi Shimbun* explained the 'catastrophic situation in Kosovo' in terms of the 'unilateral arrogation' by NATO of humanitarian principles.[9]

Does this mean that we should give up our attempts to identify universal values, that the very idea of human rights unaffected by race, culture, religion, sex or age should be abandoned? By no means. The founders of humanism have taught us that tyranny is a scourge anywhere in the world. I am not suggesting here that one should establish, alongside 'Western' human rights, other forms of right—natural, group or divine rights—suited to non-Western traditions ('Asian rights', for example), with a claim to equal legitimacy.[10] The question being debated is not the universality of rights and values, but that of their practical implementation in concrete societies; it is a question of means, not goals. We should stop contrasting the beauty of theory with its disfiguring implementation—telling ourselves 'Christianity undoubtedly failed, communism failed, but let's give liberal democracy a try'—and devote ourselves, instead, to observing the march of contemporary history.

There is another reason why we might prefer national sovereignty to the right to intervene. Sovereignty takes the form of state institutions; intervention destroys the nation-state. Now, the inhabitants of a country—democratic or non-democratic—enjoy many more rights as citizens of a state than they do as members of the human race. A human right not guaranteed by the laws of a country and its state apparatus is not good for much. The destruction of a state in the name of the rights of man therefore remains problematic; we are liable to gain the shadow by destroying the substance. Anarchy is worse than tyranny, since anarchy, the absence of a state apparatus, replaces the tyranny of the few by the tyranny of the many. Even unjust laws have the merit of predictability.

This is a lesson that we learned with the downfall of the communist regimes; in several countries, it revealed the weakening, in some cases the disappearance, of all state structures. Power then fell to *mafiosi*, to armed criminals: might became right. The UN protectorates being set up today in Bosnia and Kosovo, in a bizarre replay of the colonial past, have not escaped these difficulties. How can international bureaucrats replace the failing institutions of the nation-state? If this argument is accepted, the question then arises: is intervention legitimate where a country has already descended into a state of anarchy? No doubt anarchy should be opposed; but it seems unlikely that an order imposed *vi et armis* from without will ever appear legitimate to the people of that country. Negotiation with the relevant factions, indirect pressure and charm offensives may well prove more effective than war.

Let us now leave for a while the question of national sovereignty and consider the very principle that justifies intervention: universal values, and their concomitant, one justice for all. One is immediately struck by the fact that the right to intervene is, in fact, exercised in highly selective manners: here yes, there no. What explains these differences of treatment? A first set of examples is all too clear: in these, the countries suspected of wrongdoing are too powerful. Though the papers inform us that China violates human rights in Tibet, that India occupies Kashmir, and that the Russians are waging an unjust war in Chechnya, no one suggests bombing these countries to put an end to their misdeeds. The cost in human terms would be too great. The right to intervene should therefore be subject to a restrictive clause, that it is valid only against countries noticeably weaker than those that inflict the punishment. This situation irresistibly reminds one of the witticism Charles Péguy directed at the then President of the French League of Human Rights, Francis de Pressensé: 'Pressensé backs right against might only where might is *not* might.'[11]

There may be nothing to be proud of here, but we must take account of reality as it is. Fine. But there are other cases that cannot be explained merely by the relative strength of the countries incriminated. If we confine ourselves to the geographical context of Yugoslavia, where the initial crime was the persecution, deportation or expulsion of a minority of the population, the examples of Israel's relation to the Palestinians, or of Turkey's measures against the Kurds, immediately spring to mind. Each case is admittedly different, and requires sensitive judgement. Nevertheless, why intervene in one case and not in another? Justice as we understand it today is universal or nothing. If it condemns one individual and not another when their misdeeds are similar, we perceive some other principle at work in the judgements. Should one respond by contending that one has to begin somewhere? Our incapacity to apply the rule of law universally cannot, it might be argued, justify our failure to apply it wherever we can. Very well, but the violation of humanitarian principles is of longer standing in these countries than in Yugoslavia, and it is difficult to see why the Western powers do not intervene in these cases, were it only on the political and economic fronts.

Or, to be frank, one sees exactly what prevents such intervention—and justice has nothing to do with it. The USA and the NATO states deem Israel and Turkey 'friendly' states with shared military and political interests. The lesson to be learnt from recent history is therefore less glorious than the Secretary-General of the UN, the President of the United States, or President Havel would like us to think. Human rights violations will be prevented, but only in countries with

**35**

which we are not allied: our allies can do as they like with their minorities. The lesson is, in short, that you do well to side with the mighty. Yugoslavia's error, according to this cynical line of thought, was not to persecute its minorities, but to overestimate its forces, or to believe that Russia was still able or willing to assist: a familiar lesson in international relations. The right to intervene is now restricted by a second clause: it doesn't apply to our strategic allies.

A still different case is presented by the genocide in Rwanda. Let me offer a brief reminder about the West's non-intervention. In 1993, the UN sent an observation mission to Rwanda, comprising 2,500 men under the command of the Canadian General Romeo Dallaire. In early 1994, Dallaire submitted the first of a succession of alarming reports to his superiors. Inter-ethnic hatred, stirred up by Hutu propaganda, was reaching dangerous heights, while his own capacity to intervene was minimal. Dallaire's missives and telegrams were not, however, acted on. In early April, ten Belgian UN soldiers were killed and Dallaire found himself an impotent witness as massacre raged around him. His anguished reports were still ignored; the Security Council's only response was to withdraw a part of its contingent from Rwanda, since the lives of the UN soldiers were now endangered. The exact number of those who died over the following three months is unknown, but the latest estimates suggest that some 800,000 Tutsis were slaughtered, to whom should be added the tens or hundreds of thousands of Hutus who were either killed in reprisals by the Tutsi forces after the initial genocide, or died for lack of medical care.

A report entitled 'The Avoidable Genocide', commissioned by the Organization for African Unity (OAU), drafted by a commission of experts and published in July 2000,[12] states that the Security Council deliberately chose not to intervene. And what explains the Council's attitude? The answer is: the lack of political will on the part of the Council members most directly concerned. The United States was immediately informed of the nature of events in Rwanda, but President Clinton and his Secretary of State Madeleine Albright knew that an intervention in Rwanda would be exceedingly unpopular with the US electorate. In a previous operation, in Somalia, 18 Americans had been killed, and American public opinion was not about to forget the fact. The leaders of the Council member states therefore took care that the word 'genocide' should never pass their lips, since the treaties that they had signed obliged them to intervene should genocide occur. They therefore spoke bashfully of acts 'akin to' genocide.[13] When the Security Council *did* decide to send a further mission, American delaying tactics ensured that not a single extra soldier, not a single arm arrived in Rwanda before the genocide had run its course.

Not that the United States preferred the Hutu executioners to their Tutsi victims. It was simply that domestic policy considerations took priority over humanitarian concerns. The same priority has been observed on other occasions. Clinton has always opposed official recognition by the US Congress of the genocide of Armenians perpetrated by the Turks, arguing that to vote its recognition would 'run counter to our national interests'.[14] The right to intervene here suffers a further restriction: it is not to be exercised if one has nothing to gain from it materially, politically or in terms of moral prestige. The non-intervention of the international community in other African conflicts, notably that of Sudan, where the situation is nonetheless intolerable, also seems to pertain to this third exception to the rule of intervention.

Relative to Rwanda, the position of France was, ultimately, little different. In order to maintain its good relations with the Hutu authorities and other African states prior to the genocide, France failed to condemn the racist propaganda seething through Rwanda. Nor was any intervention planned during the genocide itself, although this part of Africa is traditionally considered a zone of French influence. Only when the massacres had been interrupted by the advance of the Tutsi Rwanda Patriotic Front, and were coming to an end, did France send in forces. This was 'Opération Turquoise', theoretically intended to come between the two warring armies. In fact, it allowed the Hutu murderers to escape into neighbouring Congo. Since then, Washington has expressed its regret that it did not act more energetically, and Paris has set up a parliamentary committee to look into the matter. General Dallaire, meanwhile, having testified many times over, has made two suicide attempts and suffers long spells of depression.

All these events belong to the recent past. They do not predate the Second World War; they are indeed subsequent to the 'just war' in Iraq. The genocide was predicted, and immediate military intervention was possible. Had the resources been made available, intervention might well have been effective. The international community knew that genocide was occurring and did nothing to prevent it. How can one ever trust these political actors again?

The objections that we have raised so far, relating to national sovereignty and the universality of justice, question not the right to intervene but its imperfect application (why here and not there?) and its undesirable side-effects (it may be productive not of human rights but of anarchy and a colonial mindset). We should now go one step further and ask: even supposing that the right to intervene could be exercised to perfection, should it be generalized? Do we wish to live in a world founded on this principle?

One reason why one might hesitate to establish the right to intervene as a universal precept is that human rights violations, not to mention disregard for the law in general, are far too widespread. If all violations were to be prevented or punished, war would never end. No country and no continent is beyond criticism. Péguy, who saw the implications of this attitude for what they were, wrote that 'In the Declaration of the Rights of Man . . . there is good reason to wage war on everyone for as long as this world lasts.'[15] Consequences of this kind seem less than desirable. Before such good intentions were realized, the road to Hell would have been paved twice over. If we cannot generalize the principle of intervention, it does not, of course, follow that no intervention is ever justifiable. But it does follow that we cannot justify intervention simply by reference to the Declaration.

Now, it is not merely the means of this enterprise that are questionable, it is also the goal. To attempt to eradicate evil from the surface of the earth, or merely to put an end to human rights violations, to seek to establish a new world order from which war and violence have been banished, these are projects that resemble the totalitarian utopias in their efforts to perfect mankind and establish a paradise on earth. They also require us to be convinced that right is embodied solely and exclusively in ourselves, an attitude reminiscent of the wars of religion. Such wars ended, of course, when it was finally acknowledged that several different conceptions of religious truth could coexist. Evil, moreover, is no contingent addition to human history, nor can we easily be rid of it; it is attached to our very identity. We cannot be free of it without changing species.

Put simply, the promotion of universal justice implies the construction of a universal state. For justice to be enacted, we need a police force that arrests the accused and collects evidence; if justice is to be universal, so too must the police. But a police force is subordinate to the orders of a government, and thus government, too, has to become universal. Indeed, unity is an indispensable plank in the doctrine of scientism, the philosophical underpinning of totalitarian regimes. Since we are sure that we have identified the objectives proper to humankind, the reasoning here goes, since we are sure that we have discovered the best possible form of government, why should we not extend its benefits to everyone, by unifying laws, institutions and police forces? But would this universal state be the perfect state? By no means— its drawbacks would be substantially greater than its advantages.

Such terms are not, of course, much used at present. Yet evidence of the tendency they represent is not lacking. We note, for example, the return of medical metaphors applied to the body politics, metaphors that one might have thought thoroughly discredited by the intensive usage they have received in totalitarian regimes. We speak of surgical interventions, and argue that prevention is better than cure—as if social defects could be analysed in terms of illness. Imagery of the body implies that we conceive of society as a single being, with one brain and one heart, and their agents as the inevitable 'arms of the law'. As a being, moreover, in which there may be zones of corruption and malady from which the body must be protected, if necessary by excision. This prophylactic perspective would also justify combating *potential* genocides and virtual crimes, and thus legitimate pre-emptive strikes—even where it subsequently emerges that the danger was illusory.

The fact that the totalitarian objective of a universal state was inherited from scientistic doctrine is only one of the reasons why we should mistrust projects tending towards such a state. In the eighteenth century, a famous controversy took place between Condorcet and Montesquieu on precisely this issue. Montesquieu, after analysing the laws of various countries, concluded that all laws referred to the same principles of justice, but that diversity of historical experience, cultural tradition and geographical location meant that it was better that diversity in laws and forms of government and religion be preserved. The crime of the *conquistadors*, he argued, was not that they rejected the rule of law, nor that they had abandoned morality; it was rather that they had acted as if the countries of the world were in fact one and the same. 'The height of stupidity', Montesquieu remarked of the trial of the Inca Emperor Atahualpa, 'was that they condemned him not according to the political and civil laws of *his* country, but according to those of their own'.[16] It is better that the world be shared among, say, five religions; for were there only one, even if that religion were the best, it might become oppressive. By acknowledging their plurality, on the other hand, religions provide for their own mutual restraint. Pluralism is a benefit in and for itself, independent of the value of the different options of which it is comprised. This is true both within a country (maintaining a plurality of powers) and in the relations between countries.

Thirty years later, Condorcet wrote a commentary on the *Esprit des lois*, in which he assailed the need for pluralism advanced by Montesquieu. If we had already discovered the best solution, the best law, the best government, why not dispose of the inferior ones? If politics was a science, its choices were the right choices. Now truth and pluralism make uneasy bedmates—truth is one, error is multiple: 'A good law must be good for all men, as a true proposition is true for all.'[17] Once all laws had been brought into uniformity, we should proceed to the unification of institutions and trade; in due course, the languages of the most enlightened peoples, the French and the English, would be universally adopted. In the last analysis, mankind, guided by reason, would 'form a single whole and tend toward a single goal'.[18]

Why is Montesquieu's pluralist ideal preferable to the unitary ideal of Condorcet? Why is the humanist project superior to the one derived from the cult of science? Because human knowledge can never be complete, and because it cannot in any case discover humanity's ideals; a science of politics will therefore never exist. In its absence, balances of powers, mutual tolerance, and a plurality of centres of decision are more valuable than unity. And this remains true even if the country seeking to impose unity currently possesses the best government, for plurality ensures liberty and the possibility of enquiry. Translated into international relations, this means that mutual deterrence among several groups of countries or several superpowers may be more advantageous than the exclusive domination of a single power. A dominant superpower is liable to seek to police the world and impose its rules universally. We may have rejoiced when the Soviet Empire fell, but that does not make the exclusive dominance of the United States any the more desirable. The danger does not simply disappear when the superpower realizes that it lacks the resources to play universal policeman, and confines its intentions to those situations where its economic interests are at risk. For all these reasons, equilibrium is preferable to unity. The economic globalization that we are experiencing today should not be followed by political globalization; autonomous states or groups thereof are needed to contain the negative effects of this unifying movement.

To escape the universal state and the temptation to build paradise on earth, it is better not to take upon ourselves the task of curing humanity of its ills. Does this mean that we should look on impassively when others are overwhelmed by catastrophe? No. What we should question is precisely sterile alternatives of the kind 'You must choose between craven inaction and carpet-bombing'. It is possible to resist evil without succumbing to the temptations of righteousness.

Military intervention in a foreign country, to the detriment of its national sovereignty, is justifiable in one extreme case— on condition, of course, that the intervention is not likely to cause more victims that it saves. For the last few decades, this extreme case has had a name, that of genocide. But we are not speaking now of potential genocide, which might justify preventive strikes, nor of civil war, horrible as its attendant massacres may be. This is precisely why it would have been illegitimate to declare war on Nazi Germany in 1936: the policy of genocide had not yet been implemented. Other forms of intervention, however, would not have been ruled out: trade pressure, firm diplomacy, political propaganda and a generous welcome for refugees. Similarly, even if the West had been sufficiently well informed about the genocide inflicted on the Ukrainian and Kazakh peasantry in 1933, no military intervention would have been justified. War with the USSR would have resulted in an even greater number of fatalities. When Soviet tanks crushed the Hungarian uprising of 1956, though no genocide occurred, an immense wave of moral

**43**

indignation swept through East and West blocs alike. I remember how at the time, we adolescents of Eastern Europe dreamed of American tanks coming to liberate us. I now think that any such intervention would have been a terrible mistake, since it would inevitably have set off a Third World War.

Intervention in the case of genocide presents the same dangers as other forms of intervention. But these risks must be accepted, given what is at stake. If we act to save the victims of genocide, how can we foresee the number of dead that our actions will cost? We cannot. How can we distinguish accurately between collective massacres and embryonic genocide? We cannot. How can we be sure that, in our reluctance to intervene before potential genocide has become real genocide, our actions will not come too late, while real individuals daily become virtual, that is, statistics of fatality? We cannot. We can only concede that life will never be as clear as a mathematical demonstration or an insurance policy; that it is closer to the 'imperfect garden'[19] of which Montaigne speaks; and that, facing the extreme, we must resist. Error cannot be eliminated; but if we take as our principle that genocide alone justifies military intervention, we are permitted to hope that interventions will be few and far between.

The two genocides that have taken place since the Second World War—those of Cambodia, beginning in 1976, and of Rwanda in 1994—have not produced the faintest hint of intervention on the part of the international community. They were interrupted, belatedly, by a military force stationed close by; in Cambodia by the Vietnamese army, and in Rwanda by the Rwanda Patriotic Front, based in Uganda. These precedents might lead us to think that the most effective reaction in such cases is not recourse to the UN. The

UN is inevitably torn between the conflicting interests of its member states, and paralysis can easily ensue. It is no accident that the USA has, over the past few years, fought shy of paying its UN dues while continuing to justify its own policies on moral grounds. The weight of bureaucracy at the UN is excessive. Moreover, the UN has no armies in the field, which is just as well, as it would otherwise tend to become a world government. The neighbours of a country in which a genocide is occurring have, by contrast, good reasons for intervening. They are informed of developments not merely by television but directly, by the influx of refugees. Finally, proximity makes for empathy and justifies the inevitable risks for intervention. One risks death more readily for one's neighbour than for a people that inhabits the ends of the earth. This solution is no panacea. There is some danger that it will favour regional powers to the detriment of universal principles; but I believe that, when it comes to stopping genocide, it is preferable.

From this point of view, the European Union and the Organization for Security and Cooperation in Europe were well placed to concern themselves with events in Kosovo (they did not). But what occurred there was not genocide, which would have justified military intervention. It was 'only'—although I realize that this 'only' involved a couple of thousands of victims—a civil war characterized by massacres, irreconcilable and visceral nationalism, and the misdeeds of Milosevic's corrupt and authoritarian regime. The military intervention, on the other hand, came close to provoking a genocide, by transforming the two million Albanian-speaking inhabitants of Yugoslavia into hostages, if not indeed enemies.

The formula 'right to intervene' is objectionable on two different counts. First and foremost, one must ask whence this 'right' derives. The right is not, we take it, of divine origin, as Havel appears to suggest; we speak of rights being granted to us by virtue of our belonging to a particular state. That is clearly not the case with the right to intervene. We also speak of human rights, to which we are all entitled simply by virtue of belonging to the human race. But is not an abusive extension of the sense of that term to find in it an excuse for meddling in others' affairs? If it is we ourselves who take on this responsibility, then it is not a right, but a duty, and voluntarily assumed. Furthermore, this duty should be determined not by the form that our intervention will take (military interference) but by the needs of those who request intervention. Those who suffer do indeed have a right to assistance (an unwritten right, a human right); we who are willing to aid them can have only a *duty to assist*.

In French, the notion of *assistance* can be understood in a confined sense, that of merely being present at the scene. This duty is one that we all share: we should not remain ignorant of what happens around us, we should, at the very least, accept our roles as witnesses of our time. But 'assistance' has, in either language, a stronger sense, that of aid, which the more energetic political or humanitarian activists among us will take upon themselves.

The duty of assistance is exclusive of military intervention, since it is oriented toward the benefit of the victims, and war, ethical or not, is rarely of assistance to the victims of human rights abuse. The benefits achieved by some are generally paid for by the suffering of others. This should not be taken to mean that military intervention is necessarily illegitimate. Only the Red Army could force the gates of Auschwitz, and we can only be thankful that it did. But its action was not essentially humanitarian. It is vital that the distinction between military intervention and humanitarian assistance remains clear. Nor does the duty of assistance require us to impose a commercial blockade on countries whose policies we condemn. After all, the rulers of the country will find it easy to stave off the consequences to themselves, leaving all the effects—deprivation and black-market prices—to be suffered by the population, which is already the victim of its own government. Yet, to our everlasting shame, this is precisely the thrust of the measure currently taken against Iraq.

The forms of assistance are not, however, limited to such things as blockades. They can be political (pressure put on foreign governments), just as they can be legal, humanitarian or economic in form. It is obvious that if the West had not invested in ever more expensive and effective weaponry, but in the economies of the Balkan states, much conflict could have been avoided. Assistance has the further merit that it is offered and not imposed; it can therefore be refused by those to whom it is offered, and this again distances us from the colonial situation.

The duty to assist cannot, then, be confused with the temptation to impose 'Right' universally or to cure humanity of its chronic maladies—or worse still, prevent them by humanitarian bombardment, another Orwellian expression coined by Havel. It is quite possible that we shall practise the duty to assist in the same way as we have until now exercised the right to intervene, that is, in selective fashion; and that we shall do so for reasons that happen also to serve our own interests. But this limitation should at least prevent us from resorting to force and multiplying the number of victims. We should not expect miracles. Assistance will, at times, be prevented by the national government in question. And we should add that, even if we assume this new duty, the world will not become a perfect place. Evil will be reduced, here and there, but not eliminated forever. Nevertheless, this may be a good place to call a halt. The temptation of righteousness, on the other hand, is dangerous because it puts abstract goals before individuals. Goodness and love have this merit above all, that they are always felt for a particular being, and prohibit our using that individual as a means to an end, however sublime that end.

The current state of the world teaches us that power is an integral factor in international relations. But we are not obliged to accept that power-relations be tricked out as the magnanimous bestowal of some transcendent or practical benefit, as they were in the 'good old days' of the Crusades or the colonial conquests. The defence of the national interest is a legitimate aim in any government, but it should not be presented as a struggle for universal justice. We must champion right over might, but when faced with two powers, if one frankly avows its objectives and the other sports a mask of virtue, we should know which to choose.

# Introduction to Michael Ignatieff

*Timothy Garton Ash*

It is a great pleasure to introduce Michael Ignatieff's lecture. If I had to sum up Michael in one word it would be 'intellectual'. He is in fact one of our leading liberal intellectuals. Now 'intellectual' is a word viewed with some suspicion in Britain. It is regarded as strange and intrinsically foreign. I remember an obituary of Karl Popper, which began with the sentence, 'Like most British intellectuals of his generation, Karl Popper was born in Vienna.' Michael wasn't born in Vienna. He was born in Canada. His education was initially in Canada, then in Cambridge (England), then Cambridge (Massachusetts). He was a Fellow of King's College, Cambridge, and then became a freelance writer and an extremely well-known broadcaster. He held a number of visiting fellowships, not least the Alastair Horne Fellowship at St Antony's College, Oxford, while he was writing his biography of Isaiah Berlin. He is currently at the Carr Center for Human Rights at the John F. Kennedy School at Harvard.

Michael is a public intellectual, a *spectateur engagé*. His work has always been on the frontier between moral philosophy and politics, for example in his early book *The Needs of Strangers* (1984). He has also written two novels: *Asya* (1991) and *Scar Tissue* (1993), novels with a good deal of real life in them. He is, of course, the biographer of Isaiah Berlin, arguably the greatest of all recent Oxford intellectuals. But perhaps most relevant to his lecture, he has written what has become a trilogy of books: *Blood and Belonging* (1993), *The Warrior's Honour* (1998) and *Virtual War: Kosovo and Beyond* (2000), which are a really original mixture of reportage, essay and a sort of moral and philosophical enquiry. If one looks at the subjects of the enquiry, they also lie on the frontiers between genres and disciplines and subjects. It is an enquiry into nationalism and citizenship, into the role of the media, into civil and human rights, into the nature of modern war and not least into the criteria for what is called 'humanitarian intervention'. This is a subject on which Michael has written a great deal in recent years. He has served as a member of a very interesting Swedish Commission enquiring into the NATO intervention in Kosovo and is currently on a Canadian sponsored international commission on state sovereignty and intervention.

The following lecture, however, is perhaps his most systematic attempt thus far to address the linked issues of human rights, sovereignty and intervention. Like Tzvetan Todorov in the preceding lecture, he sees the full moral complexity of deciding the rights and wrongs of any intervention. But much more than Todorov, he comes down in favour of the need for humanitarian intervention even where a full consensual need for humanitarian legitimacy is unobtainable. Using the traditional six requirements of Just War theory, he comes close to arguing that the sixth requirement, Proper Authority, may have to be foregone if the first five obtain. Or at least, that Proper Authority cannot be taken to mean 'UN Security Council authority and only that'. The best can be the enemy of the good.

Perhaps the most difficult issue that he addresses is what happens after a 'successful' intervention. The immediate repression and atrocities that prompted the intervention have been stopped, but can this place—this East Timor, Kosovo, Bosnia or Afghanistan—be returned (if 'returned' is the right word) to a condition of civilized life in which the people who live there can peacefully govern themselves? This, it seems to me, is the hardest test for all liberal internationalist advocates of humanitarian intervention, and one that in most of these places still remains to be passed in practice. Here is the largest open question that Michael Ignatieff leaves us with, at the end of a lecture that combines history, philosophy and contemporary examples in a lucid and scrupulous argument.

# 2

# Human Rights, Sovereignty and Intervention

## Michael Ignatieff

## Human Rights and Sovereignty: the History of an Antagonism

From 1945 until the end of the Cold War, human rights remained subordinate to state sovereignty within the framework of the UN Charter. Articles 2.1 and 2.7 of the Charter defined sovereignty in strict terms of inviolability and non-interference. The prohibition on internal interference was peremptory, while the language that urged states to promote human rights was permissive. States were encouraged to promote human rights, not commanded to do so.

The UN Charter's emphasis on sovereignty and bias against intervention reflects the chapter of European history which the drafting powers believed they had been lucky to escape. Even in death and defeat, Adolf Hitler remained the ghost at the drafters' feast. His manipulation of the grievances of the Sudeten Germans in Czechoslovakia in 1938 was uppermost in the minds of those who wanted to outlaw such 'interventions' in the future. Hitler had justified the intervention—i.e. the destruction of Czech sovereignty—on humanitarian grounds, as a foreign power's protection of an oppressed national minority. In a similar vein, the outright ban on the waging of aggressive war responded to Hitler's violation of Polish sovereignty in September 1939.

There are thus good historical reasons that united the drafting powers of the Western and communist bloc in redefining sovereignty in terms of the twin pillars of the non-intervention rule and the ban on aggressive war. The primacy of sovereignty also appealed strongly to Latin American nations, and newly emerging nations of Africa and Asia, with colonial and neo-colonial legacies to overcome, and with the challenge of nation building ahead of them.

It was Hitler the warmonger, not Hitler the architect of European extermination, who preoccupied the drafters. Their sense that aggressive war across national frontiers was the more salient risk than the extermination of peoples within national frontiers helped frame the priority given to sovereignty over human rights. Had genocide and mass extermination of political opponents been at the forefront of the drafters' minds, they might have been less absolute in their prohibition of intervention in the domestic affairs of states and more peremptory in the language chosen to encourage the promotion of human rights. The Charter was drafted in an interregnum when the Holocaust and the Red Terror existed in a kind of suspended animation, not yet the defining crimes they were to become in the 1970s and 1980s. The coercive prestige of Western communism blocked the European reckoning with Stalinism until the dissolution of Euro-communism in the mid-1970s. The Holocaust's return to the Western imagination is a more complicated story, and only its barest outlines can be suggested here. The returning survivors either kept silent or went to Israel to devote their energies to the construction of the future. It was the generation of the 1960s who rediscovered the Holocaust, by talking to the survivor generation, by seeking in a rediscovered Jewish identity a substitute for the collapsing political identities of the 1960s and 1970s. Israel itself, as its founding Labourite and Zionist ideologies waned in credibility, found in the Holocaust a new legitimizing justification. For the Germans of the 1960s, the reckoning with the Holocaust formed part of a much deeper intergenerational confrontation over parental war guilt. For other non-Jews of the 1960s generation, the Holocaust returned as the symbol of the dangers of inhuman technical reason and as a warning of the moral nihilism that lurked just beneath the apparently solid framework of bourgeois liberalism. The rediscovery of the central moral significance of the Holocaust formed part of the whole challenge that the 1960s generation mounted to their parent's legacy.

Like the Holocaust and the Red Terror, human rights lived in the shadows of the Cold War world, between 1945 and the mid-1970s. It was given a subordinate place in the institutional architecture of the United Nations system. UN bodies, like the Human Rights Commission, for example, had no powers to investigate the performance of member states, and after the successful passage of the Universal Declaration in 1948—a declaration only—no formal human rights conventions were ratified by states until the 1970s.

It is unsurprising that human rights should have occupied a marginalized place in the institutional order of the Cold War. No group of nations had any interest in encouraging domestic scrutiny of their human rights performance. The Americans had Jim Crow to hide. The Russians' dirty secret was the Gulag. The ruling elites of newly emerging nations of Africa and Asia exploited the new language of non-interference to prevent external scrutiny of their domestic records.

What broke the log-jam and turned human rights into a powerful critique of state sovereignty was not the advocacy of states, but the pressure of NGOs and non-state actors. The creation of the first mass-based human rights organization,

Amnesty International, in 1961, was a harbinger of the huge international human rights movement that was to develop in the next 40 years. A key moment in the history of that movement was the development of the campaign to free Soviet Jewry in the 1970s, out of which eventually emerged such organizations as Human Rights Watch. These organizations transformed the language of human rights, from a quiet accomplice of the propaganda campaigns of state adversaries in the Cold War, into the most powerful critique of the non-interference rule in relation to sovereignty.

Here the simultaneous historical rediscovery of Red Terror and the Holocaust proved important. The memory of these terrible events focused the moral imagination of activists, intellectuals and foreign policy specialists on the emerging reality that sovereignty was frequently an instrument and an alibi for unconscionable human rights abuse. As aggressive war between states within the North Atlantic area was banished, and the Hitlerian nightmare receded, the challenge that gradually became salient was the oppression of an increasingly regressive, economically inefficient Eastern bloc.

The renaissance of human rights in the 1970s has to be seen in the context of détente and the increasing dependence of the Soviet bloc on Western trade and investment. Human rights concessions were made in return for access to the capitalist market. The Helsinki Final Act marked the moment in which the rulers of the Soviet empire conceded that there were not two human rights languages—one socialist, one capitalist, one putting primacy on social and economic rights, the other on political and civil—but one integrated, global rights language to which all nations, at least in theory, were obligated to conform.

None of this would have happened had it not been for the

emergence of international and domestic NGOs, linking up across the Iron Curtain to demand the observance of this new global norm. These NGOs drew on the intrinsic appeal of human rights as a language of conscience. Its very individualism, its affirmation that each individual human life is entitled to protection and respect, proved a powerful stimulant to civic courage and defiance in the Soviet bloc and in emerging nations with authoritarian regimes.

With the collapse of the Soviet Union in 1991—in large measure a long-detonating result of the human rights revolution and its diffusion through the Eastern bloc—the moment arrived in which human rights ceased to be subordinate to the language of sovereignty and became a fundamental challenge to its legitimacy. The elements of this new post-Cold War context that favoured the hegemony of human rights include the dissolution of the superpower rivalry, the consolidation of the European Union, together with the spread of democracy and ethnic self-determination in Eastern Europe. Peace in Western Europe, combined with the emergence of transnational institutions of co-operation within the European Union, diluted the exercise of Westphalian sovereignty in the continent that had been its home. With peace at home, European powers found a new role for themselves promoting human rights abroad. The new Russian state, desperate for Western help, believed its interests lay in 'returning to Europe', by embracing human rights norms it had previously scorned. Ex-communist countries, once under Soviet rule or influence, now also took the path back to Europe, which meant enshrining human rights principles in their constitutions.

Outside of Europe, Western aid agencies, international banks and UN organizations increasingly 'mainstreamed' human rights considerations in their aid and lending packages for developing nations. These nations, some of whom had depended entirely on Soviet support, now felt obliged to comply with these new human rights and governance conditions. Moreover the international institutions began imposing them because they believed that they would address the problems of bad governance, corruption and civil repression.

As this summary suggests, the ascendancy of human rights in the post-Cold War world has complex causes. Those who see its rise as the simple story of progress, of an idea whose time finally came, are missing the key political dimensions: the weakness and collapse of the Soviet Union; the emerging salience of governance—and therefore of human rights—as development issues in the states of Africa and Asia; and finally, the pacification of Europe, and its search for a new legitimizing ideology. A final feature—common to all Western societies—is the coming to power of the 1960s generation, nurtured in anti-Vietnam politics, in anti-imperialist causes, disillusioned with socialism and Marxism, awakening to the moral reality of the Holocaust and the Red Terror and discovering in human rights a redemptive cause 'above politics', a moral vernacular supposedly unsullied by the compromises and equivocations of power.

Once in power, these new elites, now in charge of states, UN agencies and NGOs, began to talk seriously of reconceiving sovereignty itself in terms of compliance with human rights norms. The idea of sovereignty as responsibility—which has found its way into the speeches of the UN Secretary-General himself—implies that the legitimacy of a state depends on the extent to which it protects the basic rights of its citizens. This assumes, in turn, that the right of governments resides in the will of the people, and that their assent is secured by the protection of their rights. All of this, which is proclaimed as an emerging consensus, is actually highly problematic. Many states—authoritarian regimes, monarchies and kingdoms—do not derive their constitutional legitimacy from consent, but from force or tradition. So the basic problem with the idea of sovereignty as responsibility is that it does not happen to apply to many members of the United Nations. Moreover, the negative corollaries of sovereignty as responsibility are decidedly unwelcome to most states. These negative corollaries imply that a state that persistently violates the human rights of its people loses the right to demand their obedience and loses immunity from external interference.

All that we can say about sovereignty as responsibility is that we are not there yet, and are not likely to be there for a long time to come. Even democratic governments are uneasy about its implications. Governments with relatively good human rights records are suspicious of claims that their legitimacy is dependent on some internal or external report card of compliance with universalist norms. Any government with substantial minority populations will be uneasy about international reporting on the conditions of these minorities and will resist the claim that denial of their rights constitutes legitimate grounds for civil disobedience or unrest.

Up to a point, all this is as it should be. Human rights principles and state sovereignty are, and should be, antagonists, and government officials and human rights activists and reporters are, and should be, on opposite sides. This antagonism is actually conducive to the stability and effectiveness of modern states. Human rights oversight helps responsible governments face problems before they become crises.

Accepting human rights scrutiny, from national and international bodies, is not the same thing, however, as accepting that the legitimacy of a state depends on human rights compliance. States that tolerate external human rights scrutiny, will refuse the negative corollary that when human rights violations are persistent and gross, outside powers may intervene to put a stop to them. Nor is opposition to the emerging hegemony of human rights confined to authoritarian and repressive states. Not even democratic states want international law to construe the legitimacy of states in terms of their accountability to basic human rights norms. The greatest champion of human rights overseas, the United States, is simultaneously an uncompromising defender of a highly unilateralist definition of its own sovereignty. American leaders of all political stripes regard foreign criticism of its domestic human rights norms—the persistence of capital punishment, for example—as either irrelevant or impudent.

So, to sum up at this point, we are in a half-way house, no longer in the world of 1945 where sovereignty was clearly privileged over human rights, and yet equally, we are nowhere near the world desired by human rights activists, namely one in which sovereignty is conditional on being good international citizens. We are somewhere in between, negotiating the conflicts between state sovereignty and international human rights as they arise, case by case. Certainly, all modern states are now bound by a set of international human rights covenants. For most states, ratifying these covenants is like paying dues to a club, and they are easy to ratify precisely because they confer membership without conferring onerous obligations.

In their foreign relations, most democratic states do promote democracy and human rights. But equally, in the customary practice that governs recognition of new regimes, states accept that legitimacy continues to be defined by whether a particular regime has effective control over a given territory. In international law, therefore, legitimacy remains a matter of power not a matter of ethics. Human rights have not essentially changed the international law governing relations between states, at this most basic level.

The ethical legitimacy of states remains less important than their effective control of territory simply because other states within the international system place a higher priority on order than they do on justice. All states have an interest in ensuring that territories do remain under the effective control of a government, regardless of its human rights record. Indeed, some states perceive that the promotion of democracy and human rights—especially in fragile, newly emerging states with complex mixtures of minorities and religions—may actually fragment the state internally, and by promoting secession, fragment the international state system. This preference for order has been reinforced by the disintegration of multi-ethnic states like the former Yugoslavia. When democracy came to the former Yugoslavia, it came in the form of demands for national self-determination on ethnic lines, with catastrophic consequences for the state order left behind by Tito. Where democracy means self-determination for the ethnic majority, ethnic cleansing and massacre of minorities as a method of state consolidation usually accompany it.

## The Fifth Wave of State Formation

Mention of Yugoslavia brings into focus the chief reason why the conflict between sovereignty and human rights came out into the open in the 1990s: the process of state formation and state fragmentation that is convulsing the international state system. There is a cluster of 'bad neighbourhoods' where states are either fighting losing battles against insurgents, where civil wars have become endemic, or where state authority has broken down altogether. These 'bad neighbourhoods' include:

- Colombia, Bolivia, Peru, and Venezuela
- South Balkans: Macedonia, Montenegro and Kosovo
- South Caucasus: Georgia, Azerbaijan
- West Africa: Liberia and Sierra Leone
- Central Africa: the Congo
- East Africa: Sudan and Somalia
- Pakistan and Afghanistan
- Indonesia

It would be impossible to assemble all the reasons why this convulsion is under way, but it seems clear that it is a widening tear in the system of state order, analogous to the hole in the global ozone layer. Historically, this episode of state fragmentation and formation recalls at least four previous ones:

- the dismantling of the European empires after Versailles in 1918
- the creation of the so-called people's democracies after the Soviet victory of 1945
- the decolonization of Africa and Asia, 1945–60
- the independence of former Soviet satellites after 1991.

In these previous waves, the dominant process was state formation and the dismantling of defeated or discredited empires. In the current wave, processes of fission and disintegration predominate. In part, fragmentation may represent an attempt to correct the failure of these previous episodes of state formation. Yugoslavia's disintegration in the 1990s, for example, represents the culmination of the failure of the two previous attempts at unification of the south Slavs, the Kingdom of the Croats, Slovenes and Serbs created after Versailles in 1918, and the Titoist people's democracy of brotherhood and unity created in 1945. Both of these two previous attempts at state formation suppressed ethnic self-determination. Once democracy returned in 1990, each dominant ethnic majority set themselves the task of abolishing both the Versailles and the Titoist versions of the federal state. Doing so required them to expel, terrorize and massacre their minorities.

Many of the disintegrative state conflicts in Africa—the Congo and Angola, for example—represent the continuing struggle of competing tribal and regional groups to consolidate state authority on the ruins of incompetent, rapacious and territorially incoherent colonial regimes. State order has proven inherently difficult to establish in sub-Saharan Africa because the departing colonial powers failed to create legitimate and effective administration, because the territory over which they ruled had forcibly consolidated many different languages, traditions, ethnic groups and religions, and because, above all, the regions were poor.

Some further causes for this wave of state disintegration are obvious: the collapse of the Soviet Union simultaneously withdrew support from a host of client or satellite states. These states are now disintegrating. Another cause is the inherited effects of 40 years of misrule by local elites. This would be the case in Sierra Leone. In other cases, the disintegration is the consequence of destructive post-imperial interventions during the Cold War. Consolidating stable state order in Latin America has been bedevilled by aggressively anti-communist meddling by American foreign policy: the overthrow of legitimate regimes, like Allende's Chile, the support of violent forms of counter-insurgency by authoritarian regimes on the one hand, and support for right-wing insurgents on the other. In another strategically sensitive part of the world, north Asia, Afghanistan has been torn apart, first by the Russian intervention, then the American counter-intervention, both of which introduced heavy weapons into a tribal warfare culture—with catastrophically destructive results. In the case of Indonesia, a highly diverse archipelago composed of different religions and ethnic groups was held together from 1945 by an authoritarian postcolonial regime commanding a single national institution—the army. Over time, this regime has begun to decompose, and the component parts of the archipelago are now seeking self-determination.

The systemic property of all these different examples is state failure, although the extent to which these states are failing differs in each case. Sometimes the state is struggling, sometimes disintegrating; in a few cases, Somalia being an example, it has collapsed. Sometimes the cause is an inadequate colonial legacy; sometimes it is the result of maladministration by an indigenous elite; sometimes it is the consequence of Western or communist interference. Finally, and most importantly, many of these failed or failing states are in poor regions of the world and have suffered from the steadily more adverse terms of trade in a globalized economy. As the developed world has accelerated into the fourth industrial revolution of computers and information technology, some parts of the developing world—for example, sub-Saharan Africa—remain stuck at the bottom of the international division of labour as primary producers.

Given the unrelenting pressure of poverty—made worse by mismanagement—it is unsurprising that state institutions begin to break down. Ruling elites lose their capacity, when their states are poor, to buy off or conciliate marginal regions or minorities. When these minorities pass from disobedience to rebellion, the elites lack the resources to quell revolts. As these revolts spread, the central government loses the monopoly of the means of violence. Where state order disintegrates, basic economic infrastructure also begins to collapse. As it does so, a new economic order begins to take root. As authority disintegrates at the centre, armed ethnic groups, bandits and guerrilla forces take over, using violence to enforce the allegiance of the local population and to extract the remaining surplus. As the weakening government struggles to regain control, it engages in more and more egregious attempts to terrorize the population into obedience, and rebel groups use more and more egregious forms of counter-terror to demoralize government forces and to coerce the local population. This process of state fission may then spread beyond the borders of the state itself, as populations take refuge across the border, and as insurgent groups use frontier zones for their base camps. A collapsing state thus has the capacity to metastasize and to spread its problems through the region. These poor neighbourhoods present a cluster of human rights catastrophes: forced population displacement, ethnic or religious massacre, genocide, endemic banditism, enslavement and/or forced recruitment of child soldiers. All of these proceed from the incapacity of a state to secure and maintain order or to contain a struggle for ethnic self-determination.

All of these conditions differ sharply from the human rights dilemmas of the Cold War period. Then abuses were not caused by weak or collapsing states, but by strong, intolerant and oppressive ones. To be sure, the problem of tyranny remains. China, North Korea, Iraq and Libya are strong states, not weak ones, and their human rights abuses fit into a more classical pattern: arrest of activists, detention without trial, extra-judicial murder, torture and disappearances. Yet the most dangerous places in the world are now places where there is not too much state power, but too little. Now the human rights dilemmas of the twenty-first century proceed more from anarchy than from tyranny.

If disorder rather than oppression, or rather the oppression that follows from disorder, is the chief cause of human rights abuse in the twenty-first-century world, then the traditional antagonism between state sovereignty and human rights needs to be re-thought. For it seems clear that the chief prerequisite for the creation of basic rights regimes for ordinary people is the re-creation of a stable national state with a classic Weberian monopoly on the legitimate means of force. Without the basic institutions of a state, no human rights protection is possible. As long as populations are menaced by banditism, civil war, guerrilla campaigns and counter-insurgency by beleaguered governments, they cannot be safe and secure. In such conditions, international human rights and humanitarian organizations can do no more than bind up the wounded and protect the most vulnerable. These Hobbesian situations do teach the message of the Leviathan itself: that consolidated state power is the very condition for any regime of rights whatever. In this sense, state sovereignty, instead of being the enemy of human rights, has to be seen as their basic precondition. Protecting human rights in zones where state order is embattled or collapsed altogether has to mean consolidating or recreating a legitimate state. Nation-building thus becomes, for the first time since the Allied occupation of

Germany and Japan, a critical instrument for the creation of rights regimes, although unlike Japan and Germany, where total defeat and unconditional surrender gave the Allies the authority to create new democratic institutions from scratch, the conditions for modern nation-building, in states recovering from civil war, are much less auspicious.

## Humanitarian Intervention: the False Debate

If, as has been argued, the human rights abuses of the twenty-first century have their roots in this process of state fragmentation or formation, then the debate over humanitarian intervention needs to be re-thought. This debate conceives the challenge of intervention to be framed by a series of essentially unrelated moral crises, in which differing populations of civilians in desperate need appeal to us to be rescued. The intervention problem then consists in determining whether wealthy western nations can mobilize the will and the resources to rescue them in time and create sufficient conditions of stability afterwards to prevent the recurrence of the crisis.

What an essentially 'humanitarian' and 'moral' analysis misses is that we are looking at a crisis of state order and governance in a zone of 'bad neighbourhoods' throughout the developing world. An occasional humanitarian intervention here or there will do little or nothing to address the root causes of this crisis which lie in the legacy of colonial misrule, the incompetence of local elites, the terms of international trade and economic backwardness. The first requirement for an adequate response is to understand that the crisis is political, not just moral or humanitarian, and that a response has to mobilize political, and not just humanitarian, resources.

Focusing the problem in this way should also focus motives for action. For as long as the chief motive to get involved is conscience alone, we can only expect sporadic action from a few responsible actors. Once it is realized that we are looking at a crisis in international order, states that would otherwise remain uninvolved would understand that their long-term interest in stability compel them to commit resources to the problem.

Marshalling the resources of the developed world to address the governance problems of the developing world is a huge task, but at very least the task must be identified. The debate about when and how to intervene, usually with military force, strikes many people from poorer countries as a lurid exercise in emotional self-gratification—an attempt to demonstrate the power of conscience—when the real tasks that rich Western nations need to address are much harder: stabilizing states in the developing world; helping them to increase the competence of local institutions; conciliating ethnic conflict; building up a functioning economy.

The promotion of human rights in the developing world thus requires something more than a politics of protest and something more than acts of rescue. It needs to be connected to a sustained development strategy, focusing on building legitimate, representative and competent states capable of maintaining basic rights regimes for all their citizens. Yet as is well known, methodology and ideology divide the 'development community' and the 'human rights community'. The experts who think about 'humanitarian intervention', likewise, are a sub-specialty of political theorists and international lawyers, with little grasp of the dynamics of how to create and sustain rights-observant states. All of these divisions—and the false debates that they engender—make it more difficult even to realize the comprehensive character of the crisis of state order in a few critical zones of the developing world.

It is equally true that development itself is impossible, if civil wars are under way, if states have collapsed, if the society in question is in the middle of a humanitarian catastrophe. Thus those who think about development need to think hard about how to stop civil wars and bring basic state order back to a poor society.

## Intervention: the Illusion of Neutrality

The word 'intervention' implies interposition, placing oneself between two contending parties and keeping them apart. Thus intervention is connected to the idea of neutrality. In international law, the neutrality of an intervener is critical to the legitimacy of an intervention. Yet this neutrality is fictitious. What is meant, in reality, is that states will only accept an intervention if the intervening party takes no steps to encourage insurgents against the ruling regime. Thus neutrality means taking the state party's side. Sometimes this makes an intervener complicit in repression. At other times, neutrality makes the intervener the hapless plaything of contending parties to a civil war.

In reality, as the conflict in Bosnia cruelly showed, neutrality can become discreditable as well as counterproductive. Once the decision is taken to introduce humanitarian aid into a war zone, backed up with peacekeepers, the aid itself becomes a focus of combat, and its provision, even to unarmed combatants, becomes a way not to damp down the fighting, but to keep it going. Neutral humanitarian assistance can have the perverse effect of sustaining the fighting it seeks to reduce.

Neutrality can certainly help to protect civilians, and it respects the humanitarian principle that in war there are no good and bad, no reputable and disreputable victims. All victims have some claim to mercy, assistance and aid from those bystanders who can provide it. But if that is all that bystanders do, they may help to keep civil wars going, by sustaining the capacity of a civilian population on either side to absorb more punishment. Moreover, when mediators impose a ceasefire in an ongoing civil war, they invariably draw the line in such a way as to reward the side that has waged the conflict with the most aggression and the most success. Hence, when peacekeepers are deployed to enforce the ceasefire, they are usually viewed by the party that has lost most in the conflict as colluders in aggression. For this reason, such ceasefires rarely hold.

Neutral humanitarianism, when viewed more cynically, is a kind of hedged bet, in which intervening parties salve their consciences while avoiding the kinds of political commitments that might actually stop civil war. For the key dilemma in civil wars is: which side to back? Unless one side is helped to win, and win quickly, nothing serious can be done to reduce the humanitarian cost of the violence. The basic issue is whether external intervention should be aimed at preserving the existing state or at helping a self-determination claim succeed.

In Bosnia, Western interveners failed to respond adequately to the humanitarian challenge because they failed to understand the political dimensions of the catastrophe, namely that a recognized member of the UN—Bosnia Herzegovina—was being torn apart by armed insurrections aided and abetted by outside powers, Serbia and Croatia. The crisis was seen as an entirely internal affair when, in fact, its chief determinants were illicit foreign subversion: the arming and training of insurgents, the provision of safe bases of operation in both Serbia and Croatia. The war within Bosnia was only brought to an end when foreign intervention was directed, not at the internal combatants, but at the external instigator, Serbia. Three years of studious humanitarian neutrality nearly enabled Serbia to realize its war aims. It was only when outside interveners took sides—bombed Serbian installations, forcing it to exert pressure on its internal proxies, the Bosnian Serbs—that the civil war stopped. The international community intervened to sustain the unity of a state—Bosnia Herzegovina—and to defeat a self-determination claim by the Bosnian Serbs. Taking sides worked.

The case of Afghanistan also illustrates the fact that the key choice is not to provide humanitarian aid to all parties, but to decide who should win. If Western powers had recognized the Taliban, they would have helped consolidate Taliban rule over the entire territory and thus help bring an end to a devastating civil war. Order would prevail, but it would be an order most human rights activists would deplore: the despotism of rural Islam at its most obscurantist. In such a situation, Afghan women would pay the price of a Western preference for order over justice. If, on the other hand, Western support continued to reach the Taliban's opponents, the civil war would continue and Afghanistan would continue to bleed to death. From 1996 to 2001, Western governments did both: tacitly working both with the Taliban and with the Northern Alliance. After September 11, 2001, this strategy fell apart, and at last, the outside powers took sides.

Taking sides is not the only dilemma. The other real dilemma is triage. Since these processes of fragmentation and formation are taking place in so many regions of the world, the obvious problem is to determine which conflicts to take on and which ones to ignore. Once triage is involved, issues of ethical and political consistency, inevitably follow. The moral commitments implied in human rights are universal; the resources available to meet these commitments are finite. In practice, universalistic commitments are rationed by the realities of power. Interventions occur where they are possible, not necessarily where they are most needed.

Intervention occurs, in general, where states are too weak, too friendless, to resist. They do not occur where the violators in question have the military might to deter and dissuade. The Chinese occupation of Tibet goes unsanctioned. The Russians reduce Grozny to rubble with impunity. Yet the Serbs receive 78 days of bombardment for their human rights violations in Kosovo. These inconsistencies mean that intervention in the domestic affairs of states will never rest on unassailable grounds. Yet the fact that we cannot intervene everywhere is not a justification for not intervening where we can. Prudence requires us to be inconsistent, but the inconsistency means that no intervention is ever going to be universally accepted as legitimate, since anyone can say: 'If here, why not there?'

## Intervention: the Responsibility to Protect

When all of these problems are added together it becomes clear why states have practical reasons to be wary of intervention and resistant to the idea of it becoming normal state practice in international affairs. Even though human rights has influence, the bias of the international system remains firmly set against the use of military force to enforce human rights norms across international borders. Indeed, from the point of view of human rights activists, the chief problem in the international system is not that there is too much intervention, but that there is too little. We are living in genocidal times, plagued by a system of state power that makes it exceedingly difficult to save people in time.

Moreover, UN bodies can report on abuses by states, and NGOs can bring the abuses to the notice of what is called 'world public opinion', but there are no explicit rules mandating sanctions or coercive measures if states fail to discharge their responsibilities. The remedies, such as they are, are a continuum of soft interventions that states commonly use to exert pressure on other states, a continuum that ranges from diplomatic reproof, through public criticism in international forums, up to economic sanctions, aid cut-offs, withdrawal of military and other forms of co-operation, withdrawal of diplomatic recognition and finally full-scale blockade. The softer end of the continuum remains within the prerogatives of states. The harder end generally requires international approval.

The moral basis of this inchoate state practice of soft intervention, which has evolved since the early 1970s, is sometimes called 'good international citizenship' by the Australians and sometimes called 'international solidarity' by the French. The Canadians have pioneered the use of the term 'human security', to emphasize that international involvement in the human rights situations of other states promotes common security by enhancing state stability. 'Human security' is also intended to create an agenda for multilateral problem-solving, like the ban on land mines. But its language of mutual interdependence cannot entirely conceal a legitimation for democratic states like Canada getting involved in the human rights predicaments of other states.

The most ambitious rationale for intervention has been the enunciation of a 'responsibility to protect' by the Canadian sponsored International Commission on Sovereignty and Intervention. Building on ideas of good citizenship and human security, the Commission has argued that all states have a responsibility to protect their citizens. In certain limited cases, such as genocidal massacre or ethnic cleansing, other states have a responsibility to step in. The international responsibility to protect is therefore a default obligation that comes into play only when a domestic state proves incapable or unwilling to act, and where the resulting situation is genuinely catastrophic.

The idea of a responsibility to protect also implies a responsibility to prevent and a responsibility to follow through. Action, of a coercive kind, lacks legitimacy unless every effort has been made to avert the catastrophe; and once action is taken, its legitimacy depends on staying the course until the situation is on the mend. Thus the responsibility to protect is intended to provide a rationale for constructive engagement by rich countries through an intervention continuum that begins with prevention and ends with sustained follow-up.

## Intervention: Threshold Conditions

Many states facing intractable insurgencies learn that it is in their interest to invite outside intervention, in the form of mediation, preventive deployment of peacekeepers and so on. 'Internationalizing' an intractable internal conflict is sometimes a way of solving it. Thus the British in Northern Ireland gradually learned that it was in their interest to involve the Americans. By engaging the American administration, the

British were able to gain their assistance in shutting off financial support and arms supplies to the Irish Republican Army. By engaging in the good offices of American officials, the British were able to enlist interlocutors of sufficient prestige to drive a stalemated process towards the Good Friday Agreement. States only 'internationalize' their internal problems when they feel they can control the process and emerge with their sovereignty enhanced. Most states fear that internationalization will weaken their control over opponents. Serbia was one such example. Her leaders could have internationalized the Kosovo problem after 1989, and had they done so, they might have kept an autonomous Kosovar region within the federation. But they feared that if international interlocutors became involved, they would legitimize domestic Kosovar activists, provide them with an international platform, and create a dynamic in which Serbia would lose effective political control of the province. Yet by refusing voluntary intervention, they exposed themselves to coercive intervention and in the end lost the very objective they had hoped to secure.

Coercive military intervention arises as an option, therefore, when states refuse a range of soft interventions aimed at preventing a conflict from exploding. States bring hard interventions upon themselves when they refuse soft ones. Still, a coercive intervention is not just the hard end of a continuum: it is a decisive break. Soft interventions form part of the normal to and fro of bilateral and multilateral relations between states. A coercive intervention, using force, is outlawed under the UN Charter, except where authorized by the Security Council.

What is the threshold of violence and abuse that must be crossed before coercive military force across a national border can be justified on moral and legal grounds? The assessment that has to be made is whether a state has crossed the line that separates repression from barbarism, that divides justified counter-terror, for example, from indiscriminate attacks on civilian populations. Where all state order has collapsed, the assessment problem is whether there is an armed group that bears more responsibility than any other for the gravest human rights abuses. In both cases, where states are repressive and where states have collapsed, the further assessment problem is how to know, in advance, whether the killing is likely to get worse. Decisions about whether the threshold has been crossed are difficult precisely because they are, by nature, anticipatory and extrapolative. Policy-makers must anticipate the worst, and the worst can exceed all expectations.

In practice, two rough and ready principles seem to have emerged in state practice in the 1990s. Use of external military force may be justified where there is clear evidence of large-scale loss of life—either actual or apprehended—which can be attributed to genocidal intention by state or non-state actors. This was the situation in eastern Bosnia in 1992 and Rwanda in 1994. Coercive military action might also be justified where the collapse of state power threatens populations with wholesale loss of life. Such was the case in Somalia in 1993.

Military action might also be justified in a case where, though the actual killing has not reached genocidal proportions, there is clear evidence of a concerted attempt at mass deportation of populations, combined with rape and other acts of terror. Such would be the case in Bosnia in 1992, and also in Kosovo in 1998 and 1999.

It is impossible to codify, with greater precision, where state repression crosses the line and descends into barbarism. All that can be said is that large-scale killing or ethnic cleansing must be a sustained, rather than occasional or infrequent state practice; that the populations at risk must be substantial; and that the attack on them must be genocidal in character, that is, aiming at their physical elimination or displacement from homelands or locations that have been theirs for a considerable period of time.

These threshold conditions need to be applied consistently. As has already been said, they rarely are. The inhabitants of Sarajevo were eventually rescued. The citizens of Grozny were left to their fate. If some groups under attack receive international protection and support, while others do not, then the legitimacy of humanitarian protection is undermined.

Another threshold principle sometimes advocated is that attacks on civilian populations must also constitute a threat to international peace and security as defined under Chapter VII of the UN Charter. Adding such a condition would make the claim that a humanitarian crisis only warrants international action when it spills over a national frontier, destabilizing an important region of the world. In actual fact, in the 1990s the Security Council was prepared to authorize coercive action in cases, like Somalia and Haiti, where the crisis in question was entirely confined to the borders of a particular state.

There are principled grounds to argue that the threshold conditions within a state should be assessed independently of the threat they pose to external peace and stability in the region. The core meaning of the threshold for coercive action should be that the events inside a particular country 'shock the conscience of mankind'. In practice, of course, internal repression or disintegration within states almost always spills over borders, destabilizing neighbourhoods and regions.

Neighbouring states risk being dragged in, as guerrillas and insurgents use their territory as bases and staging posts for military action, and the beleaguered or repressive state makes cross-border incursions to contain the threat. Yet these sequelae to humanitarian and human rights catastrophes are distinct from the atrocities themselves. The question of whether these atrocities reach a threshold requiring action can be assessed independently of whether they have a destabilizing effect on international peace and security.

Another question about thresholds is whether coercive military action might be warranted in cases of military coup, where a population, having clearly expressed its desire for a democratic regime, is denied its democratic rights by a military takeover. The Security Council did authorize a coercive military action in reaction to a military coup in Haiti. In Africa there have been unilateral military actions by states to overthrow despotic governments in neighbouring states. While the overthrow of a democratic government is a grave matter, requiring concerted international action, most states seem to believe that coercive military intervention should be restricted exclusively to those situations where massive loss of civilian life, genocide or forced population displacement is threatened or taking place.

Essentially, the emerging consensus on intervention is limited. Sovereignty rules, until the abuses of states rise to a genocidal standard. Only then can a military action be justified. No state is prepared to envisage a new customary rule of international law that would justify coercive military action to change governments, to take sides in civilian uprisings, or provide covert or overt support for armed insurgencies. Coercive military action should not be used to alter borders or revise the internal composition or character of states. Nor is it justified as a response to systematic, yet non-genocidal abuse of human rights, as for example in Burma.

While this may preserve appearances, the consensus is neither satisfactory nor clear. It is unsatisfactory, at least for human rights activists, because it leaves odious regimes—Iraq, Myanmar, North Korea—essentially immune from reprisals provided they keep their repression just below the type of genocidal standard described above. Equally unsatisfactory, from a human rights point of view, is the prohibition on taking sides in self-determination claims, or internecine struggles between a state and an insurgent party. As has been said earlier, taking sides is often the only way to bring civil wars to rapid conclusions, but such exercises in partiality are explicitly excluded in the present fragile consensus. In essence, the genocide standard raises as many problems as it solves.

## Precautionary Principles: the Return of 'Just War' Theory

Besides these two threshold principles, which define the level of horror at which intervention becomes necessary, certain crucial precautionary principles also govern any just use of force. According to long-standing moral ideas, encapsulated in the Western 'Just War' tradition, but not restricted only to Western traditions, the use of military force can only be justified if it is undertaken

1. as a last resort
2. with the right intention
3. for a just cause
4. with a reasonable hope of success
5. using means proportional to the ends in view, and
6. if ordered by proper authority.

## Last Resort

The responsibility to react—with military coercion—can only be justified when the responsibility to prevent has been fully discharged. International support for military action depends on evidence that every diplomatic avenue for a peaceful resolution of the humanitarian crisis has been explored. If the crisis in question involves a conflict between a state party and an insurgent minority, the parties must be induced to negotiate. Ceasefires, followed, if necessary, by the deployment of international peacekeepers and/or observers, are always a better option, if possible, than coercive military responses. The long-term solution for ethnic minority conflict or secessionist pressures within a state is always some kind of devolutionist, federationist compromise that guarantees the minority its linguistic, political and cultural autonomy, while preserving the integrity of the state in question.

The 'last resort' principle is self-evident, but it is not easy to apply. It is always possible to claim that peaceful alternatives are not exhausted. This is essentially what has been claimed in respect of the Rambouillet negotiations prior to the Kosovo war in 1999. Opponents of the war claim that the Allied side failed to make a good faith effort to avert hostilities, and that instead of genuine negotiations, they sought to impose a settlement, backed by threat of force. Those who defend the Kosovo military action reply with the claim that no genuine negotiation over Kosovo was possible with the leadership of Serbia. The 'last resort' principle, in other words, encounters the appeasement problem. When does negotiation in search of a solution to gross human rights abuses shade into appeasement? When is enough enough?

## Right Intention

The intentions underlying a coercive military action must be restricted to the humanitarian end in view. The purpose of military action must be to relieve or avert gross physical harm to non-combatant civilians. Any use of military force that aims at conquest of territory, alteration of borders, interference on one side or the other of a civil war is illegitimate. A humanitarian use of military force should preclude long-term occupation of territory. It should aim, instead, either at returning the territory to the state that claims sovereignty over it, or if that is not possible, to turn it over to an interim civilian administration, under UN auspices, whose purpose would be to prepare the territory for effective self-government, in some form that is negotiated with the sovereign state in question.

The self-limiting character of coercive military action for humanitarian purposes is supposed to distinguish this use of violence from traditional wars of conquest and aggression. Needless to say, this distinction may seem more persuasive to the force intervening than to the state that is the object of intervention.

## Just Cause

Coercive military action across a state border can only be justified if the aim is to save human life or prevent large-scale human suffering. The justice of the cause depends on strict observance of the threshold principles already discussed. Again, the Kosovo war indicates that there are significant difficulties assessing whether these thresholds have been met, and whether, even if they are not actually met, they are likely to be met in the future.

## Reasonable Hope of Success

Military action can only be justified if it stands a reasonable chance of success, i.e. preventing or stopping the atrocities that triggered the intervention in the first place. Furthermore, a military action for humanitarian purposes cannot be justified if in the process it triggers a larger conflict. A coercive military action by Western governments to save the citizens of Grozny would have risked a full-scale military conflict with Russia. Some victims cannot be rescued except at the unacceptable cost of a larger regional conflict, involving major military powers. In such cases, however painful the reality, coercive military action is no longer justified. This precautionary principle, necessary as it may be, has the inevitable effect of restricting coercive military action to those weak states that lack the firepower to fight back.

## Proportional Means

Just war theory holds that even just wars can be betrayed by the use of unjust or disproportionate means. Coercive military action to protect human populations must employ military strategies and tactics that do not violate humanitarian law and do not entail such substantial harm that they worsen the condition of the population they were intended to protect. All combat operations must comply with the provisions of the Geneva Conventions—especially non-combatant immunity and military necessity—and given that the aim of the operation is rescue and protection of civilians, they must be conducted in such a way as to avoid damage to non-military installations and objectives. Observance of the laws of war is especially necessary in conditions of modern media war, where real-time television news-gathering permits the transmission of mistakes and crimes to the audiences whose support is essential to the continuance of the operation.

The very visibility of modern media war—when coupled with the normative obligations to the Geneva Conventions—make for a very conservative combat strategy aimed at avoiding damaging mistakes. Moreover, since national survival is not at stake, countries committing troops to coercive humanitarian operations are reluctant to accept casualties. All of these pressures combine to make coercive military action slow and deliberate rather than violent and decisive.

Modern weapons technology—precision missiles, high-altitude bombers, stand-off weapons delivery platforms, ships and submarines—all serve to reduce the risks of military engagement, while transferring the mortal costs on the adversary.

## Proper Authority

The current international consensus is firmly in favour of retaining the UN Security Council as the proper authority of first and last resort. The question is whether it should be the *only* source of legitimate authority, whether the Security Council must in every case approve coercive interventions beforehand. The Kosovo operation bypassed explicit Security Council authorization, in order to avoid a Russian veto. An international commission on the Kosovo intervention concluded that it was both illegal and legitimate, beyond what international law actually permits and yet justified on grounds of moral necessity. Other interventions in the past—Tanzania in Uganda, India in Bangladesh, North Vietnam in Cambodia—also bypassed the Security Council. In retrospect at least, all three of these interventions have come to be regarded as legitimate, even though they were, in strict terms, illegal. The question is whether this gulf between legality and legitimacy can be bridged.

It is unlikely that the Security Council can ever fully unite legitimacy and legality. The Council itself is a relic of the victors' peace of 1945. It is unrepresentative of the developing world. Two of its members—Russia and China—are recurrently guilty of serious and sustained human rights abuses. Another of its members—the United States—reserves the right to observe some human rights standards but not others, and to exercise its power unilaterally in its own backyard. Reform of the Council—enlargement of the permanent membership to include Latin America, Africa and south Asia, together with a limitation on the veto power—is as necessary as it is politically unlikely. For the foreseeable future, the world will attempt to enforce human rights norms in the twenty-first century with an outdated institution inherited from the twentieth century.

The requirement of Security Council authorization by the permanent members is designed, of course, to eliminate the unilateral exercise of military force by any one of them. In actual fact, the veto has had no such effect. The Soviet Union 'intervened' in Hungary and Czechoslovakia. The Chinese intervened in Tibet. The Americans intervened in Grenada and Panama. Unilateral military action by great powers is an inescapable feature of a world of unequal states. These interventions will be both illegitimate and illegal, but the Security Council cannot stop them happening.

Moreover, there are cases where unilateral military action will be the only way to stop genocidal massacre. This was the case when the North Vietnamese invaded Cambodia and put the Khmer Rouge regime to flight. It was also the case when the Indian army drove out the Pakistanis from East Bengal in 1971. Some limited exercises in unilateral action may be essential to protect populations from massacre, in situations where coalitions cannot be assembled in time, or where a Security Council veto blocks concerted international action. While it is always desirable to seek Security Council approval, it is not always possible, and in the choice between sticking by the letter of international law and breaking it in order to rescue human beings in need, it seems evident that policy should pay more attention to what is strictly right than to what is strictly legal.

## Nation-building

Getting in—intervening to stop genocidal massacre—is difficult enough. The ensuing problem, once an intervention has occurred, is staying in long enough to stop its recurrence. Nation-building is the term that has come to be used for all longer-term attempts to create the institutional infrastructure necessary to prevent the return of genocidal human rights violations. Despite the fact that the N-word is used in entirely negative terms in American political and strategic debate, 'nation-building' interventions have become steadily more frequent in the 1990s. A huge exercise was mounted in Cambodia to create the conditions for a democratic election. The same was attempted, with less success, in Haiti. In East Timor, a UN transitional administration successfully prepared the territory for self-rule. A similar exercise is under way in Kosovo. In Bosnia, a nominally independent international state remains under international trusteeship until such time as the three major ethnic groups can live in peace. Unlike the empires of the past, these UN administrations are designed to serve and enhance the ideal of self-determination, rather than suppress it.

The moral legitimacy of intervention depends on keeping an occupying force from becoming an imperial oppressor. The precautionary principle of 'right intention' outlaws conquest, territorial acquisition or permanent occupation. Hence all interventions presume an exit strategy, based on a progressive handover of security, local administration and ultimate political control to locally elected representatives. Creating and enhancing local capacity, without at the same time confiscating it, is the balance international administrators have to strike, and it is not easy. Whether they want to or not, they become the chief source of power in a post-conflict situation, and local actors find it only too easy to slough off responsibility for peace-building to the internationals, rather than assuming it themselves. The most successful transitional administrations are ones that force local political actors to assume administrative and security responsibility as quickly as possible. This is not always possible. The legacy of bitterness in places like Kosovo and Bosnia is so intense that international administration has to remain in place, simply in order to protect minorities from the vengeance of the victorious majority. Controlling the culture of vengeance may take longer than the timeframe dictated by most modern exit strategies.

For all the talk of exit strategies, the fact is that once Western forces intervene, they are usually committed to patrol post-conflict societies for a long period of time. It takes time to create responsible political dialogue in shattered communities, still longer to create shared institutions of police and justice, and longest of all, to create the social trust between warring communities necessary for development and co-existence. The initiative for these developments has to come from the local people. Internationals can hold the ring—provide relatively impartial administration, some inward investment and aid, some basic security protection—but the work has to be done by the political elites who inherit the victorious intervention. Nation-building takes time, and it is not an exercise in social work. Its ultimate purpose is to do something long-term to the instability of state structures in 'bad neighbourhoods' around the world.

## Conclusion: the Elusiveness of Legitimacy

This survey of what has happened to the interaction between sovereignty and human rights since 1945, necessarily ends with sceptical conclusions. Human rights do not trump state sovereignty, as many human rights activists either believe or hope. The default settings, both of international law and state practice, are firmly set against intervention, except in the case of the most grievous genocidal massacres, and even here, we have failed more often than we have succeeded.

If we survey the interventions of the recent past, the story is decidedly mixed. In Bosnia, intervention prevented the creation of a Bosnian Serb state annexed to Serbia, but it did not prevent the deaths of more than 300,000 people and the expulsion of nearly a million from their homes. In Kosovo, intervention put a stop to an endemic civil war that, had intervention not occurred, might still be going on. In East Timor, intervention has managed to deliver self-determination to the people, but not before thousands were massacred for seeking their rights. In Iraq, Kurds remain under the protection of Allied air power, but they do not have the resources to become genuinely self-governing. In places like Cambodia and Haiti, where we intervened to guide societies towards democracy, power remains in the hands of discredited and unrepresentative elites. In other places like Angola, where the UN intervened with high hopes of moving the society out of a semi-permanent civil war, the UN has now withdrawn altogether. In still other places, ranging from Chechnya to Tibet, no intervention whatever took place, and the failure showed that universal principles still lack universal practices of consistent enforcement. Worst of all, 800,000 dead Rwandans bear silent witness to our incapacity—even when no insurmountable obstacle exists, either in state sovereignty or Security Council veto—to do the right thing when we have the capacity to do so. The most that can be said about the emerging practice of intervention is that at its best it prevents the very worst from happening. At its worst, it compromises and betrays the very values it purports to defend. More generally, this survey seems to demonstrate something important about legitimacy itself. The use of military violence in defence of human rights will never have anything more than conditional legitimacy, even when the cause is just and the authority right.

# Introduction to Peter Singer

## John Broome

Peter Singer is probably the world's best-known living philosopher. This is not just because he is an excellent philosopher. Of course, he is that, and his work includes a great deal of important, perceptive, tightly argued, analytical writing about many of the difficult theoretical problems of moral philosophy. This part of his work engages with the concerns of professional philosophers. It has contributed to and stimulated a great deal of intellectual debate within the philosophy departments of universities. However, I am not thinking of Singer's recognition within the profession of philosophy, but of his recognition amongst the public at large. More ordinary people around the world know of Singer's work than any other philosopher's.

It is not Singer's analytical, theoretical writing that has gained him this extensive recognition. That comes from his other achievement, which is to make his philosophy practical. He does not engage only with the concerns of philosophers, but also with the crucial, practical concerns of ordinary people when they wonder how they should live their lives. The range and quantity of Singer's writing is vast. It includes dozens of analytical articles in academic journals. But as well as those, it includes books of practical philosophy that have influenced millions—the best known are *Animal Liberation* (1975) and *Practical Ethics* (1979), each of which has had two editions and translations in any number of languages—and it also includes a multitude of articles in newspapers and magazines. As a special expression of gratitude from an academic philosopher, I must add that in the midst of all this writing, Singer has even found time to edit some truly excellent anthologies—collections of other people's writings—in ethics. His collection *A Companion to Ethics* (1991) is perhaps the most useful book that a student, and indeed a professor, of moral philosophy can own.

Singer makes his philosophy practical, and it is so widely known because it goes to the heart of what people care about. For the very same reason, it arouses passion and controversy. Singer is famous and controversial for two of his philosophical views amongst others. One is his championing of the moral status of animals. Some people find this offensive, and think it is somehow degrading to human beings. But those people are making a mistake. Singer wishes to raise the moral status we accord to animals. This is quite different from lowering the moral status we accord to human beings, and it is a mistake to confuse the two.

A second famous and controversial view of Singer's is his uncompromising utilitarianism. Utilitarianism in moral philosophy is the view that morality should be aimed at promoting wellbeing. Singer's morality is aimed at promoting the wellbeing of people and of animals. This has led him to challenge some traditional moral notions that he believes are damaging to wellbeing. Amongst them is the idea of the sanctity of human life.

Utilitarians traditionally do not give much importance to the idea of rights. At best, they think them derivative. Assigning particular rights to people may be a way to promote wellbeing, and when it is, utilitarians favour doing it. But they see no inherent value in rights. Singer himself has expressed some scepticism about rights, which gives a special interest to his Amnesty Lecture on Human Rights.

The lecture starts with a frightening reminder of human beings' natural propensity for genocide, and how easily it can be explained by natural selection. Singer doubts this propensity can be controlled by the progress of education and civilization, so our only recourse is to control it by law. Law implies rights, of course. But the rights Singer recommends are intended to promote people's wellbeing—specifically, to prevent the dreadful harm and suffering caused by genocide.

Law must be enforced, which means that the United Nations must on occasions be entitled to intervene in the internal affairs of a country, to prevent genocide. Singer considers what the framework of international law should be, in order to legitimate intervention on appropriate occasions. He argues that a government has a full claim to sovereignty only if it is democratic, so intervention in an undemocratic country may be justified. He concludes with a vision of a democratic international order that is able to prevent genocide in the future.

# 3

# How Can We Prevent Crimes Against Humanity?

### Peter Singer

## Introduction

I dedicate this lecture to my grandparents. My father's parents, Albert and Philippine Singer, were deported from Vienna in 1941 and sent to Poland, to the Jewish ghetto in Lodz. I do not know what happened to them there. They may have died of starvation or disease. If they did not, they would, like most of the other elderly people in the ghetto, have been taken to Chelmno and murdered by carbon monoxide poisoning in the back of a truck. My mother's parents, David and Amalie Oppenheim, were sent from Vienna to Theresienstadt, or Terezin, in what is now the Czech Republic. There David soon succumbed from illness and malnutrition. Amalie survived and, after long suffering, was reunited with her children in Australia, and was able to get to know her grandchildren.

If the work of Amnesty International can to any degree reduce the likelihood that others will suffer a similar fate, then I am pleased and proud to give my support to that organization.

About David Oppenheim, I want to say just a little more. By profession a teacher of Greek and Latin language and literature, his real vocation was to understand human beings. To that end he worked first with Sigmund Freud and then with Alfred Adler, and wrote several articles and a book, *Dichtung und Menschenkenntnis* [Fiction and the Understanding of

Humanity] in which he drew on his reading of literary works to enhance our understanding of why people behave as they do. In one sense, therefore, in this lecture I will not only be asking how we can prevent others suffering his fate, I will also be continuing his work. Yet my grandfather's scholarship did not enable him to grasp fully the nature of Nazism when, in 1938 or 1939, he and Amalie could have followed their children to Australia. Whether, with all of our improved understanding of human nature, we can do better today in foreseeing—and most importantly, preventing—genocide and other atrocities is still an open question, and is the subject of this lecture.

## Human Wrongs

I begin, in the true manner of a preacher, with a text from the Bible, though perhaps not one of those that is most commonly quoted. It is from the Book of Numbers. An earlier chapter of that book has told how some Israelite men have been succumbing to the charms of women of a neighbouring tribe, the Midianites. Worse still, it seems that these Midianite women were so adept at religious pillow-talk that they succeeded in persuading their Israelite lovers to follow the Midianite religion. Now here is the text:

And the LORD spake unto Moses, saying, Avenge the children of Israel of the Midianites . . . And Moses spake unto the people, saying, Arm some of yourselves unto the war, and let them go against the Midianites, and avenge the LORD of Midian. Of every tribe a thousand, throughout all the tribes of Israel, shall ye send to the war. So there were delivered out of the thousands of Israel, a thousand of every tribe, twelve thousand armed for war . . . And they warred against the Midianites, as the LORD commanded

Moses; and they slew all the males . . . And the children of Israel took all the women of Midian captives, and their little ones, and took the spoil of all their cattle, and all their flocks, and all their goods. And they burnt all their cities wherein they dwelt, and all their goodly castles, with fire. And they took all the spoil, and all the prey, both of men and of beasts. And they brought the captives, and the prey, and the spoil, unto Moses, and Eleazar the priest, and unto the congregation of the children of Israel, unto the camp at the plains of Moab, which are by Jordan near Jericho. And Moses, and Eleazar the priest, and all the princes of the congregation, went forth to meet them without the camp. And Moses was wroth with the officers of the host, with the captains over thousands, and captains over hundreds, which came from the battle. And Moses said unto them, Have ye saved all the women alive? Behold, these caused the children of Israel . . . to commit trespass against the LORD . . . and there was a plague among the congregation of the LORD. Now therefore kill every male among the little ones, and kill every woman that hath known man by lying with him. But all the women children, that have not known a man by lying with him, keep alive for yourselves.[1]

For much of the past century it has been widely believed that people commit crimes of violence because they are poor, ignorant, oppressed, abused or exploited; or if none of these adjectives apply to them at the time they commit these crimes, then one or more of them must have applied to them at a formative period of their individual psyche, such as their childhood. This was supposed to be true not only of individual crimes, but also of those who take part in crimes on a larger scale. It follows that trying to prevent crimes by more effective policing is treating the symptoms and not the causes. To get at the roots of the problem we must end injustice and exploitation, improve and reform education so that it teaches the importance of respecting our fellow human beings, irrespective of race, religion or politics, prevent the corruption of the democratic process by the arms manufacturers and others who profit from war or genocide, and ensure that no child is brought up in poverty or by abusive parents.

We would, presumably, all like to end injustice and exploitation, and see that no child lives in poverty or is abused. Nor would I disagree with those who would like to see our schools do whatever they can to encourage an attitude of respect for others. We ought to do this, if we can, for its own sake. But will it be enough to put an end to violence? I do not think so, and the text that I have quoted above suggests why it will not.

First, the text shows that the Holocaust that engulfed my grandparents was new only in that modern technology and communications enabled the Nazis to murder far more people in a relatively brief period of time than had ever happened before. Even within the Bible, there is nothing unique about the act of genocide perpetrated against the Midianites by the Israelites, supposedly at God's behest—there are passages in the Books of Deuteronomy, the first Book of Samuel, the Book of Joshua, and the Book of Ezekiel describing other slaughters, no less ruthless.[2] There is, it is true, a terrible irony in reading today, in a text sacred to religious Jews, of genocide carried out by Jews, but that is of no relevance to my argument. I could have used many other ancient examples of genocide. There is, for example, an oft-quoted passage in Thucydides describing how the Athenians, those noble people whose philosophical discussions are still read with great admiration today, refused to allow the inhabitants of Melos to be neutral in the war between Athens and Sparta. When the Melians would not submit to Athenian rule, the

Athenians conquered them, killed all the men and sold all the women and children into slavery.[3]

Second, the text very clearly suggests that the Israeli motivation for wiping out the Midianites had nothing to do with their own poverty, or with any injustice they had suffered at the hands of the people they attacked. In fact the Midianites appear to have committed no crime at all except consenting to sexual relations—to which, presumably, the Israelite men also consented—and having a religion that was, to at least some Israelites, more attractive than that followed by Moses.

Third, and most significantly for my argument, the text shows that if the Lord had commanded Moses to do everything possible to maximize the number of genetic descendants that the Israelite males leave and to minimize the number that their rivals leave, and if he had given Moses a twenty-first century text in genetics so that he would know what he needed to do in order to achieve that goal, then Moses might have acted exactly as he is portrayed as doing in the Book of Numbers. Since women can have only a limited number of children, and the Israelite men are capable of providing them with all the sperm they need for that purpose, Midianite males are potential competitors and of no genetic use to the Israelis. So Moses ruthlessly eliminates them, mature men and children alike. He even orders his soldiers to kill all the Midianite women who are not virgins, thus ensuring that there are no pregnant women who might carry male Midianite children. This is, admittedly, not the only possible strategy—he might have waited to see which of these women were pregnant, killed their children later, and then dealt with them as he does with the virgins. But for someone in a hurry, the command was an effective way of ensuring that no

Midianite males could survive. Finally, Moses allows his troops to keep the young Midianite females for themselves, presumably to use them, when they are old enough, as concubines or wives, thus increasing the number of their own descendants.

Here we have an example of genocide in which the genetic advantage to the perpetrators is as clear as anything can be. What does this mean for us? We are all the descendants of beings who succeeded in leaving their genes in subsequent generations. Other past human beings did not. The prospects of success in leaving one's genes in subsequent generations can be enhanced in many different ways. One is by killing rival groups with whom one does not share any genes. Don't be misled by the thought that the killing of some humans by others cannot be good for the species. Species come in and out of existence too slowly to be the dominant unit of evolution. It is better to think of evolution as a competition between individuals, and perhaps between small, genetically related groups, than between species.

That, presumably, is why war and massacre have been such a central part of human history, and for that matter, of the much longer period of human pre-history. As Lawrence Keeley has shown in *War before Civilization* (1996), war has been a regular part of the existence of the overwhelming majority of human cultures, and male prisoners were usually not taken, although women and children sometimes were. Massacres of entire groups—men, women and children— seem not to have been unusual. The mass graves of Europe— burial pits containing people of all ages who have met violent deaths—go back at least 7,000 years, to the neolithic grave at Talheim, in Germany. At Crow Creek, in South Dakota, more than a century before Columbus sailed for America, 500 men, women and children were scalped and mutilated before being thrown into a ditch. It is a sobering thought that in many tribal societies, despite the absence of machine guns and high explosives, the percentage of the population killed annually in warfare far exceeds that of any modern society, including Germany and Russia in the twentieth centuries.[4]

Nor is killing members of one's own species something only humans do. Chimpanzees, who together with bonobos are our closest nonhuman relatives, go on raiding parties across the borders of their territory in which they deliberately—if you read a description of how they do it, you will be forced to agree that there is no other word for it—seek out and kill vulnerable chimpanzees, usually males, from another group. In one instance the chimpanzees that Jane Goodall was observing at Gombe completely wiped out, over a three-year period, a neighbouring group, killing at least four adult and adolescent males and one adult female, driving away all the other adults, and 'keeping alive for themselves', if I may here use the biblical expression, the two young daughters of the adult female they had killed. Similar behaviour has been observed in other chimpanzee groups, widely dispersed across Africa.[5]

Are we, then, all potential perpetrators of genocide? That goes too far. There are many ways in which one can do better than others in leaving one's genes in later generations. One of them is being particularly good at forming mutually beneficial, co-operative relationships.[6] The circumstances in which this is likely to be advantageous are much more common than the circumstances in which genocide is likely to be advantageous. Thus we would be more justified in saying that we are all potential co-operators than to say that we are all potential perpetrators of genocide. But that a significant number of human males have the potential to be perpetrators of genocide is—in view of the evidence from ethology, anthropology and history—highly plausible. It is also plausible to believe that although this potential may be more likely to be acted upon in the presence of poverty, injustice, exploitation or a lack of education, it may also be acted upon without these factors, and hence it is not something that will be overcome by their elimination.

If we bring our gaze forward from biblical times to the century that has just ended, we find terrible confirmation for that bleak statement. In 1915–17 Turks massacred perhaps 1.5 million Armenians; in the 1930s Stalin ordered the deaths of somewhere between 7 and 10 million people; the Nazi Holocaust has already been mentioned; it was followed by the killings in Cambodia, in Rwanda, and as the century neared its end, in Bosnia, Kosovo and East Timor. Some of these killings were perpetrated by people who were poor and uneducated, but others were not. Germany in the 1920s was among the most highly educated nations in the world. The peoples of the former Yugoslavia were also by no means uneducated, and the country had, since 1918—with the exception of the war years in Croatia—been striving to educate its citizens to think of themselves as Yugoslavs, not as Croats, Serbs, Muslims or other nationalities. Timothy Garton Ash asks, in his *History of the Present* (1999), what we have learnt from the events during the last decade of the twentieth century in that region. He answers: 'We have learned that human nature has not changed. That Europe at the end of the twentieth century is quite as capable of barbarism as it was in the Holocaust of mid-century.'[7] He might have also said: and for millennia before that, and not only in Europe.

So although overcoming poverty, eliminating injustice and improving education may help to make genocide less likely, we cannot rely on them to prevent it. What else can be done? Just as, at the domestic level, the last line of defence against individual crimes of murder, rape and assault is law enforcement, so too the last line of defence against genocide and similar crimes must be law enforcement, at a global level.

## The Development of International Criminal Law

Can international law reduce, if not entirely prevent, genocide and mass murder? The charter of the International Military Tribunal set up by the Allies to try the leading Nazi war criminals at Nuremberg gave it jurisdiction over three kinds of crimes: crimes against peace, war crimes, and crimes against humanity. In promulgating this charter, the Allies declared it a 'crime against peace' to plan, prepare or initiate a war of aggression; a 'war crime' to violate the 'laws or customs of war', by murdering, ill-treating or deporting either civilians or prisoners of war; and a 'crime against humanity' to murder, exterminate, enslave or deport any civilian population, or to persecute them on political, racial or religious grounds. These acts, the charter of the Tribunal stated, are crimes 'whether or not in violation of the domestic law of the country where perpetrated'.[8]

Though the Allies were able to draw on earlier precedents and conventions to justify their claim that crimes against humanity were already recognized in international law, the Nuremberg Tribunal gave new impetus to the idea that certain acts are so horrendous that they are crimes, no matter what the prevailing law at the time in the country in which they are perpetrated. Subsequently the United Nations General Assembly asked the International Law Commission to formulate principles of international law relating to crimes such as those dealt with by the Nuremberg Tribunal. In 1954, the International Law Commission recommended that there should be international criminal responsibility for crimes against humanity committed at the instigation or the toleration of state authorities. The 1984 Convention against Torture, signed by 110 states, accepted this principle. That Convention was central to the House of Lords decision on whether the United Kingdom government could extradite Senator Auguste Pinochet to Spain, to be tried there for crimes he was alleged to have committed in Chile. Chile had ratified the Convention against Torture, and this was sufficient for Lord Browne-Wilkinson and other law lords to find that Pinochet could be extradited to Spain.[9] But that case also raised the question of what is called 'universal jurisdiction', that is, the right of any country to try a person who has committed crimes against humanity, irrespective of whether the country in which the crime was committed is a signatory to a convention that provides for international criminal responsibility in respect of that crime. This was a crucial issue in the legal proceedings in Britain on whether Senator Auguste Pinochet should be extradited to Spain for crimes he committed in Chile.

At the time of the Pinochet hearing, Amnesty International made a strong case that international law recognizes universal jurisdiction for crimes of humanity.[10] A precedent for this view is the decision of the Supreme Court of Israel in *Attorney General of Israel v. Eichmann.*[11] Eichmann was in charge of the implementation of the murder of European Jews under Nazi rule, serving under Heydrich and Himmler.

He was kidnapped in Argentina and flown to Israel, where he was tried and subsequently executed. Though the method by which he was brought to Israel was of doubtful legality, there has been general acceptance that Israel had the right to assert jurisdiction over offences committed in Germany. Moreover, the Supreme Court of Israel claimed this jurisdiction, not on the grounds that Israel was the legal representative of Eichmann's victims, but on the ground of universal jurisdiction over crimes against humanity. Eichmann's crimes against non-Jewish Gypsies, Poles and others were thus also germane to the proceedings in Israel.[12]

In the Pinochet case, Lord Phillips of Worth Matravers discussed the question of universal jurisdiction, and concluded:

I believe that it is still an open question whether international law recognises universal jurisdiction in respect of international crimes—that is the right, under international law, of the courts of any state to prosecute for such crimes wherever they occur. In relation to war crimes, such a jurisdiction has been asserted by the State of Israel, notably in the prosecution of Adolf Eichmann, but this assertion of jurisdiction does not reflect any general state practice in relation to international crimes. Rather, states have tended to agree, or to attempt to agree, on the creation of international tribunals to try international crimes. They have however, on occasion, agreed by conventions, that their national courts should enjoy jurisdiction to prosecute for a particular category of international crime wherever occurring.[13]

The alternative to universal jurisdiction mentioned by Lord Phillips is perhaps, in the long term, a better way to go. Like the Nuremberg Tribunal, these more recent international tribunals have arisen in the wake of tragic events: the wars that followed the break-up of the former Yugoslavia, the massacre of Hutus in Rwanda, the Serbian attacks on the

Albanian inhabitants of Kosovo, and the killings in East Timor by militia supported by the Indonesian armed forces. By strengthening the resolve of all decent people not to allow such tragedies to continue, they are pushing us toward a global system of criminal justice for such crimes. For war criminals arrested in Bosnia by NATO troops and taken to trial by the International Tribunal in The Hague, there now is 'one world' in the sense that there is no place to escape the jurisdiction of the tribunals set up to try them.[14] Those tribunals were, however, one-off arrangements, specially set up to try particular crimes. To make this a permanent feature of international law, representatives of 160 states met in Rome in 1998 and agreed, by an overwhelming majority, to set up an International Criminal Court (ICC), to be associated with the United Nations and situated in The Hague. The Court will have a prosecutor who can bring charges of genocide, crimes against humanity, and war crimes against individuals, irrespective of their nationality or the consent of the state in which the crime occurred. Thus crimes internal to a country will fall under international law. This makes the International Criminal Court quite different from the under-used International Court of Justice (ICJ), which deals only with states, not with individuals, and can issue binding judgements only when all parties have accepted its jurisdiction. An international statute establishing the International Criminal Court has, at the time of writing, been signed by 139 states, and ratified by 32.[15] The Court came into existence after the statute had been ratified by 60 states. Thus we have become a global community that has at least some global criminal law, with no national boundaries standing in the way of its jurisdiction.

## Criteria for Humanitarian Intervention

Punishing the criminals after an atrocity has occurred is something that most people would support, if only because it will, hopefully, put those contemplating committing such crimes on notice that they will have no refuge from justice. Preventing the crimes taking place, however, is much better. It would seem, then, that if punishment can be justified, so can intervention to stop the crime. But under what circumstances should humanitarian intervention take place?

For philosophers to take up this question is not a new idea. Kant wrote a 'philosophical sketch' entitled *Perpetual Peace*, in which he argued that no state should, by force, interfere with the constitution or government of another state. He also thought that states preparing for war should seek the opinions of philosophers on the possibility of peace.[16] John Stuart Mill said that few questions are more in need of attention from philosophers than the issue of when a state that is not itself under attack may go to war. He thought that philosophers should seek to establish 'some rule or criterion whereby the justifiableness of intervening in the affairs of other countries, and (what is sometimes fully as questionable) the justifiableness of refraining from intervention, may be brought to a definite and rational test.'[17]

What rule or criterion would satisfy Mill's 'definite and rational test' of when intervention is justified and when it is not? One phrase often heard in this context is that used by Lassa Oppenheim in the following passage from his influential treatise on international law, first published in 1905:

There is general agreement that, by virtue of its personal and territorial supremacy, a State can treat its own nationals according to discretion. But there is a substantial body of opinion and practice in support of the view that there are limits to that discretion; when a state renders itself guilty of cruelties against and persecution of its nationals in such a way as to deny their fundamental rights *and to shock the conscience of mankind*, intervention in the interests of humanity is legally permissible.[18] [emphasis added]

Michael Walzer has taken up this criterion in the context of intervention. In *Just and Unjust Wars*, he wrote:

Humanitarian intervention is justified when it is a response (with reasonable expectations of success) to acts 'that shock the moral conscience of mankind'. The old-fashioned language seems to me exactly right . . . The reference is to the moral convictions of ordinary men and women, acquired in the course of their everyday activities. And given that one can make a persuasive argument in terms of those convictions, I don't think that there is any moral reason to adopt that posture of passivity that might be called waiting for the UN (waiting for the universal state, waiting for the messiah . . .).[19]

Those words date from 1977; though the intervening years have not seen the arrival of the Messiah, the UN has shown that it can act, even if its actions are open to serious criticism and have not always been as effective as one would fervently wish.[20] Walzer has continued to support the 'shock the conscience' criterion, and has pointed out that in an age in which 'the camera crews arrive faster than rigor mortis' and we are all instant spectators of every atrocity, the acts that do shock the conscience of humankind are more shocking than they used to be, because we are so intimately linked to them.[21] Nevertheless, Walzer insists on retaining a strong presumption against intervention. He specifically rejects the idea that the violation of human rights is in itself a sufficient justification for intervention, or that it is legitimate to intervene for the sake of democracy.[22] Sometimes he argues for the strong presumption against intervention in terms of the importance of protecting the sovereignty of states in which people can live a communal life, and struggle for freedom in their own way, within their own communal structures.[23] At other times his argument is more pragmatic: ever since Roman times, he reminds us, imperial powers have sought to expand their empires by intervening in civil wars. Intervention can too easily become an excuse for annexation, in one form or another. Although Walzer does find some examples of justified intervention—by India in what was then East Pakistan, now Bangladesh, in 1971; by Tanzania in 1979 against the regime of Idi Amin in Uganda; and by the Vietnamese in Cambodia in the same year—he thinks that, in general, it is best if people 'should be allowed to work out their difficulties without imperial assistance, among themselves'.[24]

The problem with Walzer's appeal to the 'conscience of mankind' criterion is that this conscience has, at various times and places, been shocked by such things as homosexuality, atheism and mixed bathing. We know that when international lawyers talk of acts that shock the conscience of humankind, they don't mean things like *that*, but how can we more precisely specify what they do mean? United Nations Secretary-General Kofi Annan has suggested that intervention is justified 'when death and suffering are being inflicted on large numbers of people, and when the state nominally in charge is unable or unwilling to stop it'. He defends this view by saying that the aim of the United Nations Charter is 'to protect individual human beings, not to protect those who abuse them'.[25]

Annan's criterion is more specific than 'shocking the conscience of mankind', and for that reason is to be preferred to it. In order to make it more precise still, however, the reference to 'suffering' should be replaced by an enumeration of more specific harms. This is done in various international legal documents, including the 1948 Convention on the Prevention and Punishment of the Crime of Genocide, which is followed by the 1998 Rome Statute of the International Criminal Court. Article 2 of the Convention defines the crime of genocide as follows:

. . . genocide means any of the following acts committed with intent to destroy, in whole or in part, a national, ethnical, racial or religious group, as such:

(a) Killing members of the group;
(b) Causing serious bodily or mental harm to members of the group;
(c) Deliberately inflicting on the group conditions of life calculated to bring about its physical destruction in whole or in part;
(d) Imposing measures intended to prevent births within the group;
(e) Forcibly transferring children of the group to another group.[26]

While I have no doubt that all of these acts should count as crimes, and those who carry them out should be prosecuted and charged whenever possible, it is possible to draw distinctions between them. Since military intervention risks widespread casualties, the imposition of measures intended to prevent births within a group, or the forcible transfer of children from one group to another, is arguably insufficient in itself to justify military intervention. Of course, such measures will generally cause serious mental harm to members of the group, thus bringing the situation under one of the other clauses of the definition of genocide, and opening the way for the possible justification of intervention.

We can now draw on Walzer and Annan's criteria, as well as the first three elements of the widely accepted definition of genocide, to say:

*Humanitarian intervention is justified when it is a response (with reasonable expectations of success) to acts that kill or inflict serious bodily or mental harm on large numbers of people, or deliberately inflict on them conditions of life calculated to bring about their physical destruction, and when the state nominally in charge is unable or unwilling to stop it.*

Admittedly, there is still a large element of imprecision in this definition. How many people is a 'large number'? How serious does the bodily or mental harm have to be? Who will decide when conditions of life that bring about the physical destruction of large numbers of people have been deliberately inflicted upon them? Beyond these questions, we could also ask: is it only things done to human beings that count? Might we one day see the destruction of a unique ecosystem, bringing with it the extinction of many species that exist nowhere else, as grounds for intervention?

These questions are difficult, but perhaps, in trying to make the test for intervention more precise, we have come as far as we can for the moment. Instead let us switch our attention to whether it is possible to establish a procedure to decide when the test has been satisfied. We can begin with the United Nations, the only global body that could conceivably develop an authoritative framework for specifying when intervention is justifiable.

## The Authority of the United Nations

In a speech to the United Nations General Assembly in September 1999, Secretary-General Kofi Annan referred to the genocide in Rwanda as indicative of the consequences of inaction, and to the intervention in Kosovo as an example of action taken by 'a regional organization [NATO] without a United Nations mandate'. He then went on to pose a dilemma:

To those for whom the greatest threat to the future of international order is the use of force in the absence of a Security Council mandate, one might ask—not in the context of Kosovo—but in the context of Rwanda: If, in those dark days and hours leading up to the genocide, a coalition of States had been prepared to act in defence of the Tutsi population, but did not receive prompt Council authorization, should such a coalition have stood aside and allowed the horror to unfold?

To those for whom the Kosovo action heralded a new era when States and groups of States can take military action outside the established mechanisms for enforcing international law, one might ask: Is there not a danger of such interventions undermining the imperfect, yet resilient, security system created after the Second World War, and of setting dangerous precedents for future interventions without a clear criterion to decide who might invoke these precedents, and in what circumstances?[27]

Annan made his own position clear, saying that state sovereignty is being redefined by the forces of globalization and international co-operation: 'The State is now widely understood to be the servant of its people, and not vice versa.' As we have seen, he reads the United Nations Charter as authorizing intervention to protect individual human beings, rather than those who abuse them. In saying this, Annan may have in

mind Article 55 (c) of the Charter, which refers to the promotion of 'universal respect for, and observance of, human rights
and fundamental freedoms for all', and Article 56, which reads:
'All members pledge themselves to take joint and separate
action in co-operation with the Organization for the
achievement of the purposes set forth in Article 55.' The
problem with interpreting these Articles as justifying humanitarian intervention to protect individual human beings whose
rights are being violated within a sovereign state, however, is
that the same Charter states, in Article 2 (7):

Nothing contained in the present Charter shall authorize the
United Nations to intervene in matters which are essentially within
the domestic jurisdiction of any state or shall require the Members
to submit such matters to settlement under the present Charter; but
this principle shall not prejudice the application of enforcement
measures under Chapter VII.

Chapter VII does not refer to human rights, but only to
'threats to the peace, breaches of the peace, and acts of aggression'. If we take this at face value, it would seem that the
United Nations cannot set up procedures to authorize
humanitarian intervention, because in doing so, it would be
violating its own Charter.

How can these different sections of the Charter be rec-
onciled? The Charter places two sets of obligations on its
members: to respect human rights, and not to interfere in the
internal matters of another state. As Brad Roth puts it: 'the
Organization and its Members are pledged to observe and
promote, but bound not to impose, wholesome internal
practices.'[28] The 'Declaration on Principles of International
Law Concerning Friendly Relations and Co-operation
among States in Accordance with the Charter of the United

Nations', adopted by the General Assembly in 1970 on the 25th anniversary of the United Nations, gives some support to this view. This Declaration elaborates on Article 2 (7) of the Charter as follows:

armed intervention and all other forms of interference or attempted threats against the personality of the State or against its political, economic and cultural elements, are in violation of international law . . . Every state has an inalienable right to choose its political, economic, social and cultural systems, without interference in any form by another state . . .[29]

So does humanitarian intervention violate the UN Charter's acceptance of the principle of non-intervention in the domestic affairs of another sovereign state? We could reconcile the Charter with humanitarian intervention if we could defend at least one of the following claims:

1. That the violation of human rights, even in one country, is itself a threat to international peace.
2. That the existence of tyranny itself constitutes a threat to international peace.
3. That the rights of domestic jurisdiction retained by the states in Article 2 (7) do not extend to committing crimes against humanity, nor to allowing them to be committed within one's domestic jurisdiction.

I shall discuss these claims in order.

## 1. The violation of human rights is itself a threat to international peace.

The first of these arguments is one that Annan himself has put forward. In referring to the United Nations Charter in his September 1999 speech, he said:

The sovereign States who drafted the Charter over half a century ago were dedicated to peace, but experienced in war. They knew the terror of conflict, but knew equally that there are times when the use of force may be legitimate in the pursuit of peace. That is why the Charter's own words declare that 'armed force shall not be used, save in the common interest'. But what is that common interest? Who shall define it? Who will defend it? Under whose authority? And with what means of intervention? These are the monumental questions facing us as we enter the new century.

Taking these remarks in their context, Annan can be read as suggesting that the common interest should be defined so as to include an interest in preventing a tyrant from violating the rights of the citizens of the country over which he rules, even if the tyrant poses no threat to other states. Though this may seem far-fetched, Annan could have pointed to several decisions of the Security Council that carry the same implication. With regard to Iraq, the Security Council resolved in 1991 that the repression of the civilian population, including that in Kurdish-populated areas, had consequences that were a threat to international peace and security. Since the Council mentioned the flow of refugees to other states, it is arguable that this repression did have some consequences outside the borders of Iraq.[30] In authorizing intervention in Somalia, however, the Council simply determined that 'the magnitude of the human tragedy caused by the conflict in Somalia, further exacerbated by the obstacles being created to the distribution of humanitarian assistance, constitutes a threat to international peace and security.'[31] No further explanation was offered, and since the conflict was purely a civil one, it is not easy to guess how international peace would be threatened if the Somalians were simply left to starve, terrible as that might be. Similarly, in Haiti the overthrow of the democratically elected president Jean-Bertrand Aristide was seen as a threat to 'international peace and security in the region' and thus as justifying the use of Chapter VII powers.[32]

Given the human tragedies in Iraq, Somalia and Haiti that the Security Council was trying to overcome, it is understandable that it should have been willing to stretch the language of its Charter to breaking point, and it might seem that a consequentialist ethic would lead us to support whatever stratagems offer the best prospect of preventing such tragedies. Taking a long-term view, however, a consequentialist cannot be content with the use of such blatant fictions as the idea that the overthrow of the president of Haiti is a threat to international peace. Once that is accepted, anything goes, and effectively the Security Council has an unconstrained mandate to interfere wherever it sees fit. That may not be the best outcome.

## 2. Democracies are the best guardians of peace.

A second strategy would be to invoke the argument that no war has ever occurred between two democratic states.[33] That thesis is controversial, and much depends on the definitions of 'war' and 'democracy'. If there has not yet been a counterexample, there no doubt will be one eventually. But the existence of one or two counter-examples does not refute a more cautiously stated version of the thesis, namely that democratic states are less likely to go to war with one another than are states that are not democracies. If this is the case, then Article 2 (7) no longer stands in the way of intervention for the sake of establishing or restoring democracy, since such interventions do reduce the general 'threat to the peace' posed by non-democratic regimes. But should so vague and indefinite a threat to peace be sufficient reason for military intervention? If not, we are again using a pretext to cover intervention that is really motivated by another purpose altogether.

## 3. The rights of domestic jurisdiction retained by the states in Article 2 (7) do not extend to committing crimes against humanity, nor to allowing them to be committed.

The third strategy draws on the body of international law which, as we have already seen when discussing the Eichmann and Pinochet cases, holds that there is universal jurisdiction over those who commit crimes against humanity. In granting domestic jurisdiction to the states the United Nations Charter cannot have intended, so this argument runs, to set aside this doctrine of customary international law.

The definition of a 'crime against humanity' is less well settled than the definition of genocide, but the Rome Statute of the International Criminal Court uses the following definition:

'crime against humanity' means any of the following acts when committed as part of a widespread or systematic attack directed against any civilian population, with knowledge of the attack:

(a) Murder;
(b) Extermination;
(c) Enslavement;
(d) Deportation or forcible transfer of population;
(e) Imprisonment or other severe deprivation of physical liberty in violation of fundamental rules of international law;
(f) Torture;
(g) Rape, sexual slavery, enforced prostitution, forced pregnancy, enforced sterilization, or any other form of sexual violence of comparable gravity;
(h) Persecution against any identifiable group or collectivity on

political, racial, national, ethnic, cultural, religious, gender as defined in paragraph 3, or other grounds that are universally recognized as impermissible under international law, in connection with any act referred to in this paragraph or any crime within the jurisdiction of the Court;

(i) Enforced disappearance of persons;

(j) The crime of apartheid;

(k) Other inhumane acts of a similar character intentionally causing great suffering, or serious injury to body or to mental or physical health.[34]

The problem with interpreting the acceptance of domestic sovereignty in the United Nations Charter as limited by international law recognizing such acts as crimes, is that the report of the International Law Commission that there should be international criminal responsibility for crimes against humanity was not made until 1954, long after the Charter had been written and accepted by the original member states of the United Nations. Thus the Charter could well have been formulated and signed in the absence of any such belief. This argument is inconclusive, for there is some evidence for the idea that the doctrine was part of customary international law prior to the Nuremberg Tribunal.

This is the most plausible and promising of the three strategies so far considered. It does not rely on a fiction, or even on an unproven theory about the link between democracy and peace. Moreover it has built-in limits to the grounds on which intervention may take place. It may therefore be what we need. Nevertheless, before settling on it as the best justification for humanitarian intervention, I want to consider a fourth, less obvious but more far-reaching strategy for reconciling humanitarian intervention with the principle of nonintervention in the domestic affairs of another sovereign state.

This fourth strategy questions the traditional view of what it takes to constitute a sovereign state, and hence needs a more extended discussion.

## Democracy and Legitimacy

In international law, the standard view has long been that the recognition of a government as legitimate has nothing to do with how that government came to power, or for that matter with how it governs. 'The Law of Nations prescribes no rules as regards the kind of head a State may have', wrote Lassa Oppenheim in his influential 1905 text on international law, and he added that every state is 'naturally' free to adopt any constitution, 'according to its discretion'.[35] The sole test is whether it is in effective control of the territory. As Brad Roth puts it:

In such a conception, the international system regards ruling apparatuses as self-sufficient sources of authority—or rather deems their authority to derive from their characteristic ability to secure the acquiescence of their populaces, by whatever means . . . a government is recognized simply because its existence is a fact of life.[36]

There is, however, an alternative view. In November 1792, in the wake of the French National Convention's declaration of a republic, Thomas Jefferson, then United States Secretary of State, wrote to the representative of the United States in France: 'It accords with our principles to acknowledge any government to be rightful which is formed by the will of the people, substantially declared.'[37] That a government cannot be legitimate unless it can show, presumably by free elections, that it represents the will of the people, is still very much the view of a dissenting minority in international law, but it has been gathering support in recent years. Its defenders can point to the opening words of the United Nations Charter, 'We the peoples . . . ' as an indication that the signatories of the Charter regard themselves as representatives of, and derive their authority from, the peoples they govern. They can refer to the Universal Declaration of Human Rights, which in Article 21 (3) states:

The will of the people shall be the basis of the authority of government; this will shall be expressed in periodic and genuine elections which shall be by universal and equal suffrage and shall be held by secret vote or by equivalent free voting procedures.

The Universal Declaration of Human Rights is not a treaty with explicit legal force, but the International Covenant on Civil and Political Rights is. Its first article states:

All peoples have the right of self-determination. By virtue of that right they freely determine their political status and freely pursue their economic, social and cultural development.

In the second article, the parties to the Covenant undertake to ensure that each individual in its territory has the rights it contains, 'without distinction of any kind, such as race, colour, sex, language, religion, political or other opinion, national or social origin, property, birth or other status.' The inclusion of 'political or other opinion' is important here, since Article 25 reads:

Every citizen shall have the right and the opportunity, without any of the distinctions mentioned in Article 2 and without unreasonable restrictions:

(a) To take part in the conduct of public affairs, directly or through freely chosen representatives;

**117**

(b) To vote and to be elected at genuine periodic elections which shall be by universal and equal suffrage and shall be held by secret ballot, guaranteeing the free expression of the will of the electors;

(c) To have access, on general terms of equality, to public service in his country.

What, however, of the seemingly unequivocal words of the 'Declaration on Principles of International Law Concerning Friendly Relations and Co-operation among States in Accordance with the Charter of the United Nations', which as we saw earlier, gave to every state 'an inalienable right to choose its political, economic, social and cultural systems'? These words do not, however, settle the crucial question: in what does the state consist? For the same Declaration goes on to say:

The establishment of a sovereign and independent State, the free association or integration with an independent State or the emergence into any other political status freely determined by a people constitute modes of implementing the right of self-determination by that people.

Every State has the duty to refrain from any forcible action which deprives peoples referred to above in the elaboration of the present principle of their right to self-determination and freedom and independence. In their actions against, and resistance to, such forcible action in pursuit of the exercise of their right to self-determination, *such peoples are entitled to seek and to receive support in accordance with the purposes and principles of the Charter.* [emphasis added]

These words were written against the background of the assertion of independence by countries that had been, and in some cases still were, colonies of other nations. Nevertheless, the right of self-determination cannot be restricted to that

**118**

context. It cannot be the case that people have a right of self-determination against colonial rulers, but have no right of self-determination against a local gang of thugs who seize power and keep the population subdued by beating, torturing and shooting anyone who opposes them. If peoples are entitled to seek and receive support 'in accordance with the purposes and principles of the Charter' in asserting their right to self-determination against a colonial ruler, they should also be entitled to seek and receive support against domestic tyrants. Similarly, if the colonial rulers are not regarded as possessing sovereignty in the territories over which they have effective control, why should the fact that the ruling gang of armed thugs have effective control over the territory mean that they are regarded as holding sovereignty over it?[38]

As we have seen, Annan has suggested that the state 'is now widely understood to be the servant of its people, and not vice versa'. This statement is too vague to play a role in international law, but it could be made more precise, in terms of Article 21 (3) of the Universal Declaration of Human Rights, which insists that the will of the people is the basis of the authority of government, and that this will must be expressed in 'periodic and genuine elections which shall be by universal and equal suffrage and shall be held by secret vote or by equivalent free voting procedures'.

The principle that legitimate government must rest on the will of the people steps around the apparent prohibition of intervention in domestic matters, in Article 2 (7) of the Charter, because it takes seriously the opening words of the Charter, 'We the peoples'. If the Charter is an agreement between peoples, then a statement that nothing in the Charter other than a threat to peace 'shall authorize the United Nations to intervene in matters which are essentially within

the domestic jurisdiction of any state' will only prevent intervention where there is a legitimate state in existence. If there
is no such state, there is no entity that has domestic jurisdiction, and the provisions of Articles 55 and 56—pledging joint
and separate action to promote observance of human rights
and fundamental freedoms—are, at least in theory, able to
come into play. A further step in this direction was taken at
the Millennium session of the United Nations, where the
General Assembly resolved to 'spare no effort to promote
democracy' and 'to strengthen the capacity of all our governments to implement the principles and practices of democracy and respect for human rights'. Nor was this left to each
government to do on its own; rather the Assembly resolved
'to work collectively for more inclusive political processes,
allowing genuine participation by all citizens in all our
countries'.[39]

How are we to decide when a government is sufficiently
democratic to be recognized as sovereign? A minimalist concept of democracy is needed here, for otherwise intervention
will become permissible everywhere. During the counting
and recounting of votes in the United States presidential election in November 2000, jokes circulated to the effect that the
United Nations—or in another version, it was Russia—was
about to send in a team of observers to ensure that the elections were fair and democratic. The jokes had a serious point
to make. Put aside the many allegations of irregularities in
voting and counting, and the extraordinary decision of the
United States Supreme Court refusing to allow a proper
count of all votes. Forget about the fact that candidates must
raise hundreds of millions of dollars to have any chance of
success, thus ensuring that the rich have far more influence on
the political process than the poor. Even without any of those

blemishes, the use of the electoral college, rather than the popular vote, to elect the President gives greater value to the votes of people living in states with small populations than to those living in states with large populations, and hence fails the basic 'one vote, one value' requirement of democracy, and the 'equal suffrage' stipulation of Article 25 (b) of the Universal Declaration of Human Rights. Nevertheless, the evident imperfections of democracy in the United States are not of the kind that should lead us to withdraw recognition of the sovereignty of the United States government. That must be a remedy of last resort, to be used only against regimes that rule by force, have no colour of consent, and do not allow the will of the people to be expressed in any open and recognizable form.

Even with a minimalist interpretation of democracy, the democratic concept of sovereignty would make a huge difference to the way we conduct world affairs. Here is one important way in which the concept might be used: when transnational corporations trade with governments, buying from them the oil, diamonds, fish, or timber that are their country's most marketable assets, they are implicitly accepting the government's right to sell these resources. An illegitimate government would not be recognized as having that right, any more than a robber who overpowers you and takes your watch would be recognized as the owner of the watch. For a private citizen to buy that watch, knowing or reasonably suspecting it to be stolen, is to commit the crime of receiving stolen goods. Under a democratic concept of sovereignty, it would similarly be a crime under international law for anyone to receive goods stolen from a nation by those who have no claim to sovereignty other than the fact that they exercise superior force.[40]

If this seems like fantasy, it was brought a stage nearer to reality by the inaugural meeting of the 'Community of Democracies', held in Warsaw in June 2000. Representatives of the governments of 106 countries signed the 'Warsaw Declaration', recognizing 'the universality of democratic values', and agreeing that:

The will of the people shall be the basis of the authority of government, as expressed by exercise of the right and civic duties of citizens to choose their representatives through regular, free and fair elections with universal and equal suffrage, open to multiple parties, conducted by secret ballot, monitored by independent electoral authorities, and free of fraud and intimidation.

The Declaration then pledges respect for a list of democratic and human rights, and concludes by stating that the signatories:

will collaborate on democracy-related issues in existing international and regional institutions, forming coalitions and caucuses to support resolutions and other international activities aimed at the promotion of democratic governance. This will help to create an external environment conducive to democratic development.[41]

Among the caucuses that the members of this community of democracies agreed to form, was one at the United Nations. Since a group of 106 nations constitutes a clear majority of the 189 members of the UN, such a group could be effective in promoting the idea—which it has already accepted—that only democratic governments have the authority to rule over their territory.

A similar link between democracy and participation in trade and other links was made by the 2001 Summit of the Americas meeting held in Quebec. There the leaders of 34

American states agreed that 'Any unconstitutional alteration or interruption of the democratic order in a state of the hemisphere constitutes an insurmountable obstacle to the participation of that state's government in the Summit of the Americas process.' This means that a country that ceased to be a democracy could not take part in continuing talks on the free-trade pact or receive support from the major international institutions like the Inter-American Development Bank.[42]

How far should this go? One possible scenario is that the United Nations would appoint a tribunal consisting of judges and experts in the conduct of free elections to scrutinize the credentials of each government on a regular basis. If a government could not, over time, satisfy the tribunal that it had held elections allowing the will of the people to be expressed, it would not be recognized by the United Nations. Arguably, though, if the United Nations is to be able to carry out its role of maintaining peace, it should remain the most all-encompassing of world bodies, and not exclude any government in effective control of its territory. It might be better if the minimal democracy test were applied by other world bodies like the World Bank and the World Trade Organization, but not made into a requirement of United Nations membership. Nevertheless, in situations in which crimes against humanity are being committed within the borders of a state, either by the government of that state or with its connivance, the fact that the state was not a democracy could be taken into account, lowering the threshold of imperative reasons that needed to be passed before intervention could be regarded as legitimate.

## Objections

## Avoiding Cultural Imperialism

It is sometimes said that to use a preference for democracy, or an appeal to the Univeral Declaration of Human Rights, as the basis of intervening in other countries is a form of cultural imperialism. By what right, those who take this view ask, do we in the West impose on other peoples our view of the kind of society that they should have? Is not this the same mistake made by the Western missionaries who sailed out to Africa, or the South Sea Islands, and told the 'primitive' people that they found there to cover their nakedness, to practise monogamy, and to have sex only in the missionary position? Have we not learnt from this experience that morality is relative to one's own society, and our morals are no better than theirs?

This objection is confused. The claim that morality is relative, far from implying that cultural imperialism is wrong, actually undermines any ethical case that can be made against cultural imperialism. For if morality is always relative to one's own society, then you, coming from society A, have your moral standards and I, coming from society B, have mine. It follows that when I criticize your moral standards, I am simply expressing the morality of my own society, but it also follows that when you condemn me for criticizing the moral standards of your society, you are simply expressing the morality of your society. There is, from this viewpoint, no way of moving outside the morality of one's own society and expressing an objective moral judgement about anything, including respect for the culture of different peoples. Hence if we happen to live in a society that holds the view that it is good to expand, and impose its ideas on the rest of the world—and there is plenty of evidence that this *is* the morality of modern Western civilization—then that is our morality, and the cultural relativist can offer no cogent reason why we should not simply get on with our imperialist plans.

We should reject ethical relativism, and with it both the confused notion that it can provide a ground for opposition to ethical imperialism, and the idea that our expansionist Western culture leaves no basis for criticism when we ride roughshod over other cultures. A much better case against cultural imperialism can be made from the standpoint of a view of ethics that gives scope for rational argument beyond the boundaries of one's own culture. Then we can argue that cultural autonomy and the preservation of distinctive cultures are values that ought not be carelessly destroyed. On that basis we can criticize the nineteenth-century missionaries for their insensitivity to cultural differences, and for their obsession with sexual behaviour, an area in which human relationships take a wide variety of forms without any one pattern being clearly superior to others. We can also argue that we should be doing much more to preserve indigenous cultures before they disappear. But once we accept that there is scope for rational argument in ethics, independent of any particular culture, we can also ask whether the values we are upholding are sound, defensible or justifiable.[43] Although reasonable people can disagree about many areas of ethics, and culture plays a role in these differences, acts of the kind carried out by Nazi Germany against Jews and gypsies, by the Khmer Rouge against Cambodians they considered to be their class enemies, and by Hutus against Tutsis in Rwanda, lack the element of consideration for others that is required of any justifiable ethic.[44]

Still, it may be said, these are extreme examples, and hence make my case too easy. The same can be said of the example I gave earlier, when I asked why, if colonial powers are not regarded as having legitimate sovereignty in virtue of the power they wield over a territory, a ruling gang of armed thugs should be seen as any more legitimate. What of a regime like that of Saudi Arabia, a hereditary monarchy that claims to be ruling in accordance with Islamic law, over a people who are—resident foreigners aside—almost entirely Muslim and appear to accept the monarchy's right to rule? Is such a form of government illegitimate because it does not hold elections? Or is it possible that the people of Saudi Arabia, like those of other neighbouring states like Kuwait, Oman and the United Arab Emirates, are not interested in democracy? Have they, in fact, chosen not to choose their rulers? If so, on what grounds can others tell them that they must have elections?

The first point to make here is that, as we shall see shortly, the fact that a regime is not democratic does not mean that any form of intervention *should* take place. If the regime is not engaging in genocide or other crimes against humanity, the question of intervention does not arise. Second, however, if the people of Saudi Arabia or other hereditary monarchies prefer their form of government to a democracy, that preference ought to be testable. Hence it is possible to envisage a country choosing, at a free and open referendum, not to have elections for political office. This could then itself be seen as giving legitimacy to the non-democratic regime.

Nevertheless, the ultimate question has not been solved. What if the monarchy, though expressing confidence that it is supported by its people, does not wish to hold a referendum on its own existence? How can we give reasons, independent of our culture, for the view that legitimacy requires popular support, rather than resting on, say, Islamic law as interpreted in Saudi Arabia? Attempts to argue for the separation of church and state will not work, since that begs the question against the defenders of the Saudi interpretation of Islamic law, which rejects such a separation. In the end, the challenge cannot be met without confronting the basis for belief in Islamic law, and that will in turn require undermining the religious beliefs on which it rests. This is not a path on which we can go further here.

## Can Democracy Really Provide Protection Against Genocide?

In the first section of this essay, I argued that at least some human beings may be biologically predisposed to take part in massacres, and hence we should not hope that achieving greater prosperity, or higher levels of education, will provide a sufficient safeguard against genocidal violence. But if that is so, it may be objected, how can we have any faith in democracy as a means of preventing, rather than promoting, genocide? If the genes of violence are in many of us, why are they less likely to be in democratically elected rulers than in dictators?[45]

Democracy, in the sense of the rule of the majority, does not provide a guarantee that human rights will be respected. But it is part of a democratic process that policies must be publicly defended and justified. They cannot simply be implemented from above. Although some of us may have the capacity to commit terrible crimes, many of us also have a moral sense, that is, a capacity to reflect on the rights and wrongs of what we are doing, or what our rulers are doing. That capacity emerges in the public arena. A small group may plot genocide, and inspire or terrify their followers to carry it out, but genocide will be rarer if it has to be defended on prime-time television. Even when the Nazis had been in power for eight years, ruling without opposition and making use of all the means of propaganda that Goebbels could devise, they did not dare to be open about what they were doing to the Jews. Himmler told a group of SS leaders that their work in exterminating the Jews was 'an unwritten, never-to-be written, glorious page of our history'.[46] If it had been possible to ensure that every page of Nazi history were written as it took place, and offered for discussion to the German people, it is hard to believe that the Holocaust would have taken place. Open procedures and public scrutiny may not be a perfect bulwark against genocide, but they do help.

Admittedly, whether this is correct is an empirical question, and we cannot claim to know the answer. The worst genocides of this century have been carried out by governments that were very far from being democracies: Ottoman Turkey at the time of the Armenian genocide, Nazi Germany, the Soviet Union under Stalin, Cambodia under the Khmer Rouge. But Rwanda was moving towards a multi-party democracy at the time of the massacres, and since 85 per cent of the population was Hutu, it is possible that more democracy would not have stopped the massacres of the Tutsis. The most difficult counter-example for the view I am defending, however, is the government of Slobodan Milosevic in Serbia, which bears substantial responsibility for the massacres in Bosnia and Kosovo. Milosevic was twice elected President of Serbia by large majorities, and while neither Serbia nor the Federal Republic of Yugoslavia during this period was an entirely free and open society, to raise the bar for acceptance of a state as democratic so high as to exclude them would have the result that very many other putatively democratic states would also be excluded.[47]

## Does Intervention Do More Good than Harm?

Since the link between democracy and legitimate government implies that the concept of national sovereignty carries no weight unless the state's government is minimally democratic, it would seem that intervention in countries without democratic regimes will be readily justified. However, if intervention is so easy to justify, will it not be used so often that it will be abused?

This objection forgets that even if humanitarian intervention against an undemocratic regime that commits crimes against humanity violates neither international law nor the UN Charter, it might still be wrong to intervene. John Stuart Mill argued that intervention to promote democracy is undesirable, not because there is any kind of intrinsic wrongdoing in one state coming to the assistance of 'a people in arms for liberty', but because he thought that when the tyranny is domestic, rather than that of a foreign power, such intervention is generally not justifiable:

[I]f they have not sufficient love of liberty to be able to wrest it from merely domestic oppressors, the liberty which is bestowed on them by other hands than their own, will have nothing real, nothing permanent.[48]

Mill distinguished 'merely domestic oppressors' from tyrants propped up by foreign powers, apparently believing that foreign support stacked the odds so heavily against the local freedom fighters that they might have 'sufficient love of liberty' to establish a permanent democracy, and yet not succeed in overthrowing their tyrant—whereas in the absence of foreign intervention, a similar sufficiency of love of liberty was bound to carry them to victory. Perhaps this claim had some plausibility when Mill put it forward, in 1859. Today, though, when a dictatorial regime has at its disposal weapons far more lethal, and means of surveillance far more intrusive, it seems merely silly. Nevertheless, Mill's more general point about the need to achieve something real and permanent needs to be remembered. For advocates of humanitarian intervention, the most challenging objection is the simple point that such interventions usually cost lives, and often do not achieve anything positive. This is often referred to, in terms deriving from Just War doctrine, as 'proportionality'.[49] It can also be seen simply as the application of consequentialist ethics. As Michael Doyle puts it, 'it makes no moral sense to rescue a village and start World War Three, or destroy a village in order to save it'.[50] We need to have rules and procedures making intervention difficult to justify, for as I have already noted, some states are capable of deceiving themselves into believing that their desire to expand their influence in the world is really an altruistic concern to defend democracy and human rights. But even when those rules and procedures have been satisfied, the key question must always be: will intervention do more good than harm?

Tzvetan Todorov has suggested that tyranny is not the greatest evil: anarchy is. Pointing to the downfall of the former communist regimes of Eastern Europe, he says that in some cases the collapse of the nation-state has led to a situation in which power is wielded by armed criminals. Intervention, even from humanitarian motives, can lead to the same outcome, because it too destroys the nation-state.[51] To the extent that this claim is factually correct, then intervention should not take place.

There is an important philosophical point at issue here, one that often leads to misguided objections to arguments for a right to intervene in the domestic affairs of another state. The objection runs: if it is justifiable to intervene against Serbia in Kosovo, then it must also be justifiable to intervene against Russia in Chechnya, or against China in Tibet. What this objection overlooks is that it is one thing to have the right to intervene, and a totally different thing to be justified in exercising that right. If I made a huge Christmas pudding with ingredients I bought from my own earnings, I may have the right to eat it all myself; but if I happen to be adrift in a lifeboat with a few other shipwreck survivors, and we have nothing but my pudding to keep ourselves going until we are rescued, I would not be justified in exercising my right. This distinction shows that the reason why it would not be justified to intervene against Russia in Chechnya or China in Tibet is not that (at least on one version of what the larger state is doing to the smaller one) there is no right to intervene, but rather that even though there is a right to intervene, the human costs of exercising it would make it wrong to do so. Similarly, Michael Ignatieff has suggested that some regions are 'bad neighbourhoods' in the sense that though the states there may be weak and illegitimate, and human rights violations widespread, military intervention is simply not likely to work.[52] Again, if this is true, then though we have the right to intervene, we ought not to exercise it.

## Reforming the United Nations

I have urged that the United Nations should, within the limits of its capacities, authorize intervention to stop crimes against humanity, and should promote a democratic idea of sovereignty. But this suggestion is not without its own irony: for the United Nations itself is scarcely a model of democracy. If the charge of 'cultural imperialism' can be met when it is brought against the general idea of promoting democracy and human rights, it is much harder to refute at the political level, given the present structure of the United Nations. That structure was set up after the Second World War, and the Allies made sure that they retained firm control of it. This is most evident in the Security Council, which is the body that makes all the decisions regarding matters of security, and whether to intervene in a dispute, either militarily or by means of sanctions. The Security Council has five permanent members—the United States, the United Kingdom, France, China and Russia—corresponding to the major powers that were fighting against the Axis powers. Although there are also ten additional members elected by the General Assembly for two-year terms, no substantive decision can be taken against the firm opposition of any one of the five permanent members. This gives each of the permanent members a veto power, which was frequently used by both the Soviet Union and the United States during the Cold War era. The veto power explains why during the 1960s and 1970s the Security Council effectively ignored the dominant conflict of the era, the Vietnam War.

There can be no justification today for giving special status to states that were great powers in 1945, but are no longer so today. Why should France or the United Kingdom have veto rights, and not Germany or Japan, or for that matter, Brazil or Indonesia? Why should China be a permanent member, and not India? Why should four of the five permanent members be European states, or states of European origin, when there is no permanent member from Africa, or Latin America or Southern or Southeastern Asia, or from anywhere in the Southern hemisphere? Is it desirable, if indeed we are facing a possible 'clash of civilizations', that four of the five permanent members are states with roots in Christianity, and none of them is an Islamic state?[53]

What then should be done? To expand the number of permanent members with veto rights risks making the Security Council unworkable. A better idea, therefore, would be to eliminate the veto, and perhaps even to eliminate the whole notion of permanent membership. To this it may be objected that the existing Security Council works reasonably well, and it is not clear that we would get a Council that worked better if we changed it to make it fairer. But if it is important and desirable to move towards greater global governance in a variety of areas—trade and the environment, for example, as well as peace and the protection of human rights—then the structure of the Security Council will make this difficult, because it is a constant reminder of the fact that the institutions of global governance are dominated by, and therefore very likely will primarily serve the interests of, the wealthiest and most powerful states. In the long run, it is hard to see that giving special privileges to a small group of states will be the best way to maintain either the authority of the United Nations, or world peace.

A second objection to reform of the Security Council is simply that it is unthinkable, and would be perilous, for the Security Council to take military action against the implacable opposition of the United States or whatever other military superpower may in time emerge. Hence political realism requires allowing such superpowers a veto. This claim may be true; but if it is, the veto rights of the superpowers should be seen as what it is: the exercise of might, not right.

Compared to the Security Council, the General Assembly of the United Nations, which includes all 189 member states, seems more democratic and it is certainly not dominated by the same small circle of states that dominates the Security Council. The General Assembly is, however, not able to take action, except in very limited circumstances. Moreover its appearance of egalitarianism is misleading. It is an assembly of the world's states, not of the world's people. Some of the states are not themselves democratic, but even if we overlook this vital point, we would have to ask why the democratically elected government of India, representing one billion people, is simply one state and the democratically elected government of Iceland, representing 275,000, is another. In fact, if the 95 states with small populations were to line up against the 94 states with larger populations, it is possible that a General Assembly resolution could be supported by a majority of states that represented a combined total of only 198.5 million people, while on the other side, the outvoted 94 largest states would represent 5.7 billion. In other words, states representing only 3.4 per cent of the total UN member-state population would carry the day.[54]

There is an obvious solution to this problem, and it is not a new idea. At the end of the Second World War, when Britain's House of Commons debated the plan for a new United Nations, Ernest Bevin, the British Foreign Secretary, called for the 'completion' of the UN design with 'a world assembly elected directly from the people [to] whom the governments who form the United Nations are responsible'.[55] In this respect the European Union, with its European Parliament directly elected by the people, could provide a model for a future, more democratic, United Nations. The European Parliament has, at present, only very limited powers. The plan is, however, for these to expand as the people and governments of Europe become comfortable with the Parliament playing a larger role. There are, of course, major differences between the European Union and the world as a whole. Most important to our present concerns is the fact that the European Union is in a position to set minimum standards for admission. These standards include a democratic form of government and basic human rights guarantees.[56] The United Nations, on the other hand, is at present open to all governments, democratic or not, in order to fulfil its role of keeping the peace. Thus while the General Assembly could allocate delegates to its member states in proportion to their population, it could not ensure that those delegates were democratically elected by those people, or even appointed by a government that was itself democratically elected. If undemocratic governments were not recognized as legitimate, and therefore as eligible for United Nations membership, this would no longer be a problem—but the negative aspect of this idea is that, as already mentioned, a United Nations that denied a voice to China, Saudi Arabia, and many other states could be less effective at maintaining world peace than one that was more inclusive. Hence, whatever the cogency of the argument given above for linking democracy and legitimacy, the right to exclude undemocratic governments from the United Nations may be another right that it is better not to exercise.

## Conclusion

I have argued for an ethic that is global, in the sense that it does not stop at, or even give great significance to, national boundaries. We can now imagine what the world might look like if that ethic were to become more widely accepted—although, to stay within the bounds of reality, I do not assume that human nature is any better than it is now, and I recognize the points made previously about the costs of intervention. This world would be one in which the United Nations functions rather more like the way in which the European Union functions today, but with significant differences due to the fact that it is a global, not regional, organization. Only states that meet minimum democratic standards can become members, but the overwhelming majority of states—and all the most powerful and politically significant states—do meet those standards, and are members. The remaining states are pariahs, outside not only the United Nations, but also its associated institutions, which include the World Bank, the International Monetary Fund, and a reformed World Trade Organization that sets its own standards for environmental protection and labour rights. The member states of the United Nations trade extensively among themselves, and though inequalities still exist, the gap between rich and poor has narrowed, the average standard of living is rising, and absolute poverty exists only in isolated pockets that have proven difficult for aid organizations to reach, especially in the pariah states. These states have only themselves to trade with, no major corporation will buy their goods, and their dictators know that if they visit one of the UN member states, they are liable to arrest and indictment for crimes against human rights. Their people cannot be kept entirely ignorant of this situation, and become restive. The dictators have limited means for buying weapons and paying their armies. Moreover they know that if they become too flagrant in their suppression of opposition and commit atrocities, the United Nations stands ready to intervene to overthrow them.

Is this a utopian fantasy? Perhaps. The realities of politics today, both at the United Nations itself and within the United States, the world's most powerful state, make it impossible to anticipate anything like this occurring in the near future. Nor should we blindly pursue philosophical ideals that look good, but may have unforeseen, and possibly disastrous, consequences. But to move slowly and cautiously in the direction of that distant vision might be worth trying.[57]

# Introduction to
# Geoffrey Bindman

*John Gardner*

Geoffrey Bindman's name is well known to all of us who take an interest in the protection of human rights in the UK. A practising solicitor who defies many of the popular pre-conceptions about his profession, he has played a prominent and progressive role in shaping several important areas of modern UK law (most notably the law relating to race and sex discrimination) and has acted, often to spectacular effect, in a number of landmark cases.

As an unapologetic campaigner for human rights, one would expect to find Geoffrey Bindman working for the defence rather than the prosecution when he is involved in criminal cases. And that is indeed where one often finds him. But not always. In the famous Pinochet extradition proceedings, for example, he was retained by Amnesty International to help make the case *in favour of* extradition. As the work of human rights lawyers becomes more influential in legal and political culture, the people in the dock are increasingly going to be those who are *charged* with human rights violations rather than those who are victims of them. At which point one begins to find the human rights organizations, and their lawyers, working alongside the prosecutors and not only on the defence team.

That change of perspective is, indeed, the theme of Geoffrey Bindman's Amnesty Lecture. It might be subtitled 'The Case for the Prosecution' because he reveals himself as an enthusiast not only for human rights but also for the criminal prosecution and punishment of those guilty of human rights violations. His particular concern here is with the proper way to ensure that such prosecution and punishment is undertaken, and undertaken properly, when the violations in question occur against a background of war or unrest, or under an oppressive regime that is complicit in the violations, or more generally in those times and places at which there is no local legal system that is willing and able to do the prosecuting and punishing.

In these times and places Geoffrey Bindman sees a central role for international law, conceived in its post-Nuremberg form, as a body of law enforceable not only against states but also against individual people. In particular he stands up for the principle of 'complementarity' embraced in the United Nations Charter of 1945, whereby the same international human rights standards were supposed to be enforced both by co-operative international action and by the actions of each signatory state acting alone. What he wants to see is more fidelity to this two-pronged approach: more concerted international action of the kind that the International Criminal Court has recently been set up to deliver, but also more vigorous actions in ordinary domestic courts against international human rights abusers—by which he means, in principle, prosecution and punishment of such people *wherever they may find themselves*, and not only in their own countries or the countries of their victims or the countries in which their violations were committed.

In his lecture, Geoffrey Bindman expresses some disappointment and frustration at the caution with which both routes are currently being explored. Concerning the jurisdiction of the International Criminal Court, he worries that a major loophole protects the worst offenders most. Why is it, he asks, that human rights violations committed on the territory of a non-signatory state by its own citizens cannot be prosecuted before the ICC, even when the violators leave home and travel to a signatory state? Concerning the contribution of national courts to prosecution and punishment for violations of international human rights standards, he has some harsh words for the UK's rather timid position under recent legislation designed to complement the arrival of the ICC. When the standards being enforced under this new legislation are international standards, why are prosecutions in UK courts in respect of human rights violations committed outside the UK to be available only against UK citizens or residents?

Both of these limitations Geoffrey Bindman regards, with disapproval, as the symptoms of 'a desire to cling to state sovereignty [that] impedes the development of a rational system of human rights enforcement'. To those who say that countries should be entrusted with sorting out their own pasts, and allowed to implement negotiated amnesties and similar arrangements as part of their effort to move forward, he replies that no doubt they should. But what this does not entail, he points out, is that the perpetrators of crimes against humanity should be protected by such national amnesty arrangements when they travel abroad. Their crimes were against humanity, and whatever safe haven they may negotiate with their own fellow citizens in a spirit of national reconciliation, that is no reason to think that the rest of humanity owes them a safe haven by the same token.

The main problem with this argument is that of keeping its conclusions under control. If we should overcome our 'desire to cling to state sovereignty' in respect of where and by whom crimes against humanity are tried, why shouldn't we by the same token abandon the protective shield of the law of extradition, which presupposes and affirms the importance of state sovereignty? If one would be happy to see Pinochet tried in the UK, then why would one not be equally happy to allow the Spanish police to come and arrest him and haul him off without further ado? The answer cannot be that we have to check whether Pinochet is being despatched into the clutches of a tolerably decent legal system. Why would *we* have to check this unless there is some salience in *our* state sovereignty, i.e. in the fact that Pinochet finds himself under our jurisdiction rather than that of the Spanish? And if jurisdiction matters in this respect, then why not in other respects? If we grant Pinochet the relatively safe haven of our extradition laws—procedures to control whether others can try him—then why is it any less rational to afford him, by the same token, a safe haven in respect of whether *we* can try him?

It is also hard to see why the logic of such an argument should not carry us far beyond crimes against humanity. In his lecture, Geoffrey Bindman adopts the international lawyer's view of what counts as a crime against humanity: 'murder, extermination, enslavement, torture, rape, enforced disappearance and other similar inhumane acts' when these are committed 'within the context of a widespread or systematic attack on any civilian population'. The latter limitation means that not everything that counts as a human rights violation in international law also counts as a crime against humanity. But if we want a 'rational system of human rights enforcement', why do we only want it in respect of the narrower class of crimes against humanity, and not in respect of other human rights violations? Why, in particular, don't we want it in respect of the whole gamut of murders, enslavements, rapes, kidnappings, and so on, all of which infringe the human rights of their victims? If we insist on the international law duty of all UN member states to criminalize all *torturers* under their own domestic laws, wherever in the world their crime may have been committed, why should we not also require all UN member states to criminalize all murderers and pimps and rapists and kidnappers, wherever in the world their crime may have been committed? This would mean the abolition of a jurisdictional requirement for the trial of such diverse criminal defendants as Harold Shipman, Peter Sutcliffe, Michael Tyson, Timothy McVeigh, and O. J. Simpson as well. But in these cases we would presumably want them to be tried within the jurisdiction in which they committed their crimes. What remains unclear, therefore, is how we can justify doing away with local trials for Milosevic and Pinochet while preserving existing jurisdictional requirements with respect to other violators of human rights.

These remarks of mine reflect two very different anxieties. The first concerns the way in which the idea of the 'rational' has been appropriated by tidy-minded folk who would prefer to see more uniformity and less variety in human practices and attitudes. But there are plenty of reasons for plenty of important issues to be determined by individual choice or local convention, such that they will be dealt with differently by different people in different places and at different times. It has become the norm to regard the scope of human rights as lying outside the range of issues that are subject to such rational variation. But even if the scope of human rights does lie outside that range—which I very much doubt—it does not follow that the enforcement mechanisms are similarly outside the range. It does not follow, in particular, that juris-dictional claims to monopoly of enforcement should not be respected. The reasons for respecting such jurisdictional claims, even in international law, are many. Political reasons, for example, may, as Geoffrey Bindman argues, threaten the adequate protection of human rights. But that does not stop them being valid reasons and hence does not make following them any the less rational. So a system of human rights enforcement may be none the less rational merely for the fact that it accommodates such political reasons, together with the patchy enforcement practices that they may sometimes yield.

My second—very different—worry concerns Amnesty International's own recent policy direction. Among the most important human rights are many that have the effect of inhibiting the trial and punishment of people who undoubtedly deserve to be tried and punished. Governments—democratic governments as well as undemocratic ones—commonly find these inhibitions annoying, and often attempt to short-circuit them. Amnesty International exists in part to keep an eye on these attempts and to act as a persistent nuisance to governments who make the trial and punishment, *even of the deserving*, too easy for themselves, especially by reducing the 'due process' hurdles that have to be crossed to mount an effective prosecution. This 'nuisance' role is important because trial and punishment, even of the deserving, ought to be difficult. There ought to be a large number of hoops for prosecutors to jump through, including some which are about jurisdiction, or more generally about the possession of proper standing to prosecute. It is therefore worrying to find it argued by Amnesty International and its lawyers that trial and punishment of one class of people who deserve to be tried and punished—namely those picked out as human rights abusers—ought to be made *easier* than it is already. I for one rebel at the idea of seeing the trial and punishment of *anyone* made easier than it is already, least of all in the name of human rights. If that rebellion means that Milosevic or Pinochet escapes his just deserts, then that is just the price we pay for being committed to human rights. Far from being a matter of global shame for all believers in human rights, our willingness to see a Milosevic or Pinochet go free on a 'technicality'—that is, for reasons of due process—is surely an excellent test of our convictions.

# 4

# Bringing International Criminals to Justice

**Geoffrey Bindman**

My theme is one that constantly engages Amnesty International and other campaigners for human rights: how can those who commit crimes against humanity be brought to justice? It is a topical subject. We have seen one example of international accountability pursued in Britain in the Pinochet case, and we are at last able to contemplate the reality of an International Criminal Court following the 1998 Rome Treaty. The International Criminal Court Act became law in May 2001 and will enable Britain to co-operate fully with the new court once it comes into operation. This is thus a proper moment to pause and take stock. What has been achieved in the field of international criminal justice? What remains to be done, especially in Britain? How much can and should we expect from the future International Criminal Court, and what is the present and future role of domestic courts in bringing the perpetrators of crimes against humanity to justice?

In Britain and most other countries we take for granted a judicial system that is ready and willing to try those charged with crimes against the law of the state. We know that if someone is convicted of a crime, the enforcement machinery is in place to carry out the sentence of the court. But the perpetrators of the worst crimes against humanity often escape justice because their power forestalls their prosecution within their own countries, and when they go to other countries the political will or the legal means to arrest them or put them on trial are absent.

## The Development of a System of International Justice

The atrocities committed during the Second World War stimulated the majority of states to take the first serious steps towards an enforceable international law against the violation of human rights. Before 1945, international law had been concerned with relations between states and hardly at all with the protection of individuals. Nuremberg was the starting point of the new era of international human rights law. The trials of the Nazi leaders[1] have been criticized as victors' justice, but the judges were trying not to be arbitrary. They made a serious effort to develop standards of universal application.[2] Nuremberg demonstrated the need for an agreed legal framework which included effective sanctions. Without effective enforcement mechanisms, it is obvious that legal obligations are of limited value. The task, slowly pursued since Nuremberg (and the less well-documented parallel trials in Tokyo),[3] has been to create an international legal framework matching those taken for granted within the domestic legal systems of most sovereign states. Most domestic systems have continuously functioning criminal courts, and a government which, if necessary, can assert its authority through police and armed forces under its direct control to make sure that the decisions of the courts are implemented.

Giving a comparable level of authority to an international body requires sovereign states to surrender power. The member states of the Council of Europe and the European Union have overcome their reluctance to do this to some degree in ceding jurisdiction to the European Court of Justice[4] in

Luxembourg and the European Court of Human Rights[5] at Strasbourg. But the pressure to concede jurisdiction to an international criminal court is less compelling and the struggle to achieve it has been arduous at the practical level, though rhetorically almost every state accepts its necessity in a civilized world.

Since the formation of the United Nations in 1945 it has been accepted that human rights enforcement is a task both for collective international action and for individual member states. The signatories of the United Nations Charter in 1945 pledged themselves to take *joint and separate* action to respect and observe human rights and fundamental freedoms for all.[6] The word 'separate' is crucial. The task was not to be given exclusively to international institutions. The member states, with their often sophisticated and well-resourced domestic legal systems, had to play a complementary role in enforcing international justice.

A system of international justice developed slowly over the next decades. The Universal Declaration of Human Rights[7] identified and spelled out in 1948 the rights and freedoms to be protected and declared the intention of putting into place a system of enforceable and enforced international human rights. But it took nearly 20 years to get to the next stage. The first legally binding treaty instruments of truly world-wide potential application, the International Covenant on Economic, Social and Cultural Rights (ICESCR)[8] and the International Covenant on Civil and Political Rights (ICCPR),[9] were adopted and opened for signature on 16 December 1966 and entered into force on 3 January 1976 and 23 March 1976 respectively. By guaranteeing the rights to life, liberty and security of the person, freedom from torture or cruel, inhuman, or degrading treatment or punishment, and prohibiting slavery, the International Covenant on Civil and Political Rights indirectly entrenches in international law the right to protection from the very crimes—genocide, enslavement, mass murder and torture—which have come to be categorized as crimes against humanity. At the same time it asserts, in Article 2, the obligation of all states to respect and ensure these rights to all individuals within their territory and subject to their jurisdiction, an obligation which, in the view of the Human Rights Committee, (which was set up to supervise compliance with the Covenant) includes an obligation to bring to justice the perpetrators of those crimes and to provide remedies for their victims.[10]

The weak point is the lack of any adequate judicial machinery and enforcement powers. The Human Rights Committee mainly reviews reports submitted by the member states describing what action they have taken to protect human rights within their territory. With regard to the conduct of states parties who are members of the first Optional Protocol to the Covenant, the Human Rights Committee can also receive individual complaints, but it can do no more than seek to persuade. It conducts no judicial hearings and has no judicial, let alone penal, powers. It is not a criminal court and it brings no criminals to justice.

After Nuremberg and Tokyo no more international tribunals were created until those set up by the UN Security Council in the 1990s to try war criminals from the former Yugoslavia[11] and the perpetrators of the Rwandan genocide.[12] They mark the resumption, after the end of the Cold War, of the movement towards international criminal jurisdiction over the worst atrocities. These ad hoc tribunals have heard few cases, and as yet there have been only a handful of convictions.[13] Richard Goldstone, a judge at the South

African Constitutional Court and the first chief prosecutor of both tribunals, believes that their most significant impact so far has been to dispel the fear that a court made up from and staffed by lawyers from every continent and legal system would be unable to work together to dispense justice fairly.[14] This is no mean achievement. With both tribunals conducting trials against the former heads of government who were politically most responsible for the human carnage which occurred under their rule—Jean Kambanda[15] in Rwanda and Slobodan Milosevic[16] in the former Yugoslavia—there is hope that early criticisms, based on the powerlessness of the tribunals to ensure arrest and attendance of those indicted[17] and the consequent risk of a random selection of those put on trial as not being the most guilty but the most easily available, will be put to rest. In fact, as one commentator put it, Milosevic's handover gave the International Criminal Tribunal for the Former Yugoslavia 'a badly needed boost: it was finally landing the "big fish" of the Yugoslav wars, not just the small fry charged with individual atrocities'.[18]

Like many international institutions, the tribunals have been restricted by the inadequate resources available to the United Nations and by logistical problems and bureaucratic delays.[19] Inherent also in the operation of an international tribunal is the need to rely on the co-operation of the states where the perpetrators are to be found. Those states may refuse to surrender them and the military capacity to force surrender is not usually available. Judge Goldstone strongly criticized the refusal of NATO to arrest those indicted by the Yugoslav tribunal, Karadzic and Mladic in particular.[20] Opposition came from the United States military, which the political leadership was not prepared to overrule.[21] In Rwanda a converse problem arose. The new government which came to power after the genocide there was only too eager to put those responsible on trial itself. It opposed the war crimes tribunal in part because it feared that it would impose lesser sentences than the government—and possibly the Rwandan public, too—thought appropriate. The tribunal could not impose the death penalty, which Rwandan law permitted. Nevertheless the tribunal is now working co-operatively with the government.[22]

## The International Criminal Court

What are the prospects in the light of this experience for the International Criminal Court? It was agreed by the 120 nations that participated in the United Nations Diplomatic Conference of Plenipotentiaries on the Establishment of an International Criminal Court (ICC) in Rome in July 1998 that the Court would come into being when 60 nations had ratified the Rome Treaty.[23] By the end of the year 2000, 139 had taken the preliminary step of signing the treaty, but only 27 had ratified it. By the end of 2001 the number of ratifications had reached 48, and the total of 60 was reached in mid-2002. Several of the signatory states, including the United Kingdom,[24] have enacted domestic legislation which will provide the necessary national support for the work of the new Court when it comes into being.

Within the context of a widespread or systematic attack on any civilian population, the long list of crimes against humanity which the ICC will have jurisdiction to try includes murder, extermination, enslavement, torture, rape, enforced disappearance and other similar inhumane acts, none of which can be justified in any circumstances within any civilized community.[25] Genocide[26] and war crimes[27] are covered separately, though most people would regard these as properly included in the concept of crimes against humanity.

However, even when the Court is operational, there will be major gaps in its coverage. Far from having universal jurisdiction over all crimes against humanity throughout the world, it will be unable to try crimes committed in their own countries by citizens of states that are not parties to the Rome Treaty.[28] Thus the worst offenders can escape justice wherever they travel, simply by ensuring that their states do not become a party to the treaty. Iraq, Iran, Libya and Indonesia are, perhaps unsurprisingly, among those states that have said they will stay out.[29] The hugely populous states of China and India are also among those that have opposed the Treaty. And the United States, under the Bush administration, has not only declined to ratify but has withdrawn its signature of the treaty. It is difficult to understand or defend the exemption of non-party citizens. Customary international law is universally binding, not just on those who choose to accept it, and the foundation in customary international law of the substantive criminality of crimes against humanity is, after all, the legal basis for the jurisdiction over such acts of barbarity exercised by the 'ad hoc' war crimes tribunals.[30] Obviously there are practical problems of putting people on trial if they stay at home in countries that have rejected the Court. But that practical consideration cannot, in my view, justify immunity if perpetrators choose to go abroad.

Furthermore, the Court will not have retrospective jurisdiction.[31] So neither Pinochet nor his younger henchmen need fear it, nor any of those who commit atrocities before the Treaty came into force. The Treaty also provides that even a country that has ratified it can prevent its citizens from being put on trial by the ICC by investigating and prosecuting the individual itself, or by investigating the case and deciding not to prosecute.[32] This provision in the Treaty—giving expression to the decision of the parties to grant only complementary jurisdiction to the future International Criminal Court[33]—has the sensible purpose of encouraging states to prosecute international criminals in their own courts where possible and to give them reasonable latitude in doing so. However, it is open to abuse.[34] It led Baroness Kennedy in a House of Lords debate on the International Criminal Court Bill to suggest that the criminals most likely to be put on trial at The Hague are those who have committed atrocities in a failed conflict in a country which lacks the ability to try them itself. Those who seize and retain power by violence and repression are the least likely to find themselves on trial at The Hague. Some believe that these weaknesses, especially the unwillingness of some major powers to participate at all, will destroy the value and effectiveness of the ICC completely. One can only hope that such a gloomy view is unduly pessimistic.

Undoubtedly, the Treaty also has considerable strengths. The leaders and commanders who plan and direct atrocities will be liable for the crimes committed by their subordinates.[35] The subordinates themselves are also liable[36]—it was the Nuremberg Tribunal which established that 'superior orders' cannot excuse personal responsibility for war crimes and the principle applies to all crimes against humanity. Nor is there room for the immunities that have often protected heads of state and diplomats in domestic courts. Article 27 of the ICC Statute makes it clear that it is to apply equally to all persons without any distinction based on official capacity.

Opposition to the Rome Treaty in the United States and from some British conservatives has concentrated on the fear that armed forces carrying out military operations will be vulnerable to indictment by the ICC. There are two answers to these concerns. The first is that the prohibition of war crimes is already well entrenched in international law and no civilized state could justify permitting its forces to commit them or any other crimes against humanity. Consequently one would expect all states (including the United States) to take action themselves against their own troops accused of such crimes. Second, the Treaty provides that a case is inadmissible before the ICC where it is being investigated or prosecuted by the state that has jurisdiction over it.[37] It remains true that another state might seek to try foreign troops for war crimes, but that is already possible without reference to the Treaty or the ICC.[38]

As the UN Charter envisaged, the key to the system prescribed in the Rome Treaty is 'complementarity' of jurisdiction. The role of the ICC is not to replace or make redundant the obligation of individual states to try international crimes. The ICC and national courts are to complement each other in their common task of deterring and punishing the perpetrators. The ICC, even when it becomes operational, will not excuse governments from their responsibility to enforce international human rights in their own courts.

## The Pinochet Case

The arrest of the Chilean former dictator Pinochet while on a visit to Britain for medical treatment in October 1998 dramatically illuminates the opportunities for domestic courts to enforce international justice. Pinochet was not alleged to have committed any crimes in Britain, and neither was he a citizen or resident of the UK. He was a private visitor. Despite a variety of ingenious attempts by his lawyers to challenge the validity of his arrest and detention,[39] it was only doubt about his physical fitness to stand trial which ultimately prevented his extradition to Spain and his trial there on charges of torture.[40]

To appreciate the significance of the Pinochet decision, one has to take a closer look at the legal questions raised by the case. Generally, crimes committed abroad cannot be tried in British courts. Piracy on the high seas was the time-honoured exception because the pirate belonged to no nation state: he was *hostis humani generis*, the universal enemy of seafaring nations and at the mercy of all. In other cases, extra-territorial crimes could be prosecuted only where Parliament made special provision; the Slave Trade Act of 1834 is an early example. In modern times the Suppression of Terrorism Act 1978 allows prosecution for some acts carried out abroad. In 1991 the War Crimes Act enabled prosecutions for murders committed by non-UK citizens in Europe during the Second World War. In 1988 Parliament incorporated the United Nations Convention Against Torture and Other Cruel, Inhuman or Degrading Treatment or Punishment 1984[41] (hereafter referred to as the Torture Convention) into British law in sec. 134 of the Criminal Justice Act 1988.

It was that 1988 law which justified the arrest of Pinochet. The Torture Convention obliges its member states to establish criminal jurisdiction over any person, including public officials of other countries, who are present in its territory and alleged to have committed acts of torture, regardless of the nationality of the offender or where the torture took place.[42] The British courts have universal jurisdiction over torture cases—but not over other crimes against humanity, except where similar conventions have led to legislation granting universal jurisdiction. The British authorities failed to carry out their treaty obligation to put Pinochet on trial,[43] as they had failed to do on two previous visits. It was left to Spain to seek his extradition, so that they could carry out their equivalent duty under the Torture Convention.

It is important to note that Pinochet's lawyers, supported by the Chilean government, tried to prevent his extradition by claiming that he was entitled to the traditional immunity given to heads of state against any form of criminal prosecution. They failed because the House of Lords held that this sweeping immunity 'ratione personae' did not apply to *former* heads of state. Pinochet, as a former head of state, could only claim limited immunity 'ratione materiae' with regard to official acts performed in the exercise of his functions as head of state,[44] and their Lordships held that the functions of a head of state could, properly understood, not include the commission of international crimes. A current head of state could still be entitled to immunity, and diplomatic immunity might still be available.[45]

At the time few people seriously believed that Pinochet would ever be prosecuted in Chile. Immunities granted to him both under a general amnesty law which he engineered and in his capacity of Senator were thought to prevent it, and the political mood seemed to be against it. But political influences are finely balanced. Criminal charges arising from the activities of the so-called Death Caravan, a military squad that flew by helicopter to cities all over Chile and left behind a trail of mutilated corpses, were finally brought against Pinochet early in 2001. After initially allowing the trial to proceed, the Santiago Court of Appeals on 10 July 2001 eventually halted the case by holding Pinochet physically unfit to stand trial, a ruling that is expected effectively to end further efforts to prosecute Pinochet in Chile, though formally the case remains open.

The Pinochet case exposed some of the most important weaknesses of British law with respect to human rights. If the object of deterring the most flagrant violations of human rights is to be best achieved, the domestic courts of every state should have at least the same powers to try international crimes as the proposed International Criminal Court. Indeed they should go further, for they are not bound to make the compromises that weaken the Rome Treaty. We need to remember that the nations of the world agreed in the UN Charter to defend human rights by both joint and separate action. The deterrent was designed to be cumulative. Domestic courts should have universal jurisdiction to try those within their territory wherever the crimes have occurred. The preamble to the ICC Statute reminds us that 'it is the duty of every state to exercise its criminal jurisdiction over those responsible for international crimes.' Unfortunately, the British International Criminal Court Act 2001, in contrast to many other signatories, including Canada, New Zealand and several of our European partners, fails to live up to it.

The International Criminal Court Act 2001 falls short of universal jurisdiction in two ways. First, crimes covered by the Rome Treaty committed outside the United Kingdom cannot be tried in British courts unless the person accused is a UK citizen or a UK resident. Where universal jurisdiction already exists, as in torture cases and under the Geneva Conventions Act 1957, it will continue, but the new Act does not extend it. So future Pinochets visiting Britain will be at no greater risk than now, unless they have already been indicted by the International Criminal Court.

The government's justification for rejecting universal

jurisdiction has been pragmatic. Peter Hain, the minister in charge of the ICC Bill before his move to the Department of Energy, and current posting at the FCO, said in a letter to the Chairman of Amnesty UK:

We must be practical. It would be difficult to investigate and effectively prosecute in the UK crimes committed overseas by non-British citizens. The UK legal system relies on having evidence in court, primarily given by witnesses in person, where it can be subjected to cross-examination. This would be difficult if the host state were being uncooperative.

This really misses the point. We are not talking about cases where British policemen have to roam the world looking for evidence. Obviously there can only be an effective prosecution if the evidence, including live witnesses, is available. In the Pinochet cases there was an avalanche of evidence in Britain and many witnesses here or willing to travel here. There is no logic in excluding all prosecutions because in some cases it might prove impossible to get hold of the necessary evidence.

Second, the Act does not remove immunity from prosecution in Britain for international crimes. It does so only in relation to those already indicted by the ICC. So heads of state and diplomats may enter Britain with impunity. While diplomatic contacts with perpetrators of international crimes may still be necessary, it would be preferable to make ad hoc agreements not to prosecute in particular cases rather than retain a blanket immunity as the International Criminal Court Act does. These gaps in the jurisdiction of the British courts could prove to be serious weaknesses.

The reluctance of the British government to allow British courts to be used to challenge the actions of other countries or their rulers extends also to civil proceedings. Civil proceedings, while they do not lead to punishment of the perpetrators, can at least ensure some financial compensation for the victim. However, civil proceedings by a victim against a foreign government are traditionally barred by the doctrine of state immunity.

The case of Suleiman Al-Adsani had the potential to change that, at least in cases of torture and possibly other crimes against humanity. Mr Al-Adsani was an airforce officer tortured in Kuwait by a member of the ruling family shortly after the Gulf War. Brought to England with severe burns and other injuries, he sued the Kuwaiti government in the High Court. After a series of hearings, the Court of Appeal dismissed his case on the sole ground that the government of Kuwait was entitled to immunity.[46] Although there are some exceptions in United Kingdom law to state immunity—for some commercial transactions, for example—no exception existed for violations of fundamental human rights.[47]

The ruling was challenged by Mr Al-Adsani in the European Court of Human Rights on the footing that Article 6 of the European Convention on Human Rights gives him the right to a fair trial, while he had been denied any trial at all. Furthermore, he argued that the United Kingdom violated the prohibition against torture in Art. 3 by not doing its utmost to support him in taking legal action against the state under colour of whose authority the perpetrators had acted. However, the European Court of Human Rights rejected the application on both grounds.[48] With regard to Art. 3 the Court held that, while contracting states are under a duty to refrain from taking action which has as its direct consequence the exposure of an individual to proscribed ill-treatment in a third state, they are not obliged to take any positive action with regard to the provision of remedies, within their jurisdictions, for acts of torture to which they have no causal connection.[49] Art. 6 does not provide an absolute right of access to a court, and the British laws granting states immunity from jurisdiction to the extent provided for in Part I of the State Immunity Act 1978 were considered by the majority to be consistent with customary international law on the issue, and to be proportionate restrictions of the Convention right to access to a court.[50] The dissenting minority found this a puzzling conclusion in the light of the broad consensus that the prohibition of torture is compulsory in international law and must take precedence over any immunity.

Globalization in commerce and communications is only slowly being matched by political changes. The desire to cling to state sovereignty equally impedes the development of a rational system of international human rights enforcement but, as the UN Charter envisages, international and state legal systems should be able to work in partnership rather than in conflict. Complementarity is sensible and should be workable.

## Truth, Reconciliation and National Sovereignty

Sometimes the question is raised to what extent, if at all, the international institutions and other states should refrain from prosecutions and thus effectively condone abuses because the government of the state in which they have been committed has reached a political compromise with the abusers. Internal conflicts in which abuses have occurred are often resolved by not punishing—if not pardoning—the guilty, sometimes in return for acknowledging their guilt and as far as possible reconciling the surviving victims to their loss. Truth and

Reconciliation Commissions in Chile, Argentina, South Africa and many other countries were, with varying success, created as a foundation for social cohesion in a new political system.[51]

As pointed out above, the ICC Statute allows the Court to decline jurisdiction in a case where a state, having investigated it, has decided not to prosecute 'unless the decision resulted from the unwillingness or inability of the state genuinely to prosecute'. This suggests that a decision not to prosecute for reasons of reconciliation would not exclude the ICC's jurisdiction. Nor should it. And nor should it exclude the jurisdiction of any other state that gives its courts universal jurisdiction over international crimes. The beneficiary of reconciliation within his own country has no claim to immunity if he travels abroad.

The issue was raised when Pinochet was under arrest in Britain. A number of commentators and a lobby of Pinochet supporters including Lady Thatcher and Lord Lamont said that he should be allowed to return to Chile so that he could be brought to justice there. Apart from the medical arguments which eventually got him home, this was not an option within the law of extradition. There was no guarantee that he would be tried there. Ironically the prosecution which he later faced in Chile concerned crimes for which he could not have been tried in Britain.

Human rights are universal and should be recognized as binding on all nation-states. The international community and other states should be able to enforce these rights even against the will of states that have failed to act against human rights violators in their own territories. That is what we mean by universal jurisdiction over human rights. One cannot discount the view that nations that have suffered cataclysmic evils, such as the Holocaust or apartheid, need to come to terms with them in their own way, undisturbed by outside interference into what they may wish to regard as their own internal concerns. At their extremes the two positions may be incompatible, but a balance should be possible which accepts both. The Rome Treaty has attempted to do this by limiting intervention by the International Criminal Court to cases in which there has been no domestic prosecution. Other states should, and in practice will in any event under diplomatic pressures, exercise similar restraint.

Nor should we have any illusions about the practical impact of universal jurisdiction. In the first place it is likely to be useful only when the perpetrator is physically available to be brought before a domestic court. It is not the role of states to be international policemen. However, international criminals who enter Britain should not go free, as they can now do. The point is that universal jurisdiction would discourage them from coming to Britain, or any other country where they would face arrest. We can be confident that Pinochet has made his last visit here. It must be a good thing to deprive dictators of some of the fruits of their crimes by forcing them to stay at home. By limiting the rewards of violence and repression, we may reduce the incentive to use such methods.

The prospect of an International Criminal Court is an exciting step forward in the international protection of human rights. However, it could also become a pretext for inaction by nation-states which should be using their own resources to challenge abuses. An international court can deal with only a fraction of the abuses which occur, and it will tend to concentrate on the leaders. But a universal system needs every state to complement its role by adopting universal jurisdiction over crimes against humanity. The more which do so, the more the remainder will become increasingly the bolt holes for the criminals not important enough to be indicted by the ICC.

Already this has happened. Colonel Muvunyi, a Rwandan accused of 100,000 murders, was allowed to remain at liberty for nearly two years in Britain before pressure to put him on trial here led to a hurried application for his transfer to Tanzania for trial by the ICTR.[52] There are said to be a number of other Rwandan mass murderers here but they have broken no British law by killing their compatriots. The former dictator of Sierra Leone, General Strasser, led an untroubled life in Britain for several years, before he was eventually deported. Pinochet would have had no problems in Britain had it not been for the initiative of Spanish lawyers backed by their government.

What practical steps are needed to give Britain its proper role? The War Crimes Act 1991 is a useful precedent. It was passed after powerful lobbying and initial rejection to allow British courts to try those who committed murder in Europe in the Second World War. Special units were set up to investigate cases and prepare them for trial. When the small flow of suspects dried up altogether, the Home Office and the Crown Prosecution Service dispersed their expert units instead of redirecting their expertise to the investigation of more contemporary crimes against humanity.

There is no clear administrative responsibility for the prosecution of those extra-territorial crimes against humanity which are already covered by our law. There are said to be arrangements in place to enable the police and the Crown Prosecution Service to liaise with the Foreign and Commonwealth Office and the Home Office in the investigation of such cases, but there is no unit comparable to those set up in relation to the War Crimes Act. Better co-ordination between the relevant government agencies will be essential to ensure that prosecutions take place in future. We need a much stronger commitment from the government to using our own legal system to bring international criminals to justice in Britain whenever they are found here. The International Criminal Court Act 2001 falls short of giving universal jurisdiction to British courts over all crimes, but it is nevertheless a considerable step in the right direction.

# Introduction to
# Gayatri Chakravorty Spivak

*Robert J. C. Young*

There are plenty of academics in this world, but amongst them there is no one quite like Gayatri Chakravorty Spivak. She stands alone, unique. For many years now, in her lecturing and writing, Gayatri Spivak has challenged the accepted, the assumed, the expected. In her work, *In Other Worlds* (1987), *Outside in the Teaching Machine* (1993), *A Critique of Postcolonial Reason: Toward a History of the Vanishing Present* (1999), she has contested the ways in which dominant power groups in many different fields represent the world, and assert *their* world, *their* perspectives, as the visible embodiment of humanity in general. Spivak's theoretical work is at the same time exceptional in the ways in which it crushes theory against material circumstance, against the material inequality and deprivation which every day we silently consent to allow others to suffer.

Spivak is also very well known for the ways in which she has inflected metropolitan feminism with an awareness of its responsibilities towards the emancipatory struggles of other women outside the restricted homogeneous radar screen of metropolitan concerns. Although herself a compelling performer, as a political-intellectual her politics are far removed from the contemporary preoccupation with identity as performance. Idiosyncratic, breaker of rules, focused on the dynamics of pedagogy at the local level, Spivak has been at the forefront not of the institutional study of marginalization, but of the intrusion of a radically different politics and epistemology into the academy itself. Spivak's engaged theoretical work is designed, above all, to contribute to the creation of empowering processes of ideological and social transformation. She has decisively demonstrated that it *is* possible to make effective political interventions within and beyond one's own disciplinary field by developing significant connections between the different forms of intellectual engagement and activism in the world today.

All these qualities become rapidly evident in the lecture that follows. Few issues produce such an immediate and antagonistic response in first world-tricontinental relations as human rights. Whereas the West typically identifies human rights with its central political ideologies of freedom and democracy, on the three continents the discourse and implementation of human rights are frequently criticized on the grounds of eurocentrism in conception, and instrumentalism in terms of the selectivity of focus on where (and by whom) human rights abuses are alleged to take place. This issue came to a head in May 2001, when the UN voted to unseat the United States from the 53-member Human Rights Commission (HRC).

It is in the context of such differences that in this lecture, Spivak characteristically reorients the debate about human rights towards a different perspective, suggesting that the significant distinction is not so much that between the first world and the three continents of the South as the 'class apartheid' between the elites and subalterns across the first world and three continents alike (inequality of income distribution is one defining feature of third world countries, a hidden part of the general statistic whereby the world's richest I per cent collectively earn more than the poorest 60 per cent). The problem with human rights for Spivak is that they invariably tend to operate in a top-down power structure, in which the empowered—whether political activists, aid workers or NGOs, with access to the global public sphere—are positioned as agents, and take the burden and responsibility of human rights agency upon themselves. Significant as successful challenges at the national political and legal levels are, the gap between the empowered and disempowered often remains at the point of implementation where oppressive local power structures remain intact. How, then, to theorize and implement a subaltern strategy for human rights? Spivak here defines as subaltern those without access to lines of social mobility, which leads her to focus on the rural poor—a choice that problematically excludes the urban poor, but which remains true to the original Maoist, Naxalite origins of the Subaltern Studies project. The widespread prevalence of peasant rebellion today across the three continents, whether in Assam, Bolivia, Columbia, Ecuador, Mexico, Nepal, Paraguay, Vietnam or Zimbabwe, suggests the continuing refusal of the rural poor to submit to conditions of impoverishment, exploitation and oppression, and here the demand for basic human rights, which begins not with abstract notions of freedom but with the right to basic material resources—food and water—features as central in a way that can only be chastening for anyone fortunate enough to have the means to be involved in Amnesty International.

Spivak's interest begins at that point also: specifically, with the need for a new waterpipe to deliver clean water to a community of tribals in rural India. For Spivak the ability to achieve such a humble, minimal objective—as yet unsuccessful—begins with a different kind of agency from that customarily invoked in postcolonial academia—that is, with literacy, and the forms of political agency and understanding that literacy can bring. The need to achieve effective forms of literacy drives Spivak on to a preoccupation with the processes of teaching. What she proposes here is not the liberal account of the teaching of humanities in the West or another narcissistic reflection on the role of the intellectual: instead Spivak argues for a pedagogy of the oppressed designed to enable empowerment, the righting of wrongs, through a dynamic dialogic model of education as the means to cultural and political action.

# 5

# Righting Wrongs

## Gayatri Chakravorty Spivak

*Argument*: Responsibility-based cultures are long delegitimized and unprepared for the public sphere; rights-based cultures are increasingly committed to corporatism in philanthropy. The former need supplementation for entry into democratic reflexes just as the latter need supplementation into the call of the other. Supplementation is needed by both sides. The humanities can play a role. Otherwise human rights feed (on) class apartheid.

'Human Rights, Human Wrongs', the title of this lecture series, is asymmetrical. The primary nominative sense of 'rights' cited by the *Oxford English Dictionary* is 'justifiable claim, on legal or moral grounds, to have or obtain something, or to act in a certain way'. There is no parallel usage of 'wrongs', connected to an agent in the possessive case—'my wrongs'—or given to it as an object of the verb 'to have'— 'she has wrongs'.

'Rights' entail an individual or collective. 'Wrongs', however, cannot be used as a noun, except in so far as another, as agent of injustice, is involved. The verb 'to wrong' is more common than the noun, and indeed the noun probably gets its enclitic meaning by back-formation from the verb.

The word 'rights' in the title of our lecture series this year acquires verbal meaning by its contiguity with the word 'wrongs'. The verb 'to right' cannot be used intransitively on this level of abstraction. It can only be used with the unusual noun 'wrong': 'to right a wrong' or 'to right wrongs'. Our title thus makes visible that 'Human Rights' is not only about having or claiming a right or a set of rights, it is also about righting wrongs, about being the dispenser of these rights. The idea of human rights, in other words, may carry within itself the agenda of a kind of Social Darwinism: the fittest must shoulder the burden of righting the wrongs of the unfit—and the possibility of an alibi.[1] Only a 'kind of' Social Darwinism, of course. Just as 'the white man's burden', undertaking to civilize and develop, was only 'a kind of' oppression. It would be silly to footnote the scholarship that has gone to show that the latter may have been an alibi for economic, military and political intervention. It is on that model that I am using the concept-metaphor of the alibi in these introductory paragraphs.

Having arrived here, the usual thing is to complain about the eurocentrism of human rights. I have no such intention. I am of course troubled by the use of human rights as an alibi for interventions of various sorts. But its so-called European provenance is for me in the same category as the 'enabling violation' of the production of the colonial subject.[2] One cannot write off the righting of wrongs. The enablement must be used even as the violation is renegotiated.

Colonialism was committed to the education of a certain class. It was interested in the seemingly permanent operation of an altered normality. Paradoxically, human rights and 'development' work today cannot claim this self-empowerment that high colonialism could. Yet, it is some of the best products of high colonialism, descendants of the colonial middle class, who become human rights advocates in the countries of the South. I will explain through an analogy.

'Doctors without Frontiers'—I find this translation

[*Médécins sans Frontières*] more accurate than the received 'Doctors without Borders'—dispense healing all over the world, travelling to solve health problems as they arise. They cannot be involved in the repetitive work of primary health-care, which requires changes in the habit of what seems normal living: permanent operation of an altered normality. This group cannot learn all the local languages, dialects and idioms of the places where they provide help. They use local interpreters. It is as if, in the field of class-formation through education, colonialism and the attendant territorial imperial-ism had combined these two imperatives—clinic and primary healthcare—by training the interpreters themselves into imperfect yet creative imitations of the doctors. The class thus formed—both (pseudo)doctor and interpreter, as it were—was the colonial subject.

The end of the Second World War inaugurated the post-colonial dispensation.

It was the U.N. Special Committee on Decolonization . . . that in 1965 asked the Commission [on Human Rights, created in 1946] to process the petitions that the Committee was receiving about human rights violations in southern Africa . . . [Until the mid-1960s,] particularly for the new African and Asian members, the priority was [white] racism and [against it] self-determination from colonial rule [in other words, decolonization]. Later, their enthusi-asm for the new procedures waned as the protection of civil and political [human] rights [in the new nation] emerged as the priority consideration and many of them became the targets [since they, as the new masters, were the guilty party] for the Commission's new mandate.[3]

For the eighteenth-century Declaration of the Rights of Man and of Citizens by the National Assembly of France, the 'nation is essentially the source of sovereignty; nor can any individual, or any body of men, be entitled to any authority which is not expressly derived from it.'[4] One hundred and fifty years later, for better or for worse, the human rights aspect of postcoloniality has turned out to be the breaking of the new nations, in the name of their breaking-in into the international community of nations.[5] This is the narrative of international manoeuvring. Risse, Roppe and Sikkink's recent book, *The Power of Human Rights*, takes the narrative further. In addition to the dominant states, they argue, since 1993 it is the transnational agencies, plus non-governmental organizations that subdue the state.[6]

Nevertheless, it is still disingenuous to call human rights eurocentric. This is not only because, in the global South, the domestic human rights workers are, by and large, the descendants of the colonial subject, often culturally positioned against eurocentrism. It is also because, internationally, the role of the new diasporic is strong, and the diasporic in the metropolis stands for 'diversity' 'against eurocentrism'. Thus the work of righting wrongs is shared above a class line that to some extent and unevenly cuts across race and the North–South divide.[7] I say 'to some extent and unevenly' because, to be located in the Euro-US still makes a difference. In the United Nations itself, 'the main human rights monitoring function [has been] allocated to the OSCE [Organization for Security and Cooperation in Europe]'.[8] The presuppositions of Risse, Roppe and Sikkink's book also make this clear. The subtitle, 'International norms and domestic change', is telling. In keeping with this, the authors' idea of the motor of human rights is 'pressure' on the state 'from above' (international) and 'from below' (domestic). (It is useful for this locationist privilege that most NGOs of the global South survive on Northern aid.) Here is a typical example, as it happens about the Philippines: '"Human rights" have gained prescriptive status independent of political interests . . . [We] doubt that habitualization or institutionalization at the state level have proceeded sufficiently to render pressure from societal actors futile.'9 This is pressure 'from below', of course. Behind these 'societal actors' and the state is 'international normative pressure'. I shall go on to suggest that, unless 'education' is thought differently from 'consciousness-raising' about 'the human rights norm' and 'rising literacy expand[ing] the individual's media exposure', 'sufficient habitualization or institutionalization' will never arrive, and this will continue to provide justification for international control.

Thinking about education and the diaspora, Edward W. Said has recently written that 'the American University generally [is] for its academic staff and many of its students the last remaining utopia.'10 The philosopher Richard Rorty as well as Lee Kuan Yew—the former Prime Minister of Singapore who supported 'detention without trial . . . [as] Confucianist'—share Professor Said's view of the utopianism of the Euro-US university. I quote Rorty, but I invite you to read Premier Lee's *From Third World to First: the Singapore Story: 1965–2000* to savour their accord:

Producing generations of nice, tolerant, well-off, secure, other-respecting students of [the American] sort in all parts of the world is just what is needed—indeed all that is needed—to achieve an Enlightenment utopia. The more youngsters like that we can raise, the stronger and more global our human rights culture will become.11

If one wishes to make this restricted utopianism, which extends to great universities everywhere, available for global social justice, one must unmoor it from its elite safe harbours, supported by the power of the dominant nation's civil polity, and be interested in a kind of education for the largest sector of the future electorate in the global South—the children of the rural poor—that would go beyond literacy and numeracy and find a home in an expanded definition of a 'humanities to come'.

Education in the humanities attempts to be an *uncoercive rearrangement of desires*.[12] If you are not persuaded by this simple description, then nothing I say about the humanities will move you. This is the burden of the second section of this essay. It is this simple but difficult practice that is outlined there. It is only when we interest ourselves in this new kind of education for the children of the rural poor in the global South that the inevitability of unremitting pressure as the primum mobile of human rights will be questioned. If one engages in such empowerment at the lowest level, it is in the hope that the need for international/domestic-elite pressure on the state will not remain primary forever. We cannot necessarily expect the old colonial subject transformed into the new domestic middle-class urban radical, defined as 'below' by Risse, Roppe and Sikkink and by metropolitan human rights in general, to engage in the attempt I shall go on to describe. Although physically based in the South, and therefore presumably far from the utopian university, this class is generally also out of touch with the mindset—a combination of episteme and ethical discourse—of the rural poor below the NGO level. To be able to present a project that will draw aid from the North, for example, to understand and state a problem intelligibly and persuasively for the taste of the North, is itself proof of a sort of epistemic discontinuity with the ill-educated rural poor.[13] (And the sort of education we are thinking of is not to make the rural poor capable of drafting NGO grant proposals!) It is this discontinuity, not skin colour or national identity crudely understood, that undergirds the question of who always rights and who is perennially wronged.[14]

I have been suggesting, then, that 'human rights culture' runs on unremitting Northern-ideological pressure, even when it is from the South; that there is a real epistemic discontinuity between the Southern human rights advocates and those whom they protect.[15] In order to shift this layered discontinuity, however slightly, we must focus on the quality and end of education, at both ends: the Southern elite is often educated in Western or Western-style institutions. We must work at both ends—both in Said/Rorty's utopia and in the schools of the rural poor in the global South. I shall argue this by way of a historical and theoretical digression.

As long as the claim to natural or inalienable human rights— rights that all human beings possess because they are human by nature—was reactive to the historical alienation in 'Europe' as such (the French *ancien régime* or the German Third Reich), the problem of relating 'natural' to 'civil' rights was on the agenda. Since its use by the Commission on Decolonization in the 1960s, its thorough politicization in the 1990s, when the nation-states of the South, and perhaps the nation-state form itself needed to be broken in the face of the restructuring demands of globalization; and its final inclusion of the postcolonial subject in the form of the metropolitan diasporic, that particular problem—of relating 'natural' to 'civil' rights—was quietly forgotten. In other words, that the question of nature must be begged (assumed when it needs to be demonstrated), in order to use it historically, has been forgotten.[16]

The urgency of the political calculus obliges Thomas Paine to reduce the shadow of this immense European debate—between justice and law, between natural and civil rights [*jura*], at least as old as classical antiquity—to a 'difference'. The structural asymmetry of the difference—between mental theatre and state structure—remains noticeable:

His natural rights are the foundation of all his civil rights. But in order to pursue this distinction with more precision, it will be necessary to mark the different qualities of natural and civil rights . . . Every civil right has for its foundation, some natural right pre-existing in the individual, but to the enjoyment of which his individual power is not, in all cases, sufficient.[17]

The context of the *second* Declaration brings us close to our present. To situate it historically within the thematic of the begged question at the origin, I refer the reader to Jacques Derrida's treatment of how Walter Benjamin attempts to contain this in his 1921 essay 'Critique of Violence', which deals precisely with the relationship between natural and positive law and legitimate and illegitimate violence.[18] Benjamin's consideration of the binary opposition between legitimate and illegitimate violence as it relates to the originary violence that establishes authority can be placed on the chain of displacements from Hobbes's consideration of the binary opposition between the state of nature and the law of nature, with the former split by what George Shelton sees as the difference between the fictive and its representation as the real.[19]

I will mention Ernst Bloch's *Natural Law and Human Dignity* (1961) here to give a sense of a text at the other end of the Third Reich.[20] The 1960s will witness the internationalization of human rights. The Benjamin/Bloch texts represent the European lineaments that brought forth the second Declaration.

Bloch faces the problem of the 'natural' by historicizing it. He gives an account of the ways in which the European tradition has finessed the begged question of nature. His heroes are the Stoics—especially Epicurus—and Marx. Marx contains the potential of setting free the question of nature as freedom: '[a] Marxism that was what it was supposed to be would be a radical penal theory, indeed the most radical and at the same time most amiable: It kills the social mother of injustice.' I cannot credit a 'Marxism in its proper outlines'. But I can at least suggest that in these times, when an inter-nationalized human rights has forgotten to acknowledge the begged question of nature, a non-disciplinary 'philosopher' who has been taught the value of philosophy as an 'art of living' in the Stoic style through the Nietzschean line of Foucault and Derrida might want to point out that Zeno and Epicurus were, necessarily, what would today be called 'colonial subjects'. I would also suggest that we may attempt to supplement a merely penal system by re-inventing the social mother of injustice as worldwide class-apartheid, and kill her, again and again, in the mode of 'to come', through the educa-tion of those who fell through colonial subject-formation.[21]

I have not the expertise to summarize the long history of the European debate surrounding natural/civil rights. With some hesitation I would point at the separation/imbrication of nature and liberty in Machiavelli, at the necessary slippage in Hobbes between social contract as natural fiction and social contract as civil reality, at Hobbes's debate on liberty and necessity with Bishop Bramhill.[22] George Shelton dis-tinguishes between a 'hypothetical' and a 'real' social contract in Hobbes, at a certain point calling the former a 'useful fiction.'[23] New interest in Hobbesian theology has disclosed a similar pattern in Hobbes's discussion of God as ground.[24] This is particularly interesting because Hobbes is so widely seen as the initiator of individualism. Hobbes himself places his discussions within debates in Roman law and I think we should respect this chain of displacements—rather than a linear intellectual history—that leads to the rupture of the first European Declaration of Human Rights.[25] I am arguing that such speculative lines are not allowed to flourish within today's global human rights activities, where a crude notion of cultural difference is about as far as grounds-talk will go.

Academic research may contest this trend by tracking rational critique and/or individualism within non-European high cultures.[26] This is valuable work. But the usually silent victims of pervasive rather than singular and spectacular human rights violations are generally the rural poor. These academic efforts do not touch their stagnating general cultures unless it is through broad generalizations, positive and negative. Accessing those long-delegitimized epistemes requires a different engagement. The pedagogic effort that may bring about lasting epistemic change in the oppressed is never accurate, and must be forever renewed. Otherwise there does not seem much point in considering the humanities worth teaching. And, as I have already signalled, the red thread of a defence of the humanities as an attempt at uncoercive rearrangement of desires runs through this essay.

Attempts at such pedagogic change need not necessarily involve confronting the task of undoing the legacy of a specifically *colonial* education. Other political upheavals have also divided the postcolonial or global polity into an effective class apartheid. (I expand my argument beyond postcoloniality in the narrow sense because of what I hope is the beginning of a long-term involvement with grassroots rural education in China.) All that seems possible to surmise is that the redressing work of human rights must be supplemented by an education that can continue to make unstable the presupposition that the reasonable righting of wrongs is inevitably the manifest destiny of groups—unevenly class-divided, embracing North and South—that remain poised to right them; and that, among the receiving groups, wrongs will inevitably proliferate with unsurprising regularity. Consequently, the groups that are the dispensers of human rights must realize that, just as the natural Rights of Man were contingent upon the historical French Revolution, and the Universal Declaration upon the historical events that led to the Second World War, so also is the current emergence, of the human rights model as the global dominant, contingent upon the turbulence in the wake of the dissolution of imperial formations and global economic restructuring. The task of making visible the begged question grounding the political manipulation of a civil society forged on globally defined natural rights is just as urgent; and not simply by way of *cultural* relativism.

In disciplinary philosophy, discussion of the begged question at the origin of natural rights is not altogether absent. Alan Gewirth chooses the Rational Golden Rule as his PGC (principle of generic consistency), starting his project in the following way: 'The Golden Rule is the common moral denominator of all the world's major religions.'[27] From a historical point of view, one is obliged to say that none of the great religions of the world can lead to an end to violence today.[28] Where Gewirth, whom nobody would associate with deconstruction, is important for our argument, is in his awareness of the grounding of the justification for Human

Rights in a begged question. He takes it as a 'contradiction' to solve and finds in the transposition of 'rational' for 'moral' his solution.[29] 'The traditional Golden Rule [Do unto others as you would have them do unto you] leaves open the question of why any person ought to act in accordance with it.'[30] This is the begging of the question, because the moral cannot not be normative. According to Gewirth, a commonsensical problem can be theoretically avoided because

[i]t is not the contingent desires of agents but rather aspects of agency which cannot rationally be avoided or evaded by any agent that determine the content of the Rational Golden Rule [because it] . . . focuses on what the agent necessarily wants or values insofar as he is rational.

It would seem to us that this begs the question of the reasonable nature of reason (accounting for the principle of reason by the principle of reason).[31] We would rather not construct the best possible theory, but acknowledge that practice always splits open the theoretical justification.

In fact, Gewirth knows this. Toward the end of the essay, this curious sentence is left hanging: '*Materially*, [the] *self-contradiction* [that to deny or violate the Rational Golden Rule is to contradict oneself] is *inescapable* because . . . the Rational Golden Rule [is] derived from the necessities of purposive agency' (emphasis added). If we acknowledge the part outside of reason in the human mind, then we may see the limits of reason as 'white mythology' and see the contradiction as the necessary relationship between two discontinuous begged questions as I have suggested above: proof that we are born free and proof that it is the other that calls us before will. Then the question 'Why must we follow the Golden Rule (the basis of human rights)?' finds an answer: because the other calls us. But it is never a fitting answer, it is not continuous with the question. Let us then call this a relationship, a discontinuous supplementary relationship, not a solution. Instead, Gewirth is obliged to recode the white mythology of reason as unavoidable last instance, as an '*inherent* capab[ility] of exercising [human rights]'.[32] If one enters into a sustained give-and-take with subordinate cultures attempting to address structural questions of power as well as textural questions of responsibility, one feels more and more that a Gewirth-style recoding may be something like a historical incapacity to grasp that to rationalize the question of ethics *fully* (please note that this does not mean banishing reason from ethics altogether, just giving it an honorable and instrumental place) is to transgress the intuition that ethics are a problem of relation before they are a task of knowledge. This does not gainsay the fact that, in the juridico-legal manipulation of the abstractions of contemporary politics by those who right wrongs, where a reasoned calculus is instrumentally necessary, nothing can be more welcome than Gewirth's rational justification. What we are describing is a simplified version of the aporia between ethics and politics. An aporia is disclosed only in its one-way crossing. This essay attempts to make the reader recognize that human rights is such an interested crossing, a containment of the aporia in binary oppositions.[33]

A few words, then, about supplementing metropolitan education before I elaborate on the pedagogy of the subaltern. By 'subaltern' I mean those removed from lines of social mobility.[34]

I shall continue to insist that the problem with US education is that it teaches (corporatist) benevolence while trivializing the teaching of the humanities.[35] The result is, at best, cultural relativism as cultural absolutism ('American-style education will do the trick'). Its undoing is best produced by way of the training of reflexes that kick in at the time of urgency, of decision and policy. However unrealistic it may seem to you, I would not remain a teacher of the humanities if I did not believe that at the New York end—standing metonymically for the dispensing end as such—the teacher can try to rearrange desires noncoercively (as I mentioned a few pages back) through an attempt to develop in the student a habit of literary reading, even just 'reading', suspending oneself into the text of the other. For this, the first condition and effect is a suspension of the conviction that I am necessarily better, I am necessarily indispensable, I am necessarily the one to right wrongs, I am necessarily the end-product for which history happened, and that New York is necessarily the capital of the world. It is not a loss of will, especially since it is supplemented in its turn by the political calculus, where, as Said's, Rorty's and Premier Lee's argument emphasizes, the possibility of being a 'helper' abounds in today's triumphalist US society. A training in literary reading is a training to learn from the singular and the unverifiable. Although literature cannot speak, this species of patient reading, miming an effort to make the text respond, as it were, is a training not only in poiesis, accessing the other so well that probable action can be prefigured, but teleo-poiesis, striving for a response from the distant other, without guarantees.

I have no moral position against grading, or writing recommendation letters. But if you are attempting to train in specifically literary reading, the results are not directly ascertainable by the teaching subject, and perhaps not the taught subject either. In my experience, the 'proof' comes in unexpected ways, from the other side. But the absence of such proof does not necessarily 'mean' nothing has been learnt. This is why I say 'no guarantees'.[36] And that is also why the work of an epistemic undoing of cultural relativism as cultural absolutism can only work as a supplement to the more institutional practice, filling a responsibility-shaped gap but also adding something discontinuous. As far as human rights goes, this is the only prior and patient training that can leaven the quick-fix training institutes that prepare international civil society workers, including human rights advocates, with uncomplicated standards for success.[37] This is not a suggestion that all human rights workers should have institutional humanities training. As it stands, humanities teaching in the United States is what I am describing only in the very rare instance. And the mode is 'to come'.

It is in the interest of supplementing metropolitan humanities pedagogy, rather than from the perspective of some fantasmatic cultural difference, that we can say that the 'developed post-capitalist structure' of today's world must 'be filled with the more robust imperative to responsibility which capitalist social productivity was obliged to destroy. We must learn to re-define that lost imperative as defective for the emergence of capitalism, rather than necessarily pre-capitalist on an interested sequential evolutionary model.'[38] On the simplest terms, being defined by the call of the other—which may be a defining feature of such societies—is not conducive to the extraction and appropriation of surplus. Making room for *otium* and living in the rhythm of the eco-biome does not lead to exploration and conquest of nature. And so on. The method of a specifically literary training, a slow mind-changing process, can be used to open the imagination to such mindsets.[39]

One of the reasons international communism failed was

because Marx, an organic intellectual of the industrial revolution, could only think the claiming of rights to freedom from exploitation by way of the public use of reason recommended by the European Enlightenment. The ethical part—to want to exercise the freedom to redistribute after the revolution— comes by way of the sort of education I am speaking of. This intuition was not historically unavailable to Marx: 'circumstances are changed by men and . . . the educator himself must be educated'.[40] In the event, the pedagogic impulse was confined to the lesson of capital, to change the victim into an agent. The intuition that the lesson was historically determined was of course not unavailable to Marx either.[41] My position is thus not against class-struggle, but yet another attempt to broaden it, to include the 'ground condition' [Grundbedingung] of the continued reproduction of class apartheid in ancient and/or disenfranchised societies in modernity. If the industrial proletariat of Victorian England were expanded to include the global subaltern, there is no hope that such an agent could ever 'dictate' anything through the structures of parliamentary democracy—I admit I cannot give this up—if this persisent pedagogic effort is not sustained.

(I am more than ever convinced of the need to resuscitate the lost cultural imperative to responsibility after the initial trip, mentioned above, to the lowest-level rural schools in a mountain province in China, in the company of a wonderfully enthusiastic young English teacher at the University of Science and Technology in the provincial urban center. He had never visited such schools, never thought of the possibility of restoring a failed communism with a persistent effort to teach oneself how to access older cultural habits in practice in order to suture in, in rural education, the ethical impulse that can make social justice flourish, forever in the mode of 'to

come', because forever dependent upon the qualitative education of the young.[42] Yet he has already been used by the US
industry in 'China's ethnic minority education' scholarship,
as a 'grassroots native informant' sent into 'the field' with a
questionnaire for ten days' research! A perfect candidate for
the domestic 'below', for whom the 'evils' of communism
seem to be open for correction only through the absolutist
arrogance of US utopianism, coded as an interest in cultural
difference.)

A desire to redistribute is not the unproblematic consequence of a well-fed society. In order to get that desire
moving by the cultural imperative of education, you have to
fix the possibility of putting not just 'wrong' over against
'right', with all the genealogical lines compressed within
it; but also to suggest that another antonym of 'right' is
'responsibility', and further, that the possibility of such
responsibility is underived from rights.

I will now describe a small and humble experiment that I
have tried over the last ten years, nearly every day at the
Columbia University gym and, unhappily, the rate of experimental verification is 100 per cent. There is an approximately
6 ft by 4 ft windowless anteroom as you enter the locker area.
This useless space, presumably to protect female modesty, is
brightly lit. There is a light switch by the door from the main
gym into the anteroom, and another by the door leading into
the lockers. In other words, it is possible to turn the light off as
you exit this small enclosed space. You can choose not to let it
burn so brightly for 24 hours for no one. Remember, these are
university folks, generally politically correct, interested in
health, a special control group, who talk a good deal about
environmental responsibility. (I am drawing the example from
within the cultural idiom of the group, as always.) I turn off

the light in this windowless cube whenever I enter the locker and my sciatica keeps me going to the gym pretty regularly. In the last ten years, I have never re-entered this little space and found the light off. Please draw your own conclusions.

The responsibility I speak of, then, is not necessarily the one that comes from the consciousness of superiority lodged in the self (today's quote of the month at the gym is, characteristically: 'The price of greatness is responsibility'—Winston Churchill), but one that is, to begin with, sensed before sense as a call of the other.[43]

Varieties of the Churchillian sense of 'responsibility', nearly synonymous with duty, have always also been used from within the Rights camp, of course. Machiavelli and Hobbes both write on duty. The 1793 version of the Declaration of the Rights of Man contains a section on the duties of man and of the citizen. The UN issued a Declaration of Responsibilities—little more than a reinscription of the rights as duties for their establishment—in 1997. There is a scientists' 'Declaration of Duties'. And so on. This is the trajectory of the idea of 'responsibility' as assumed, by choice, by the group that can right wrongs. I think Amnesty International is correct in saying that the UN Declaration of Responsibilities is 'no complement to human rights', and that 'to *restate . . . rights* from the UDHR [Universal Declaration of Human Rights] *as responsibilities* the draft declaration introduces vague and ill-defined notions which can only create confusion and uncertainty'.[44] Thus even a liberal vision is obliged to admit that there is no continuous line from rights to responsibilities.

This notion of responsibility as the 'duty of the fitter self' toward less fortunate others (rather than the predication of being-human as being called by the other, before will) is not my meaning, of course. I remain concerned, however, by one of its corollaries in global social movements. The leaders from the domestic 'below',—for the subaltern an 'above'—not realizing the historically established discontinuity between themselves and the subaltern, counsel self-help with great supervisory benevolence. This is important to remember because the subalterns' obvious inability to do so without sustained supervision is seen as proof of the need for continued intervention. It is necessary to be involved in the everyday working (the 'textuality') of global social movements to recognize that the seeming production of 'declarations' from these supervised groups is written to dictation and is thus no strike against class-apartheid. 'To claim rights is your duty' is the banal lesson that the above—whether Northern or Southern—then imparts to the below. The organization of international conferences with exceptionalist tokenization to represent collective subaltern will is a last-ditch solution, for both sides, if at all. And, sometimes, as in the case of my friend in Yunan, the unwitting native informant is rather far from the subaltern.

Within the rights camp, the history of something like responsibility-based cultural systems is generally given as part of the progress towards the development of a rights-based system in the type case of the European self.[45]

The Judaic articulation of responsibility, after the very war that produced the Universal Declaration, is set forth by Emmanuel Levinas.[46] Derrida has attempted to unmoor this from unquestioning support for the state of Israel by proposing a messianicity without messianism, although he acknowledges that he is caught in the traces of his own peculiar cultural production in stating responsibility just this way.[47] This history and its institutional discussions remain confined to the elite academy. If there is no direct line from rights to responsibility, there is certainly no direct possibility of supplementing the below from this discussion.[48]

It can seem at first glance that if the Euro-US mindset modifies itself by way of what used to be called, just yesterday, Third Way politics, providing a cover for social democracy's rightward swing, perhaps the dispensers of human rights would at least modify their arrogance. As George W. Bush claims Tony Blair as his chum on Bush's visit to Britain in July 2001, I believe it is still worth examining this impulse, however briefly, so that it is not offered as a panacea. Let us look at a few crucial suggestions from *Beyond Left and Right* by Anthony Giddens, the academic spokesperson of the Third Way.[49]

Giddens mentions the virtues of Third World poverty and therefore may seem at first glance to be recommending learning from the subaltern. Criticizing the welfare state, he quotes Charles Murray with approval: 'Murray, whose work has been influenced by experiences in rural Thailand, asks the question, what's wrong with being poor (once people are above the level of subsistence poverty)? Why should there be such a general concern to combat poverty?' I hope it is clear that I have no interest in keeping the subaltern poor. To repeat, it is in view of Marx's hope to transform the subaltern—whom he understood only as the worker in his conjuncture—into an agent of the undoing of class apartheid rather than its victim that this effort at educating the educator is undertaken.

Here are some of Giddens's 'practical' suggestions: 'A post-scarcity system is . . . a system in which productivism no longer rules', a 'new ethics of individual and collective responsibility need to be formed', 'traditions should be understood in a non-traditional manner', a 'pact between the sexes [is] . . . to be achieved, within the industrialized societies and on a more global level'—that hesitation between the two levels is kin to the asymmetry in our title and the invasive gender-work of the international civil society—and, best of all, 'a new pact between the affluent and the poor' is now needed. How is Professor Giddens going to persuade global finance and world trade to jettison the culture of economic growth? The question applies to all the passages I have quoted and more. He is, of course, speaking of state policy in Europe, but his book tries to go beyond into other spaces:

The question remains whether a lifestyle pact as suggested here for the wealthy countries could also work when applied to the divisions between North and South. Empirically, one certainly could not answer this question positively with any degree of assurance. Analytically speaking, however, one could ask, what other possibility is there?[50]

However utopian it might seem, it now appears to me that the only way to make these sweeping changes—there is nothing inherently wrong with them, and of course I give Professor Giddens the benefit of the doubt—is for those who teach in the humanities to take seriously the necessary but impossible task to construct a collectivity among the dispensers of bounty as well as the victims of oppression.[51] Learning from the subaltern is, paradoxically, through teaching. In practical terms, working across the class–culture difference (which tends to refract efforts), trying to learn from children, and from the behaviour of class-'inferiors', the teacher learns to recognize, not just a benevolently coerced assent, but also an unexpected response. For such an education, speed, quantity of information, and number of students reached are not exclusive virtues. Those 'virtues' are inefficient for education in the responsibilities in the humanities, not so much a sense of being responsible *for*, but of being responsible *to*, before will. Institutionally, the humanities, like all disciplines, must be subject to a calculus. It is how we earn our living. But where 'living' has a larger meaning, the humanities are without guarantees.

Speaking with reference to the Rights of Man and the Universal Declaration, I am insisting that in the European context, it used to be recognized that the question of nature as the ground of rights must be begged in order to use it historically. The assumption that it is natural to be angled toward the other, before will, the question of responsibility in subordinate cultures, is also a begged question. Neither can survive without the other, if it is a just world that we seem to be obliged to want. Indeed, any interest in human rights for others, in human rights and human wrongs, would do better if grounded in this second begged question, to redress historical balance, as it were, than in the apparent forgetting of the other one. In the beginning are two begged questions.

Surely the thought of two begged questions at the origin is no more abstract than John Rawls's interminable suppositions which, when confronted with the necessity of doing something, come up with such platitudes as

There will also be principles for forming and regulating federations (associations) of peoples, and standards of fairness for trade and other cooperative arrangements. There should be certain provisions for mutual assistance between peoples in times of famine and drought, and were it feasible, as it should be, provisions for ensuring that in all reasonably developed liberal societies people's basic needs are met.[52]

In the 'real world' there is, in general, a tremendously uneven contradiction between those who beg the question of nature as rights for the self and those who beg the question of responsibility as being called by the other, before will.

If we mean to place the latter—perennial victims—on the way to the social productivity of capital (as an old-fashioned Marxist I distinguish between capital and capitalism and do not say these words ironically), then we must acknowledge the need for supplementation there as well, rather than transform them willy-nilly, consolidating already existing hierarchies, exporting gender-struggle, by way of the greed for economic growth. I have argued above that these cultures started regressing because their cultural axiomatics were defective for capitalism. I have also argued that the socialist project can receive its ethical push not from within itself but by supplementation from such axiomatics. I have argued that in their current decrepitude the subaltern cultures need to be known in such a way that we can suture their re-activated cultural axiomatics into the principles of the Enlightenment. I have argued that socialism belongs to those axiomatics. That socialism turns capital-formation into redistribution is a truism.[53] It is by this logic that supplementation into the Enlightenment is as much the possibility of being the agent of the social productivity of capital as it is of the subjectship of human rights.

The general culture of Euro-US capitalism in globalization and economic restructuring has conspicuously destroyed the possibility of capital being redistributive and socially productive in a broad-based way. As I have mentioned above, 'the burden of the fittest'—a re-territorializing of 'the white man's burden'—does also touch the economic sphere. I hope I will be forgiven a brief digression into that sphere as well. I have prepared for this by describing the 1990s as a time 'of the restructuring demands of globalization'. The reader is urged to concentrate on the lack of intellectual connection between the people at work in the different spheres. I cannot be more than telegraphic here, but it would be a mistake to leave untouched the great economic circuits that often remotely determine the shots in the human rights sphere. I remain among the unabashed walking wounded generalist aspirants from the 1960s. Elsewhere, I have called this 'transnational literacy'.

As an introduction to this brief foray into the economic sphere, let us consider philosophers connecting Hobbes with global governance, an issue that bears on the administration of human rights in an economically restructured post-state world.[54] The question they have asked—whether the 'stronger nations might reasonably believe their prospects to be better if they remain in the international state of nature, rather than accepting some international (but nonabsolute) equivalent of Hobbes's civil sovereign . . . despite the fact that in supporting it they run the risk, along with the weaker nations, of creating a monster that may well attempt to devour them'—has no bearing on the institutive difference at the origin of the state of nature.[55]

The quotation above is from the early 1980s, when the floodgates of the current phase of globalization—the financialization of the globe with the decentred centralization of world trade attendant upon the dissolution of the Soviet Union which, in turn, allowed a fuller flow for information technology—had not yet been opened. Yet the process had already begun, through the newly electronified stock exchanges combining with what was then called postfordism, enabled by computer technology and the fax machine. And Euro-US thinkers, connecting Hobbes with human rights, were certainly ignoring the question of the relationship between 'natural' and 'civil'.

The relatively autonomous *economic* sphere of operations, worked by agents with competence restricted to this area, is explained for the *cultural* sector by other kinds of academic agents, restricted to the political sphere, in terms of a global governance story that started at the beginning of the post-colonial era at Bretton Woods. The culturalists then weigh in by endlessly pointing out that world markets are old hat. This then feeds back into the cultural difference story or the hip global public culture story.[56] Other disciplinary areas involved in this are social psychology and management. The former (as I indicate in note 14) gives us the multiculturalist cultural difference stereotypes that undergird human rights policy when it wishes to protect a 'community without individualism' against a rogue state. Cultural distance studies in management relate directly to the economic sphere and global finance, plotting the 'joint ventures' opened up by neo-liberal economic restructuring.[57] There is a compendious literature on how such ventures undermine the state and move toward the post-state world which becomes the object of global governance. In this brief compass, I refer the reader to note 25. The rogue state is disciplined by fear and pressure—the stick—with the promise of economic partnership—the carrot. My principal argument continues to be that a combination of fear and pressure, today supported by these powerful para-disciplinary formations proliferating crude theories of cultural difference, cannot bring about either lasting or real epistemic change although, accompanied by public interest litigation, they may be effective short-term weapons.

Meanwhile, the seriousness of training into the general culture is reflected by the fact that Morgan Stanley Dean Witter, Merrill Lynch, and other big investment companies are accessing pre-schoolers; children are training parents to manage portfolios. There is a growing library of books making it 'fun' for kids to invest and giving them detailed instructions on how to do so. The unquestioned assumption that to be rich is to be happy and good is developed by way of many 'educational' excuses.

Children are never too young to start grasping the fundamentals of money management . . . Even toddlers understand the concept of 'mine!' In fact, it's the idea of owning something they like that sparks their interest in investing. Rest assured, you won't turn your child into a little money-grubber by feeding that interest. Through investing you're going to teach him more about responsibility, discipline, delayed gratification, and even ethics than you ever thought possible![58]

Such a training of children builds itself on the loss of the cultural habit of assuming the agency of responsibility in radical alterity. It is followed through by the relentless education into business culture in academic and on-the-job training, in management, consumer behaviour, marketing, prepared for by the thousands and thousands of business schools all over the global South as well as the North, training undergraduates into business culture, making the supplementation of the responsibility-based subaltern layer by the ethics of class–culture difference altogether impossible, consolidating class apartheid.[59] The Declaration of the Right to Development is part of such acculturation into the movements of finance capital. Third Way talk floats on this base. Culturalist support is provided on the internet—in book digests on 'market Taoism' and 'Aristotle for capitalism'.[60] It is provided in the sales presentations of countless telecommunication marketing conferences. It connects to the laughing and frequent exhortations to 'follow the money' at women's rights meetings at the UN. We should keep all this in mind when we give Professor Giddens the benefit of the doubt.

Ethics within the corporatist calculus is also inscribed within this cultural formation. I team-taught a course with Political Science in Fall 2000. Our greatest problem was negotiating the difference between ethics as imagined from within the self-driven political calculus as 'doing the right thing' and ethics as openness toward the imagined agency of the other, responsibility for and to—a tiny radical enclave here and, as I shall argue, a compromised and stagnating conformity there.

Such a training of children is also a legitimation by reversal of our own insistence on elementary pedagogy of the rural poor. Supplementation by the sort of education I am trying to describe becomes necessary here, so that the relationship between child investors and child labourers is not simply one of righting wrongs from above. How does such supplementation work? If in New York, to stem the tide of corporatist ethics, business culture, appropriative New Age radicalism, and politically correct multiculturalism, the subterranean task is to supplement the radical responsibility-shaped hole in the education of the dispenser of rights through literary reading, and making use of the humanities, what about the education of those whose wrongs are righted?

Some assumptions must first be laid aside. The permeability of global culture must be seen as restricted. There is a lack of communication between and among the immense hetero-geneity of the subaltern cultures of the world. Cultural bor-ders are easily crossed from the superficial cultural relativism of metropolitan countries, whereas, going the other way, the so-called peripheral countries encounter bureaucratic and policed frontiers. The frontiers of subaltern cultures, which developed no generative public role, have no channels of interpenetration. Here, too, the problem is not solved in a lasting way by the inclusion of exceptional subalterns in South-based global movements with leadership drawn from the descendants of colonial subjects, even as these networks network. These figures are no longer representative of the subaltern stratum in general.

In 2000 I visited a so-called biodiversity festival, where a rural and country town audience in a 'least-developed country [LDC]' roared its derision at biodiversity songs from two neighbouring nation-states, applauding enthusiastically instead at embarrassing imitations of Bollywood (the tradename of the hugely international Bombay film industry) 'adaptations' of moments from US MTV, unrecognizable by the audience as such, of course. The embarrassment of the activist leaders, from a colonial subject's class background, was compounded by their public exhortations, which were obeyed by the rural audience as a set of bewildering orders. The historical discontinuity leading to such events is one of the reasons why, although I generalize, my example remains singular. On the practical calculus, the problem of the singular and the universal is confronted by learning from the singularity of the singular, a way to the imagination of the public sphere, the rational representation of the universal.

We must question the assumption that, if the sense of doing for the other is not produced on call from a sense of the self as sovereign, packaged with the sense of being fittest, the alternative assumption, romantic or expedient, of an essence of subalternity as the source of such a sense, denies the depradations of history. Paulo Freire, in his celebrated *Pedagogy of the Oppressed*, written during the era of guerrilla warfare in Latin America, warns us against subalternist essentialism, by

GAYATRI CHAKRAVORTY SPIVAK

reminding us that 'during the initial stages of the struggle, the oppressed . . . tend themselves to become oppressors'.[61]

In addition, in the face of UN human rights policy-making, we must be on guard against subalternist essentialism, both positive and negative. If the self-permission for continuing to right wrongs is premised implicitly on the former—they will never be able to help themselves—the latter nourishes false hopes that will as surely be dashed and lead to the same result: an unwilling conclusion that they must always be propped up. Indeed, in the present state of the world, or perhaps always and everywhere, simply harnessing responsibility for accountability in the South, checking up on other-directedness, as it were, without the persistent training of 'no guarantees', we reproduce and consolidate what can only be called 'feudalism', where a benevolent despot like Lee Kuan Yew can claim collectivity rather than individualism when expedient. In the present state of the world, it also reproduces and consolidates gender oppression, thus lending plausibility to the instant rightspeak of the gender lobby of the international civil society and Bretton Woods.

Declarations like the Bangkok NGO Declaration, entitled 'Our Voice', and cataloguing what 'their right to self-determination' would be for 'indigenous people in general',[62] may like many UN Declarations be an excellent tool for political manoeuvring but it will not touch the entire spectrum of Asian aboriginals, each group as culturally absolutist as the rural audience at the biodiversity festival. In order to make the political manoeuvrings open to the ethical, we must think the supplementation towards which we are now moving.

When the UN offers violence or the ballot as a choice, it is unrealistic because based on another kind of related mistake—

unexamined universalism—the assumption that this is a real choice in all situations. It will soon lead to military intervention in the name of righting wrong, in geopolitically specific places. For 'democratization' is not just a code name, as it so often is in practice, for the political restructuring entailed by the transformation of (efficient through inefficient to wild) state capitalisms and their colonies to tributary economies of rationalized global financialization. If it is to involve the largest sector of the electorate in the global South—the rural population below poverty level—it requires the undoing of centuries of oppression, with a suturing education in rural subaltern normality, supplementing the violent guilt and shame trips of disaster politics.

I offer here a small but representative example. I was handing out sweets, two a head, to villagers in Shahabad, Birbhum. Some of the schools I describe later are located in this area. These villages have no caste-Hindu inhabitants. Sweets of this cooked traditional variety, that have to be bought from the Hindu villages, are beyond the villagers' means. There are no 'candy stores' in either type of village. Distribution of sweets is a festive gesture, but it makes my Calcutta-bred intellectual-leftist soul slightly uneasy. I have learnt such behaviour in my decades-long apprenticeship in these areas.

A young man in his early thirties, generally considered a mover and a shaker among this particular ethnic group—the Dhekaros, straddling the Aboriginal–Untouchable divide—was opening the flimsy paper boxes that swam in syrup in flimsier polythene bags, as I kept dipping my hand.[63] Suddenly he murmured, 'Outsiders are coming in, one a piece now.' I thought the problem was numbers and changed to one, a bit sad because there were now more children. Suddenly, the guy says in my ear, 'Give her two, she's one of ours.' Shocked, I quickly turn to him, and say, in rapid monotone Bengali, 'Don't say such things in front of children; what if I should say you're not one of ours?', since I'm a caste-Hindu and technically one of his oppressors.[64]

This is the seedbed of ethnic violence in its lowest common unit.[65] You can fill in the historical narrative, raise or lower the degree of the heat of violence. Punishing Milosevic is good, human rights pressure and guilt and shame trips on rogue states should continue, I suppose, but it is on ground such as this that violence festers. This man is quite aware of party politics, the CPM (Community Party Marxist) is strong here. He certainly casts his vote regularly, perhaps even rallies voters for the party. There are two sentiments at work here. First, ethnic group competition within a corrupt quota system in the restructured state as resources dwindle. Second, the intuition of a multi-party parliamentary democracy as a species of generally homo-social competitive sport with the highest stakes available to players in the impoverished rural sector being violence and the ballot. These sentiments can co-exist in a volatile relationship, one ready to be mobilized over the other, or even in the other's interest. This is why the UN's choice—ballot box *or* 'peacekeeping mission'—is unrealistic. I shall consider an answer by way of a digression into suturing rights thinking into the torn cultural fabric of responsibility; or, to vary the concept-metaphor, activating a dormant ethical imperative.

Subordinate cultures of responsibility, then, base the agency of responsibility in that outside of the self that is also in the self, half-archived and therefore not directly accessible. I use the word 'subordinate' here because, as I have been arguing throughout this essay, they are the recipients of human rights bounty, which I see as 'the burden of the fittest', and which, as I insist from the first page on down, has the *ambivalent* structure of enabling violation that anyone of goodwill associates with the white man's burden. I will rely on this argument for this second part of my essay, which concerns itself with the different way in to the damaged episteme.

From the anthropological point of view, groups such as the Sabars and the Dhekaros may be seen to have a 'closely-knit social texture'. But I have been urging a different point of view through my concept-metaphor of 'suturing'. These groups are also in the historical present of state and civil society (human rights punishes the latter in the name of the Enlightenment). I am asking readers to shift their perception from the anthropological to the historico-political and see the same knit text-ile as a torn cultural fabric in terms of its removal from the dominant loom in a historical moment. That is what it means to be a subaltern. My point so far has been that, for a long time now, these cultural scripts have not been allowed to work except as a delegitimized form forcibly out of touch with the dominant through a history that has taken capital and empire as telos. My generalization is therefore precarious, though demonstrable if the effort I go on to describe is shared. These concept-metaphors, of suturing a torn fabric, of recoding a delegitimized cultural formation, are crucial to the entire second half of my argument.

Subordinate cultures of responsibility, as I have argued, base the agency of responsibility in that outside of the self that is also in the self, half-archived and therefore not directly accessible. Such a sentence may seem opaque to (christianized) secularists who imagine ethics as internalized imperatives; they may seem silly to the ordinary language tradition which must resolutely ignore the parts of the mind not accessible to reason in order to theorize.[66] It may be useful to think of the archived exteriority, in terms of your unmediated knowledge, of the inside of your body. The general premise of the Oxford Amnesty series *The Genetic Revolution and Human Rights*, for example, was that genes are digitalized words that are driving our bodies, our selves.[67] Yet they are inaccessible to us as objects and instruments of knowledge, in so far as we are sentient beings. (A smart reader mistook this as alterity being thoroughly interiorized. My exhortation is to try to think otherwise: that there is an other space—or script, all analogies are 'false' here—in the self, which drives us.) Think also of our creative invention in the languages that we know well. The languages have histories before us and futures after us. They are outside us, in grammar books and dictionaries.[68] Yet the languages that we know and make in are also us, and in us. These are analogies for agency that is out of us but in us—and, like all analogies, imperfect, but I hope they will suffice for now. In responsibility-based subordinate cultures, the volatile space of responsibility can be grasped through these analogies, perhaps. Please note, I'm not suggesting that they are better, just that they are different, and this radically different pair— rights and responsibility—need to relate in the hobbled relationship of supplementation.

These are only analogies, to be found in an Oxford Amnesty series collection and in Saussure. They work in the following way: if we can grasp that all human beings are genetically written before will, and if we can grasp that all human children access a language that is 'outside', as mother-tongue, then on these structural models, we might grasp the assumption that the human being is human in answer to an 'outside call'. We can grasp the structure of the role of alterity at work in subordinate cultures according to these analogies. The word 'before' in 'before the will' is here used to mean logical and chronological priority as well as 'in front of'. The difference is historical, not essential. It is because I believe that right/responsibility can be shared by everyone in the persistent mode of 'to come' that I keep insisting on supplemental pedagogy, on both sides.

In its structure, the definitive predication of being-human by alterity is not with reference to an empirical outside world. Just as I cannot play with my own genes or access the entire linguisticity of my mother-tongue, so 'is' the presumed alterity radical in the general sense. Of course it bleeds into the narrow sense of 'accountability to the outside world', but its anchor is in that imagined alterity that is inaccessible, often transcendentalized and formalized (as indeed is natural freedom in the rights camp).

I need not be more specific here. The subordinate subaltern is as diversified as the recipients of human rights activity. I need not make too many distinctions, for they are tied by a Universal Declaration.

Anticipating objections to this stopping short of distinction and specificities, I should perhaps say once again that, if these people became my object of investigation for disciplinary information retrieval as such, I would not be able to remain focused on the children as my teachers. There is nothing vague about this activity. Since this is the central insight of my essay, the reader will, I fear, have to take it or leave it. This is the different way of epistemic access, this the teacher's apprenticeship as suturer or invisible mender, this the secret of ongoing pedagogic supplementation. Writing this piece has almost convinced me that I was correct in thinking that this different way was too *in situ* to travel, that I should not make it part of my academic discourse. And yet there is no other news that I can bring to Amnesty International under the auspices of human rights.

Rewriting Levinas, Irigaray called for an ethics of sexual difference in the early 1980s.[69] That fashion in dominant feminist theory is now past. But the usefulness of the model does not disappear with a fad. Call this supplementation an ethics of class-culture difference, then: relating remotely, in view of a future 'to come', the dispensers of rights with the victims of wrongs.

With this proviso, let us consider an example of why we need to suture rights thinking into the torn cultural fabric of responsibility or, to vary the concept-metaphor, activate a dormant ethical imperative. I shall give only the bare bones.

Activists from the institutionally educated classes of the general national culture win a state-level legal victory against police brutality over the tribals. They try to transform this into a national-level legal awareness campaign.[70]

The ruling party supports the activists on the state level. (India is a federation of states. The national level is not involved here.) The ruling party on the local level is generally less answerable to the state precisely because of the discontinuity from the grassroots that I have been insisting upon all along. Indeed, this absence of redress without remote mediation is what makes the subaltern subaltern. On the local level, the police of the ruling party consistently take revenge against what is perceived as a victory over 'their' party by taking advantage of three factors, one positive, two negative:

1. The relatively homogeneous dominant Hindu culture at the village level keeps the tribal culturally isolated through prejudice.
2. As a result of this *cultural* isolation, women's independence among the tribals has remained intact. It has not been

infected by the tradition of women's oppression within the general Hindu rural culture.

3. *Politically*, the general, supposedly homogeneous rural culture and the tribal culture share a lack of democratic training.[71] This is a result of poverty and class prejudice existing nationally. Therefore, votes can be bought and sold here; and electoral conflict is treated by rural society in general like a competitive sport where violence is legitimate.

Locally, since the legal victory of the metropolitan activists against the police, the ruling party has taken advantage of these three things by rewriting women's conflict as party politics.[72] To divide the tribal community against itself, the police have used an incidental quarrel among tribal women, about the theft of a bicycle, if I remember right. One side has been encouraged to press charges against the other. The defending faction has been wooed and won by the opposition party. Thus a situation of violent conflict has been fabricated, where the police have an immediate edge over everyone, and since the legal victory in remote Calcutta is there after all, police revenge takes the form of further terror. In the absence of training in electoral democracy, the aboriginal community has accepted police terror as part of the party spirit: this is how electoral parties fight, where 'electoral' has no intellectual justification. This is a direct consequence of the educated activists'—among whom I count myself—good-hearted 'from above' effort at constitutional redress, since at the grassroots it can only be understood as a 'defeat' by police and party.

I am not asking that the women be left alone to flourish in some pristine tribality. I am also not speaking about how to stop women's oppression! The police are rural Hindus, the aboriginals are a small disenfranchised group, the situation is class–race–state power written into the caste system. Teaching is my solution, the method is pedagogic attention, to learn the weave of the torn fabric in unexpected ways, in order to suture the two, not altering gender politics from above. As for gender, I hope the parenthesis below will show why everything cannot be squeezed into this relatively short piece. I am suggesting that human rights activism should be supplemented by an education that should suture the habits of democracy on to the earlier cultural formation. I am the only person within this activist group—organized now as a tax-sheltered, non-profit organization—who thinks that the real effort should be to access and activate the tribals' indigenous 'democratic' structures to *parliamentary* democracy by patient and sustained efforts to learn to learn from below. 'Activate' is the keyword here. There is no tight cultural fabric (as opposed to group solidarity) among these disenfranchised groups after centuries of oppression and neglect. Anthropological excavation for description is not the goal here. (I remain suspicious of academic golden-agism from the colonial subject.) I am not able to give scholarly information. Working hands-on with teachers and students over long periods of time on their own terms without thinking of producing information for my academic peers is like learning a language 'to be able to produce in it freely . . . [and therefore] to move in it without remembering back to the language rooted and planted in [me, indeed] forgetting it.'[73]

As I mentioned above, I do not usually write about this activity at all. Yet it seems necessary to make the point when asked to speak on human rights, because this is a typical wake of a human rights victory. The reader is invited to join in the effort itself. In the meantime I remain a consensus breaker among metropolitan activists, who feel they can know every-thing in a non-vague way if only they have enough informa-tion, and that not to think so is 'mystical'. The consensually united vanguard is never patient.

This narrative demonstrates that when the human rights commissions, local, national or international, right state terror-ism, police brutality, or gender violence in such regions, the punishing victory is won in relatively remote courts of law.

Catharine A. MacKinnon describes this well:

The loftiest legal abstracts . . . are born . . . amid the intercourse of particular groups, in the presumptive ease of the deciding classes, through the trauma of specific atrocities, at the expense of the silent and excluded, as a victory (usually compromised, often pyrrhic) for the powerless.[74]

In the aftermath of victory, unless there is constant vigil-ance (a 'pressure' that is itself a species of terror), the very forces of terror, brutality, or violence that suffer a public defeat often come back to divide and oppress the community even further. If the community fights back, it does so by the old rules of violence. The dispensation of justice, the righting of wrongs, the restoration of human rights, is reduced to a pat-tern of abyssal revenge and/or, at best, a spirit of litigious blackmail, *if* the group that has been helped has a strong con-nection to the regional human rights agencies or commissions (the dominant pressure groups described as 'below'), which is by no means always the case. Legal awareness seminars, altogether salutary in themselves, can exacerbate the problem without the painstaking foundational pedagogy which pre-pares the subject of rights from childhood and from within a disenfranchised culture of responsibility. And, if we get away from such remote areas, human rights dependency can be particularly vicious in its neo-colonial consequences if it is the state that is the agency of terror and the Euro–US that is the saviour.

(Incidentally, this narrative also demonstrates that Carole Pateman's invaluable insight, 'that the social contract presupposed the sexual contract', has historical variations that may not always justify the eurocentrism that is the obvious characteristic of even *her* brilliant book.[75] On the other hand, today the history of domination and exploitation has reduced the general picture, especially in the clients of human rights intervention, to a uniformity that may justify Pateman's remark: '[o]nly the postulate of natural equality prevents the original [European] social contract from being an explicit slave contract.' Even so brief a hint of this historicized and uneven dialectic between past and present surely makes it clear that feminists must think of a different kind of diversified itinerary for teasing out the relationship between human rights and women's rights rather than cultural conservatism, politically correct golden-agism, or ruthless-to-benevolent eurocentrism. The suturing argument that I will elaborate below develops in the historical difference between the first two sentences of this parenthesis.)

Even if the immense labour of follow-up investigation on a case-by-case basis is streamlined in our era of telecommunication, it will not change the epistemic structure of the dysfunctional responsibility-based community, upon whom rights have been thrust from above. It will neither alleviate the reign of terror, nor undo the pattern of dependency. The recipient of human rights bounty whom I have described above, an agent of counter-terrorism and litigious blackmail at the grassroots, will continue not to resemble the ego ideal implied by the Enlightenment and the UDHR. As long as real equalization through recovering and training the long-ignored ethical imagination of the rural poor and indeed, all species of sub-proletarians on their own terms—is not part of the agenda to come, s/he has no chance of becoming the subject of human rights as part of a collectivity, but must remain, forever, its object of benevolence. We will forever hear in the news, local to global, how these people cannot manage when they are left to manage on their own, and the new imperialism, with an at best embarrassed Social Darwinist base, will get its permanent sanction.

The seventh article of the Declaration of the Rights of Man and of Citizens, following eighteenth-century European radical thought, says that '[t]he law is an expression of the will of the community'.[76] Among the rural poor of the global South, one may attempt, through that species of education without guarantees, to bring about a situation where the law can be imagined as the expression of a community, always to come. Otherwise the spirit of human rights law is completely out of their unmediated reach. The training in 'literary reading' in the metropolis is here practised, if you like, in order to produce a situation, in the mode of 'to come', where it can be acknowledged that '[r]eciprocally recognized rating [to acknowledge a corresponding integrity in the other] is a condition without which no civil undertaking is possible'.[77]

The supplementary method that I shall go on to outline does not suggest that human rights interventions should stop. It does not even offer the impractical suggestion that the human rights activists themselves should take time to learn this method. Given the number of wrongs all the world over, those who right them must be impatient. I am making the practical suggestion for certain kinds of humanities teachers, here and there, diasporics wishing to undo the de-linking with the global South represented by impatient benevolence, second-generation colonial subjects dissatisfied by the divided postcolonial polity. (This is not to limit the readership of this essay, of course. Anyone can do what I am proposing.) Only, whoever it is must have the patience and perseverance to learn well one of the languages of the rural poor of the South.

*One* of the languages. For the purposes of the essential and possible work of righting wrongs—the political calculus—the great European languages are sufficient. But for access to the subaltern episteme to devise a suturing pedagogy, you must take into account the multiplicity of subaltern languages. This is because the task of the educator is to learn to learn from below, the lines of conflict resolution undoubtedly available, however dormant, within the disenfranchised cultural system; giving up convictions of triumphalist superiority. It is because of the linguistic restriction that one is obliged to speak of just the groups one works for; but, in the hope that these words will be read by some who are interested in comparable work elsewhere, I am always pushing for generalization. The trainer of teachers will find the system dysfunctional and corrupted, mired in ritual, like a clear pond choked with scum. For their cultural axiomatics as well as their already subordinated position did not translate into the emergence of nascent capitalism. We are now teaching our children in the North, and no doubt in the North of the South, that to learn the movement of finance capital is to learn social responsibility. It is in the remote origins of this conviction—that capitalism is responsibility—that we might locate the beginning of the failure of the aboriginal groups of the kind I am describing: their entry into (a distancing from) modernity as a gradual slipping into atrophy.[78]

This history breeds the need for activating an ethical

imperative atrophied by gradual distancing from the narrative of progress—colonialism/capitalism. This is the argument about cultural suturing, learning from below to supplement with the possibility of the subjectship of rights.[79]

Now I go back to my broader argument—a new pedagogy. The national education systems are pretty hopeless at this level because they are the detritus of the postcolonial state, the colonial system turned to rote, unproductive of felicitous colonial subjects like ourselves, at home or abroad. This is part of what started the rotting of the cultural fabric of which I speak. Therefore, I am not just asking that they should have 'the kind of education we have had'. The need for supplementing metropolitan education—'the kind of education we have had'—is something I am involved in every day in my salaried work. And when I say 'rote', I am not speaking of the fact that a student might swot as a quick way to do well in an exam. I am speaking of the scandal that, in the global South, in the schools for middle-class children and above, the felicitous primary use of a page of language is to understand it; but in the schools for the poor, it is to spell and memorize.

Consider the following, the vicissitudes of a local effort undertaken in the middle of the nineteenth century. Iswarchandra Banerjee, better known as Iswarchandra Vidyasagar, a nineteenth-century public intellectual from rural Bengal, was 20 when Macaulay wrote his 'Minute on Indian Education'. He fashioned pedagogic instruments for Sanskrit and Bengali that could, if used right (the question of teaching, again), suture the 'native' old with Macaulay's new rather than reject the old and commence its stagnation with that famous and horrible sentence: 'A single shelf of a good European library [is] worth the whole native literature of India and Arabia.'[80]

Vidyasagar's Bengali primer is still used in state-run primary schools in rural West Bengal.[81] It is a modernizing instrument for teaching. It activates the structural neatness of the Sanskritic Bengali alphabet for the teacher and the child, and undermines rote learning by encouraging the teacher to jumble the structure in course of teaching at the same time. The wherewithal is all there, but no one knows (how) to use it any more.[82]

The first part of the book is for the active use of the teacher. The child does not read the book yet—just listens to the teacher, and learns to read and write by reading the teacher's writing and writing as the teacher guides. Reading and writing are not soldered to the fetishized schoolbook. In very poor rural areas, with no books or newspapers anywhere, this is still a fine way to teach. (If you have been stumped a hundred times in a lot of places by both teacher and student producing some memorized bit from the textbook when asked to 'write whatever comes to mind', you are convinced of this.) Halfway through the book, the child begins to read a book, and the title of that page is *prothom path*: 'first reading' not 'first lesson.' What a thrill it must have been for the child, undoubtedly a boy, to get to that moment. Today this is impossible, because the teachers, and the teachers' teachers, indefinitely, are clueless about this book as a do-it-yourself instrument. Well-meaning education experts in the capital city, whose children are used to a different world, inspired by self-ethnographing bourgeois nationalists of a period after Vidyasagar, have transformed the teacher's pages into children's pages by way of these ill-conceived illustrations.[83]

In the rural areas this meaningless gesture has consolidated the book as an instrument for dull rote learning. The page where Vidyasagar encourages the teacher to jumble the

structure is now a meaningless page routinely ignored. I could multiply examples such as this, and not in India alone. Most of the subordinate languages of the world do not have simple single-language dictionaries that rural children could use. Efforts to put together such a dictionary in Bengali failed in false promises and red tape. The habit of independence in a child's mind starts with the ability to locate meaning without a teacher. If the dictionary is put together by the kind of well-meaning experts who put together the pictures in the primer, it would be geared for the wrong audience.

The generalizable significance of this case is that, at the onset of colonialism/capitalism, when the indigenous system of teaching began to be emptied out of social relevance, there had been an attempt to undo this. The discontinuity between the colonial subject and the rural poor is such that the instruments of such undoing were thoughtlessly de-activated. (This relates to the concept-metaphor of activation that I am using in this part of the essay.) As note 78 indicates, the metropolitan specialist has no sense of the pedagogic significance of the instruments. My discovery of the specific pattern of the primer was a revelation that came after eight years of involvement with using the primer. Since I do not consolidate instruction for the teacher except in response to a felt need, it was only then that I was letting the teacher at one school take down hints as to how to teach the students at the lowest level. As I continued, I realized the primer had pre-empted me at every step! I hope the impatient reader will not take this to be just another anecdote about poor instruction. And I hope I have made it clear by now, in spite of all the confusion attendant upon straying from the beaten track, that the practice of elementary pedagogy for the children of the rural poor is one of my main weapons, however humble.

The interference of the state can also be a cruel negligence. That is the point of the following story. I have included two personal details to show how caste politics, gender politics and class politics are intertwined in the detail. These details are typical.

Each of the rural schools of which I speak has a tube well. This provides clean water for the entire group. Near two of these schools the tube well is broken. The aboriginals cannot mend it for the same reason that the metropolitan middle class cannot do these repair jobs. They are not used to it and Home Depot hasn't hit yet.

One of my fellow students in college occupies a leading position in a pertinent ministry on the state level. I renewed contact with this man after 31 years, in his office in Calcutta, to ask for tube wells. Not only did I not get tube wells after two trips separated by a year, but I heard through the grapevine that, as a result of his boasting about my visit, his wife had disclosed in public, at a party, that she had complained to his mother about our ancient friendship!

A near relative in the next generation, whom I had only met briefly when he was an adolescent, held a leading administrative position on the district level. I got an appointment with him, again to beg for the tube wells. I did not get them. But he did tell me that he was in line for a fellowship at the Kennedy School. Where the infrastructure for the primary education of the poor seems negligible even in the line of official duty, boasting about one's own spectacular opportunities for higher education seems perfectly plausible: internalized axiomatics of class apartheid. I use the detail to point at a pervasive problem.

The Hindu villagers insulted a boy who went to fetch water from the tube well in the main village. At night, the oldest woman was about to go and get water under cover. We sat together in her kitchen and boiled a pot of water.

The next morning, the teacher in the school could not prove that the students had learnt anything. She is a young Hindu widow from the village, who has failed her secondary school leaving exam. As a rural Hindu, she cannot drink water touched by the Aboriginals, her students. As I kept berating her, one of these very students spoke up! (She loves the students; her not drinking water from their hands is internalized by them as normal, much less absurd than my drinking hot boiled water. On her part, going back to the village every afternoon, keeping the water-rule, which she knows I abhor, compares to my standing in the snow for six hours to replace my stolen green card, I later thought.)

The student spoke up to say that all but three in the school had accompanied their parents 'east' and so had not come to school for months. Going east: migrant labour.

Just as not repairing tube wells is taken as proof of their fecklessness, taking their children on these journeys is seen as proof that they don't know the value of education. These are oral tradition folks for whom real education takes place in the bosom of the family. By what absurd logic would they graduate instantly into a middle-class understanding of something so counter-intuitive as 'the value of education'? Such lectures produce the kind of quick-fix 'legal awareness'-style lectures whose effects are at best superficial, but satisfying for the activists, until the jerrybuilt edifice falls down. When the community was addressed with sympathy, with the explicit understanding that behind this removal of the students from school lay love and responsibility, some children were allowed to stay behind next year. When I spoke of this way of dealing with absenteeism to the one hundred so-called rural teachers (stupid statistics) subsidized by the central government, one of the prejudice-ridden rural Hindu unemployed, who had suddenly become a 'teacher', advised me—not knowing that this elite city person knew what she was talking about—that the extended aboriginal community would object to the expenditure of feeding these children. Nonsense, of course, and prejudice, not unknown in the native informant.

When I saw that the three students who had not 'gone east' were doing fine, and that a year had gone by without tube wells, I said to them, write a letter. Another student, sitting back, looked so eager to write that I let her come forward as well. Each one give a sentence, I said, I will not prompt you. What they wrote is shown on p. 216.[84]

I told them the secret of alphabetization. They successfully alphabetized their first names. My second visit to this man's office, the source of the prurient party gossip in Calcutta, was to deliver the letter, in vain.

I have covered the place names because we do not want a tube well from a remote international or national philanthropic source. The water is getting boiled for me. They are drinking well water. We want the children to learn about the heartlessness of administrations, without short-term resistance talk. The bounty of some US benefactor would be the sharp end of the wedge that produces a general will for exploitation in the subaltern.[85] *Mutatis mutandis*, I go with W. E. B. DuBois rather than Booker T. Washington: it is more important to develop a critical intelligence than to assure immediate material comfort.[86] This may or may not bear immediate fruit. Let me repeat once again, although I fear I will not convince the benevolent ethnocentrist, that I am not interested in teaching 'self-help'. I am interested in being a good enough humanities teacher in order to be a conduit (Wordsworth's word) between subaltern children and their subaltern teachers. That is my connection with DuBois, who writes a good deal about teacher training.

The teachers on this ground level at which we work tend to be the least successful products of a bad system. Our

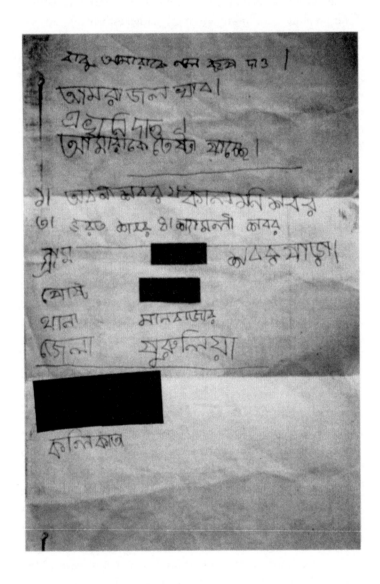

educator must learn to train teachers by attending to the children. For, just as our children are not born electronic, their children are not born delegitimized. They are not yet 'least successful'. It is through learning how to take children's response to teaching as our teaching text that we can hope to put ourselves in the way of 'activating' democratic structures.

And it is to distinguish between 'activating' and producing good descriptive information for peers (the appropriate brief for an essay such as this), that I should like to point at the difference between Melanie Klein and Jean Piaget. Attending to children, Klein's way of speaking had turned into a kind of sublime literalness, where the metaphor is as literal as reality itself. In order to flesh out Freud's intuitions about children, Klein learnt her system from the children themselves. Her writings are practical guides to people who wished to 'learn' that language. That too is to learn to learn from below.

By contrast, all the confident conclusions of Piaget and his collaborators in *The Moral Judgment of Children* would be messed up if the investigators had been obliged to insert themselves into and engage with the value-system the children inhabited. Piaget is too sharp not to know this.

[I]t is one thing to prove that cooperation in the play and spontaneous social life of children brings about certain moral effects and another to establish the fact that this cooperation can be universally applied as a method of education. This last point is one which only experimental education can settle . . . But the type of experiment which such research would require can only be conducted by teachers or by the combined efforts of practical workers and educational psychologists. And it is not in our power to deduce the results to which this would lead.[87]

The effort at education that I am describing—perhaps comparable to Piaget's description of 'practical workers' (the teachers) and 'educational psychologists' (the trainers) with the roles productively confused every step of the way—hopes against hope that a permanent sanction of the Social Darwinism—'the burden of the fittest'—implicit in the human rights agenda will, perhaps, be halted if the threads of the torn cultural fabric are teased out by the uncanny patience of which the humanities are capable at their best, for the 'activation' of dormant structures.

Indeed, this is the 'humanities component', attending upon the object of investigation as other, in all labour. Here is the definitive moment of a humanities 'to come', in the service of a human rights, that persistently undoes the asymmetry in our title by the uncoercive rearrangement of desires in terms of the teaching text described above.

The Greek poet Archilochus is supposed to have written: 'The fox knows many things, but the hedgehog knows one big thing.' This distinction between two types of thinkers was developed by Isaiah Berlin into the idea that fox-thinkers are fascinated by the variety of things, and hedgehog-thinkers relate everything to an all-embracing system.[88]

My experience of learning from the children for the last decade tells me that nurturing the capacity to imagine the public sphere and the fostering of independence within chosen rule-governance is the hedgehog's definition of democracy which will best match the weave of the torn yet foxy fabric—great variety of detail—of the culture long neglected by the dominant. The trick is to train the teachers by means of such intuitions, uncoercively rearranging *their* (most often unexamined) desires for specific kinds of futures for the children. No mean trick, for these teachers have been so maimed by the very system of education we are trying to combat, and are so much within the class-apartheid produced by it, that they would blindly agree and obey, while the trainer was emoting over consciousness-raising. Great tact is called for if the effort is to draw forth consent rather than obedience. In addition, the children have to be critically prepared for disingenuously offered cyber literacy if these groups get on the loop of 'development'.[89] The hope is that this effort with the *teachers* will translate into the teaching of these reflexes in the educational method of the children who launch *the trainer* on the path of the hedgehog. The children are the future electorate. They need to be taught the habits and reflexes of such democratic behaviour. Do you see why I call this necessary and impossible? As I remarked about humanities teaching, you cannot gauge this one.

To suture thus the torn and weak responsibility-based system into a conception of human dignity as the enjoyment of rights, one enters ritual practice transgressively, alas, as a hacker enters software. The description of ritual-hacking below may seem silly, perhaps. But put yourself on the long road where you *can* try it, and you will respect us—you will not dismiss as 'nothing but' this or that approach on paper. In so far as this hacking is like a weaving, this too is an exercise in *texere*, textil-ity, text-ing, textuality. I must continue to repeat that my emphasis is on the difficulties of this texting, the practical pedagogy of it, not in devising the most foolproof theory of it for you, my peers. Without the iterative text of doing and devising in silence, the description seems either murky or banal.

Subordinate cultural systems are creative in the invention of ritual in order to keep a certain hierarchical order functioning. With the help of the children and the community, the trainer must imagine the task of recoding the ritual-to-order habits of the earlier system with the ritual-to-order habits of parliamentary democracy, with a teaching corps whose idea of education is unfortunately produced by a terrible system. One learns active ritual as one learns manners. The best example for the readership of this anthology might be the 'wild anthropology' of the adult metropolitan migrant, learning a dominant culture on the run, giving as little away as possible. The difference here is that we learn from the vulnerable archaic (Raymond Williams's word captures the predicament better than the anthropological 'primitive'), but also without giving much away. The point is to realize that democracy also has its rituals, exaggerated or made visible, for example, when in our metropolitan life we seek to make politically correct manners 'natural', a matter of reflex.

It is because this habit of recoding ritual (always, of course, in the interest of uncoercive rearrangement of desires) for training other practitioners—rather than for production of knowledge about knowledge—has to be learned by the teacher as a reflex that I invoked the difference between Klein and Piaget. I will not be able to produce anthropologically satisfying general descriptions here because no trainer can provide satisfactory descriptions of the grammar of a language that s/he is learning painfully. This *is* the distinction I want to convey. I have such fear of derision of the detail of my work that I feel obliged to cite a self-defence that I offered at Columbia, when I presented there a talk whose London version drew forth my invitation to participate in the Amnesty Oxford Lectures.[90] What follows must remain hortatory—an appeal to your imagination until we meet in the field of specific practice, here or there. Of course, we all know, with appropriate cynicism, that this probably will not be. But a ceremonial lecture allows you to tilt at windmills, to insist that such practice is the only way that one can hope to supplement the work of human rights litigation in order to produce cultural entry into modernity.

Fine, you will say, maybe human rights interventions do not have the time to engage in this kind of patient education, but there are state-sponsored systems, NGOs and activists engaging in educational initiatives, surely? The NGO drives count school buildings and teacher bodies. The national attempts also do so, but only at best. Activists, who care about education in the abstract and are critical of the system, talk rights, talk resistance, even talk nationalism. But instilling habits in very young minds is like writing on soft cement. Repeating slogans, even good slogans, is not the way to go, alas. It breeds fascists just as easily. UNESCO's teaching guides for human rights are not helpful as guides.

Some activists attempt to instil pride in these long dis-enfranchised groups in a pseudo-historical narrative. This type of 'civilizationism' is good for gesture politics and breed-ing leaders, but does little for the development of democratic reflexes.[91] These pseudo-histories are assimilated into the aetiological mythologies of the Aboriginals without epistemic change. Given subaltern ethnic divisions, our teaching also proceeds in the conviction that, if identitarianism is generally bad news here, it is also generally bad news there.

Let me now say a very few words about the actual teaching, which is necessarily subject to restricted generalizability, because it is predicated upon confronting the specific prob-lems of the closest general educational facility to which the teachers have had, and the students might have, access. Such generalizations can be made within the framework of the undoing of those specific problems. One generalization seems apposite and relates to my parenthesis on Pateman. Whatever the status of women in the old delegitimized cultural system, in today's context emphasis must always be placed on girl-children's access to that entry, without lecturing, without commanding, earning credibility, of course. Another minimally generalizable rule of thumb in this teaching I will focus on is the one that Vidyasagar, the nineteenth-century Bengali intellectual, picked up 150 years ago: undermine rote learning.

As I mentioned at the beginning of this discussion, I am not speaking of the fact that a student might swot as a quick way to do well in an exam. I'm speaking of the scandal that, in the global South, in the schools for middle-class children and above, the felicitous primary use of a page of language is to understand it; in the schools for the poor, it is to spell and memorize. This is an absolute and accepted divide, the consolidation of continuing class apartheid I referred to above. It is as a result of this that 'education' is seen upon subaltern terrain as another absurdity bequeathed by powerful people and, incidentally, of no use at all to girl-children.

My own teachers, when I was a student in a good middle-class Bengali medium primary school in Calcutta, explained the texts. But as I have mentioned, there is no one to explain in these rural primary schools. I walked a couple of hours to a village high school in the national system and waited an hour and a half after opening time for the rural teachers to arrive. I begged them to take good care of the two aboriginal young women I was sending to the school. In late afternoon, the girls returned. Did she explain, I asked. No, just spelling and reading. An absurd history lesson about 'National Liberation Struggles in Many Countries', written in incomprehensible prose. I am going into so much detail because no urban or international radical bothers to look at the detail of the general system as they write of special projects—'non-formal education', 'functional literacy', science projects here and there. Just before I left India in January 2001, a filmmaker made an English documentary entitled something like 'A Tribe Enters the Mainstream'. My last act before departure was to make sure that the shots of my school be excised. The so-called direct interviews are risible. How can these people give anything but the expected answers in such situations? And yet it is from such 'documentaries' that we often gather evidence. I have just received news that this video will be shown at a nationwide human rights gathering in the capital city with international attendance in September 2001. What is the generalizable significance of these embittered remarks? To emphasize the discontinuity between the domestic 'below' and the grassroots before I offer the final report on the education of Gayatri Spivak.

My project seems to have defined itself as the most ground-level task for the breaking of the production and continuation of class apartheid. I now understand why, in Marx's world, Marx had come down to something as simple as the shortening of the working day as 'the grounding condition [*die Grundbedingung*]' when he was speaking of such grand topics as the Realm of Freedom and the Realm of Necessity.[92]

The discovery of the practical use of the primer was an important moment for me. Other moments would be difficult to integrate into this; they might seem inconsequential or banal. Something that can indeed be reported is that, since I presented my paper in February 2001, I have learnt how to communicate to the teachers and students—for whom the absurd education system *is* education—that it is the class apartheid of the state that is taken on in the move from rote to comprehension. I can now show that there is no connection in this absurd education (to memorize incomprehensible chunks of prose and some verse in response to absurd questions in order to pass examinations; to begin to forget the memorized material instantly) with the existing cultural residue of responsibility. (In metropolitan theoretical code, this lack of connection may be written as no sense at all that the written is a message from a structurally absent subject, a placeholder of alterity, although the now-delegitimized local culture is programmed for responsibility as a call of the other—alterity—before will. Thus education in this area cannot activate or rely on 'culture' without outside/inside effort.) For the suturing with enforced class-subalternization I had to chance upon an immediately comprehensible concept-metaphor: when there is no exercise for the imagination, no training in intellectual labour (*matha khatano*) for those who are slated for manual labour (*gatar khatano*) at best, the rich/poor divide (*barolok/chhotolok* big people/small people) is here to stay.[93] At least one teacher said, at leave-taking, that he now understood what I wanted, in the language of obedience, alas. There is more work for the trainer down the road, uncoercive undermining of the class-habit of obedience.

Perhaps you can now imagine how hard it is to change this episteme, how untrustworthy the activists' gloat. For the solidarity tourist, it is a grand archaic sight to see rural children declaiming their lessons in unison, especially if, as in that mud-floored classroom in Yunan, 6 to 9 year olds vigorously dance their bodies into ancient calligraphy. But if you step forward to work together, and engage in more than useless patter, the situation is not so romantic. Learning remains by rote.

It is a cruel irony that when the meaning of *sram* in Vidyasagar's Lesson 2—*sram na korile lekhapora hoy na*—is explained as 'labour' and the aboriginal child is asked if she or he has understood, he or she will show their assent by giving an example of manual labour. In English, the sentence would read 'Without labour you cannot learn to write and read'— meaning intellectual labour, of course.

Produced by this class-corrupt system of education, the teachers themselves do not know how to write freely. They do not know the meaning of what they 'teach', since all they have to teach, when they are doing their job correctly, is spelling and memorizing. They do not know what dictionaries are. They have themselves forgotten everything they memorized to pass out of primary school. When we train such teachers, we must, above all, let them go, leave them alone, to see if the efforts of us outsiders have been responsive enough, credible enough without any material promises. When I see rousing examples of 'people's movements', I ask myself, how long would the people continue without the presence of the activist leaders? It is in the context of earning that credibility that I am reporting my access to the new concept-metaphor binary: *matha khatano/gator khatano*: class-apartheid: *barolok/chhotolok*.

I am often reprimanded for writing incomprehensibly. There is no one to complain about the jargon-ridden incomprehensibility of children's textbooks in this subaltern world. If I want you to understand the complete opacity of that absurd history lesson about 'National Liberation Struggles in Many Countries', devised by some state functionary at the Ministry of Education, for example, I would have to take most of you through an intensive Bengali lesson so that you are able to assess different levels of the language.

Without venturing up to that perilous necessity, I will simply recapitulate: First, the culture of responsibility is corrupted. The effort is to learn it with patience from below and to keep trying to suture it to the imagined felicitous subject of universal human rights. Second, the education system is a corrupt ruin of the colonial model. The effort is persistently to undo it, to teach the habit of democratic civility. Third, to teach these habits, with responsibility to the corrupted culture, is different from children's indoctrination into nationalism, resistance-talk, identitarianism.

I leave this essay with the sense that the material about the rural teaching is not in the acceptable mode of information retrieval. The difficulty is in the discontinuous divide between those who right wrongs and those who are wronged. I have no interest in becoming an educational researcher or a diasporic golden-agist. I will ask my New York students what concept-metaphor served them best. (Dorah Ahmad told me this afternoon that what she liked best about my graduate teaching was the use of stories that made immediate sense!)

Here are some nice abstract, seemingly fighting words:

[G]enerative politics is by no means limited to the formal political sphere but spans a range of domains where political questions arise and must be responded to. Active trust is closely bound up with such a conception . . . No longer depending on pregiven alignments, it is more contingent, and contextual, than most earlier forms of trust relations. It does not necessarily imply equality, but it is not compatible with deference arising from traditional forms of status.[94]

If you want to attempt to bring this about, hands-on—for the sake of a global justice to come—you begin along the lines I have described in this paper.

I am so irreligious that atheism seems a religion to me. But

I now understand why fundamentalists of all kinds have succeeded best in the teaching of the poor—for the greater glory
of God. One needs some sort of 'licensed lunacy' (Orlando
Patterson's phrase) from some transcendental Other to develop the sort of ruthless commitment that can undermine
the sense that one is better than those who are being helped,
that the ability to manage a complicated life support system
is the same as being civilized. But I am influenced by
deconstruction and for me, radical alterity cannot be named
'God' in any language. Indeed, the name of 'man' in 'human'
rights (or the name of 'woman' in 'women's rights are human
rights') will continue to trouble me.

'Licensed lunacy in the name of the unnamable other' then.
It took me this long to explain this incomprehensible phrase.
Yet the efforts I have described may be the only recourse for a
future to come when the reasonable righting of wrongs will
not inevitably be the manifest destiny of groups that remain
poised to right them; when wrongs will not proliferate with
unsurprising regularity.

# Introduction to Gitta Sereny

## Jonathan Glover

We academics, toiling away in our libraries, writing our books, tend to use the word 'journalist' in a somewhat condescending way. We like to think that we write deep, scholarly, researched works, and that 'journalism' has a slight tinge of the superficial about it. But it has to be said that Gitta Sereny has written far more profound books than most of us academics. When I read her books, I feel I wouldn't mind my own work having a journalistic tinge. Her books are not always an unadulterated pleasure to read, because they touch on some very dark things. She asks difficult questions, particularly about the psychological roots of human cruelty.

At least a quarter of a century ago, I read her remarkable book based on interviews with Franz Stangl, the Commandant of Treblinka. One thing has haunted me ever since. She asked an extraordinarily penetrating question. She said to him, 'If they were going to kill them anyway, why the humiliation? Why the cruelty?' Franz Stangl gave an honest and illuminating answer. He said the cruelty and humiliation were necessary to make it possible for people who had to carry out the policy to do what they had to do. In other words, they were necessary to make it possible to overcome the barriers that normally inhibit people. Gitta Sereny's books are full of insights of that kind. What is so powerful about her work is that so much of it comes from direct experience. It is not abstract theorizing, but the result of talking to people directly.

She is also very interested in the roots of cruelty in childhood. I am reminded of something she said in her book on Albert Speer, the Nazi architect. In the interviews, he struggled towards some sort of truth concerning his part in the Nazi dictatorship. She said that he was missing the capacity to feel, which his childhood had blotted out. Pity and human understanding were not part of his emotional vocabulary. My own latest research involves interviewing people diagnosed as having antisocial personality disorder. I am struck over and over again, when asking questions about how they came to do the sorts of things they did, how without my prompting them, we get back to childhood. I often have the feeling that Gitta Sereny has been there before. Her book on Mary Bell, about the 11-year-old child who killed two boys, raises disturbing questions about the way in which we as a society deal with young children who have committed terrible crimes; troubling questions which are very hard to answer. One comes away thinking that there is something tremendously unsatisfactory about the current system for dealing with such people. There is a further disturbing question she raises about childhood abuse, and about how that creates the personality and the ability to do these terrible things.

One always comes away from Gitta Sereny's books with this sense of very difficult questions having been honestly investigated, with some hints at answers, but no pretence that there is an easy solution. We are left to think about it for ourselves. Her books are disturbing and a tough read. But one of the redeeming features which helps to keep one's spirits up is the extraordinary belief she has (a belief which I half-share—I wish I could fully share it) that children are fundamentally born good and that they are distorted by the terrible things that happen to them in childhood.

Those of us who give lectures spend much of our time looking into people's eyes, to see what is coming across and what is not. When Gitta Sereny gave the lecture that follows in the Sheldonian Theatre in Oxford, I've never looked into the eyes of an audience so completely taken up by what was being said.

In the lecture she brings out important links between restrictive immigration policies, xenophobia and the 'inner racism' that is widespread and yet sometimes invisible to those who harbour it. I would like to support her point with a memory of a visit to South Africa during the time of apartheid. One of the most striking things was that the cruelties of apartheid were most apparent not when we were talking about politics, but the moments when we were talking about something else. I remember talking to a woman who was part of a surgical team in a South African hospital. We were talking about the way in which male surgeons lorded it over the female and other members of their team. That was the subject of our conversation, but she happened to say that in the hospital they did lots of amputations. I asked, 'Why do you do a lot.of amputations?' She said,

Well, it's the trains. The trains have segregated coaches. The 'Whites Only' coaches usually have lots of seats in them. The 'Non-Whites Only' coaches are usually extremely crowded, and as a result, people often travel on the outside, and quite often they fall off, and suffer injuries that mean that they have to have limbs amputated.

It was at moments like this that it really hit me that I was visiting a society in which one group of people were effectively saying to another group of people, 'We would rather that you lost your limbs than came and sat next to us.'

One of the most disturbing things Gitta Sereny argues, in

the lecture that follows, concerns racism in the context of disputes in this country about asylum seekers. In keeping out so-called 'bogus asylum seekers', we are in effect saying that we would rather you went back to whatever horrors you would have to endure when you go back—whether political persecution or abject poverty—than that you came and lived next to us. We are not quite as far from the South African example as we would like to be.

## 6

# Racism Within

**Gitta Sereny**

At the end of January 2001, I participated in a conference convened by the Swedish Prime Minister, Goran Persson, on 'Intolerance and Xenophobia', the battle against which, it seems to me, is the lifeblood—the mission—of Amnesty International.[1] I cannot blame you if none of you have heard of this conference, which Mr Persson's staff worked on for months to prepare, which was attended by 400 delegates, including prime ministers and ministers of justice and foreign affairs from 42 countries, and 300 journalists—100 from countries other than Sweden—but about which hardly a word appeared in the British press, and not that much in other countries either. It is a reaction I am very familiar with, from vainly suggesting press coverage of similar, if not as extraordinarily timely events, to a number of papers I contributed over the years. Conferences such as this one are referred to by editors as representing the 'goodie-goodie factor', in which—so the media barons believe—the reading public is not interested. Newspapers and their readers can, of course, be politically categorized to the right, left or middle ground. But it is strange that even editors of the best quality papers believe they are responding to a kind of thermometer of popular feeling or need, when they downgrade the content or style of their pages. Tabloids, of course, always want us to believe that their sensationalism—no, more than that when human factors are involved—their inflammatory diatribes merely mirror the mood of the people. The truth, of course, is that what they do, and often quite horribly so, is to *create* the mood of the people. My own experience at their hands (just before the publication of my book *Cries Unheard*[2]) is thankfully limited—for I assure you that it was most unpleasant, even though I am in a position to withstand it and, with the help of other media, even to fight it. However, this does not apply to the general public, above all to the most vulnerable among them, such as nameless immigrants, of whatever colours or so-called race. How condescending some of our media can be, how wrong about how people feel and what they want to know and are prepared to learn.

## Immigration, Racism and European Governments

Just a few days after the Stockholm Conference—and a mere week or so before the European Union meeting there on immigration—the then Home Secretary Jack Straw made public his opinion that changes needed to be made to the 1951 UN Convention on Refugees which, he argued, was no longer suited to current patterns of migration. New ways had to be sought to limit or contain immigration within or into European states. It is, of course, perfectly true that the circumstances that prompted the 1951 UN Convention, i.e. the Nazi genocide of the Jews, have changed. The state is no longer the main persecutor of minorities, who are now more likely to suffer at the hands of factions, tribal gangs and the like. But the Convention only provides refuge from state persecution. International travel has become easier, and other channels of migration to Europe are now mostly closed. Above all, the gap between rich and poor countries has widened. While there are still many hundreds of thousands of potential refugees for reasons of racial, religious or ideological persecution, the real problem today is that people from poor nations of the world wish to live and work in rich countries such as Britain. It made me think of Hans Magnus Enzensberger's 1992 essay 'The Great Migration'. 'Of course', he writes, 'no nation has an absolutely homogeneous ethnic population.'

This fact is in fundamental conflict with the national feeling that has taken shape in most states. As a rule, the leading national group consequently finds it difficult to reconcile itself to the existence of minorities, and every wave of immigrants is considered a political problem. The most important exceptions to this pattern are those modern states which owe their existence to migration on a large scale; above all the United States, Canada and Australia. Their founding myth is the *tabula rasa*. The reverse of this coin is the extermination of the indigenous population, whose remnants have only very recently been conceded essential minority rights.

Almost all other nations justify their existence by a firm self-ascription. The distinction between 'our own' people and 'strangers' appears quite natural to them, even if it is questionable historically. Whoever wishes to hold on to the distinction would need to maintain, according to his own logic, that he has always been there—a thesis which can all too easily be disproved. To that extent, a proper national history assumes the ability to forget everything that doesn't fit.

However, it is not only one's own motley origin that is denied. Movements of migration on a large scale always lead to struggles over the distribution of resources. National feeling prefers to reinterpret these inevitable conflicts as though the dispute had more to do with imaginary than with material resources. The struggle is then over the difference between self- and external ascriptions, a field that offers demagogy ideal possibilities for development.[3]

We are beginning to hear increasing sounds of *Realpolitik* from our masters: these days both British and German politicians are quoted as favouring selection of immigrants, not on the grounds of their fears and troubles, but the economy's needs for immigrants with education and training. The mind boggles at the comparative image which all of us now have in our heads from photographs and films, of the often illegal arrival both over the borders of Austria, Italy, Germany, Holland, Belgium and France, and in our coastal towns, of tired young men and women, sometimes, as in the case of certainly harassed and persecuted gypsies—Romanies—also men, women and children from Eastern Europe, Afghanistan, Albania, Russia, the Balkans, Pakistan and Africa. Seeing the images I have just mentioned of the arrival of migrants, one is forcibly reminded of the writing carved on the Statue of Liberty since 1883:

Give me your tired, your poor,
Your huddled masses yearning to breathe free,
The wretched refuse of your teeming shore,
Send these, the homeless, tempest-tossed, to me:
I lift my lamp beside the golden door.

It seems to me, we, in the rich countries of Western Europe, are confronted by a strange conflict between the principles of morality and the demands of materialism. What *do* people, coming from different cultures, different standards, often—though far from always—without educational qualifications, have to offer us? I would say the strength of their bodies, the willingness of their spirits, the good hearts and, under positive educational circumstances, the intellectual potential of their existing or future children. But I would ask whether it has occurred to the leaders of Western Europe that *ours* is now 'the golden door', and that we could, without unbearable cost to ourselves, open it to those who, by undertaking the terrifying risks of this journey into the unknown, already demonstrate the individuality and strength that any progressive society can put to good use.

Writer and journalist Slavenka Drakulíc, born in Croatia, is an immigrant. When she was a schoolchild in Croatia, she told us in Stockholm, it was clear what Europe was: it was where the Soviet Union was not. But now? 'I live in Sweden, Croatia and Austria', she said at the beginning of her five-minute presentation as a panellist for the media seminars. 'And Europe is my home. But what is Europe now?' Who is European, she meant, with the rights and privileges of that term?

How far can Europe spread to the East remaining Europe? Is Turkey Europe? In that case, what about Russia? These are not abstract questions. The bottom line here is how the changes which are occurring [the challenges, she means, to the European—essentially the European Union identity] will influence the individual's life, work, income, education, language.

She spoke of the indefinable anxiety 'palpable, measurable in opinion polls, referendums, elections, reflecting doubts in the necessity of common currency, integration, enlargement, foreigners', which, in the form of increasing right radicalism, is coming to infuse the lives and the political landscape of Europe. 'The mechanism of exploiting fear', she said, 'is simple and well known.'

As an individual, you feel lost and confused. Suddenly, somebody offers you shelter, a feeling of belonging, a guarantee of a kind of security. We are of the same blood, we belong to the same territory, 'our people first', so goes the rhetoric. To frightened ears it is so soothing to hear the old-fashioned words like blood, soil, us, them. You feel stronger, you are no longer alone confronted with

'The Others': Muslims, Turks, gypsies, Africans, refugees, asylum seekers—from fear of the threat represented by the unknown to a creation of the 'known' enemy is only a small step. It doesn't need more than that vague sense of anxiety, plus a political leader who will know how to exploit it.

There is no lack of figures for the trend toward the political right and toward racism: an opinion poll undertaken by the reliable Eurobarometer in 1997 found that racism in Europe can be divided fairly evenly into three. About a third of those interviewed described themselves as 'not at all racist', a third 'a little racist' and a third 'quite or very racist'. Racism was considered moderate both in Germany and the UK, with only 6 per cent and 8 per cent 'very racist'. It was considered high in Belgium, France, Austria, Finland and Denmark, with 12 per cent in Denmark and 22 per cent in Belgium describing themselves as 'very racist'. The Eurobarometer poll also showed that *fear* of unemployment was a stronger criterion for racism than actual unemployment. Racism was found to be stronger in those of the political extreme right and extreme left, in those over 55 years old, in people who had little education, and in those who are against the European Union. The enquiry found no significant differences between urban or rural inhabitants or between genders.

On the positive side, however, 70 per cent of questioned Europeans thought immigrants should have the same rights as native citizens, 55 per cent felt that their families should be freely admitted, and 47 per cent came out for more liberal naturalization laws. Although 80 per cent of Europeans felt that immigrants who offended against the law of the host country should be excluded from it, 80 per cent also came out against the return to the birth countries of immigrants or their families, even if the wage earners lost their jobs. Nonetheless, overall 20 per cent of Europeans—i.e. comparable to the highest figure (Belgium) of admitted strong racism—felt all immigrants, legal and illegal, should be repatriated.[4]

One name that kept coming up in Stockholm was Austria's Jörg Haider, whose emergence as a major political player was, strangely enough, a spur for Austria, so long deplorably reticent about her role in Hitler's Europe, to begin to take issue with that past. Anneliese Rohrer, head of the domestic politics section of *Die Presse*, Vienna's leading conservative newspaper, is one of Austria's best-known journalists. 'I feel responsible for the developments in Austria in the last ten years', she said in Stockholm.

And I feel guilty for two reasons. We of the media never really acknowledged the problems of increasing xenophobia and intolerance in our country. We saw the signs as of 1989 and during a series of letter bombs in 1993. But we had identified the man and the party responsible for the changes: Jörg Haider and his Freedom Party, but then deliberately did not deal in our pages with the problems of minorities in any substantial way. Integration of refugees and foreigners was no issue for us; the difficulties of those who came to Austria after the downfall of the Iron Curtain and the civil war in former Yugoslavia was not given space: we looked the other way. Why did we neglect these issues? We thought that by dealing with them in the media we would support [i.e. publicize] the xenophobic politics of Haider, and therefore we blocked them out. This shows that meaning well is not always doing well. We achieved the contrary of what was intended. The lack of information on the realities of the changes in Austria became the basis for growing xenophobia and aggression against refugees and foreigners. We must accept part responsibility for this and we must change.

The British government suggests, with apparent reason-
ableness, that instead of immigration facilities, support should
be given to potential immigrants in the form of investment to
developing countries. By such means, the native infrastructure
would be improved, and citizens of those countries encouraged to stay where they are. We might all wish—if for different reasons than the government—that it was right, for it is
not easy for people, many of whom have to leave their families
behind, to become immigrants. But the sad truth is that there
is a great difference—a huge time-lag—between improving
the infrastructure of developing nations through foreign sub-
sidies, and improving the life-chances of individual human
beings. Men and women who want to improve the lives of
their families think in terms of now, not then; of the misery
they and their families live in now, not years hence; of the
physical strength for hard work they have now, but possibly not
later; of the benefits of a new life for their children while they
are small and malleable toward what can be, not later, when
they have become entrenched in what is or always has been.
The British government is probably quite right that a rethink
is necessary about the movement of people from one country
to another, but the problem is not how to stop them, for I
suspect the movement is unstoppable, but rather how to help
them go or stay where they can be most useful and most happy.

All this and far more along this line—timely, as I said—was
the subject of the Stockholm deliberations: the immorality of
colour arrogance, and prejudice on all sides; the immorality of
hate between people of different races and religions. Another
area I am involved with as a writer also emerged strongly: the
horror of allowing children to be unhappy, of allowing children to be hurt. I have attended many conferences around the
Western world, but never one that was so human. The very

beginning, before the formal opening by the Prime Minster
or any speeches, set the tone which somehow, throughout the
next days, was never lost. It was a 35-minute documentary,
showing a startlingly large number of young Swedish neo-
nazis, in black uniforms, with swastika-like insignias and flags,
marching-type music, raised arms and *Sieg Heils* wreaking
mayhem in the streets of Sweden. They were unstopped and
seemed unstoppable, until, horrified, we saw a dead little boy
of some indeterminate non-white colour whom they had
beaten up and killed. Showing us this film at the beginning of
the conference was a courageous Swedish *mea culpa*, which in
the course of the proceedings as I have said, would be echoed
in a number of presentations by representatives and panellists
from other nations.

'The greatest danger', said Sweden's Prime Minister in his
opening statement, 'is not the evil among those who are evil,
but in the silence of those who are good.' Two days later, in
his closing remarks—again a courageous act by a politician—
he deplored the lack of 'energetic and purposeful action on
the part of Sweden during the 1940s' which could have saved
Raoul Wallenberg. Wallenberg's heroism in saving many tens
of thousands of Hungary's Jews in 1944 somehow permeated
the conference. When the Soviets arrested, imprisoned and
tortured him in 1944 and, it is now believed, for many years
thereafter, it was not because he rescued Jews, but because,
possibly rightly, they believed him a scion of Sweden's richest
and most powerful family, to have been an American agent.
But when the Swedish government at the time and his uncles
(the top of the Swedish oligarchy, all of whom had successfully played off both sides—the German and the British—
during the war) did nothing to save him, it was at least in large
part because, with his humanism, and active compassion for

Jews, he made himself an outsider, an embarrassment for them. I think that Wallenberg died because he was an embarrassment to the deep-seated prejudices of the mighty. Over the years—his second great contribution—this had changed: his country, partly thanks to him, has changed. He has become a hero not only for much of the world but for Sweden's conscience. His half-sister, Nina, who worked for more than half a century to find out and expose what happened to him, sat next to me during the keynote addresses that followed the Prime Minister's Dinner on the first night. Her daughter, Nane, is married to the former Secretary-General of the United Nations, Kofi Annan, who addressed us. 'It is vital', he said, 'to do more to educate people about what immigrants are doing (in Western European countries) to explain the contributions they make; to make clear that they shouldn't be seen as a problem but as a solution.' 'Education of the young', he said 'must build on two simple truths: no one is born prejudiced, but neither is any child (responding as they do to their social environment) immune to intolerance.' As the Swedish Prime Minister admitted,

Intolerance manifests itself everywhere, in any country, with different faces. But the ugly tenet underlying it—that all human beings don't have the same value, and that human dignity doesn't need to be respected—that is a universal human phenomenon. We know the kind of answer all too often given to children who ask the questions 'Why war? Why hurt? Why death?' It is: it's the fault of the Serbs, the Albanians, the Hutus, the Tutsis, the Israelis, the Palestinians; the same answer that children have received down the ages. It is always the fault of 'Others'.

As Enzensberger reminds us, our one-time ideal in Europe was the 'melting pot' of races in North America. But the truth, we are now learning, is different. America, it is true and admirable, has somehow survived without collapsing into open ethnic conflict. But as Fergal Keane wrote some time ago in *The Independent*, 'There is in fact no blending together of the races into one nation indivisible under God.'[5] This becomes very clear when, as I have done—and it was a disturbing revelation for me—you try as a white person to step, socially, into black society in Harlem. It happened after a book of mine, on child prostitution,[6] was published in America and a well-known black psychiatrist and his wife, also a child therapist, invited me to dinner. The apartment house they lived in was not unlike ours in Kensington, and certainly better taken care of. There were books, many the same as those I read; there was a music system and classical tapes and the dinner was delicious. Our interests in children were identical. Where we began to be different, and I fear all three of us felt it, was that both their experience and their interest, naturally enough perhaps, was entirely in black children. What I'm saying is that I am allowed to be interested, involved with and write about any children of any colour, any race. They, though at the top of their profession, had never treated a white child and didn't think they ever would or could. This happened ten years ago. Since then, however, with ever more Hispanic American immigration—who, with other blacks, especially in urban America, end up living on the economic downside of society—the deep sense of exclusion I felt that night in Harlem has become much worse.

## Inner Racism

There is a challenge here for us in Europe, to create in the midst of this racially infected immigration storm, an exemplary multi-racial society. However, although little thought of and rarely mentioned, there exists an impediment to such a dream, an impediment not from without but from within. Over these three days in Stockholm we pondered how, through education, legislation and community strategies, we can combat the perilous extremes of violence: against immigrants by those who believe they threaten their livelihood; by passionate separatists in defence of their religious and ethnic cultures; and incipient violence too in massed bands of unthinking youths who confuse ideology with identity. We sought ways how, in our age of communication, that new dangerous medium, the internet, can be controlled; and how the print and television media, all too often prone to the intervention of commercial interests, can exercise the self-censorship commensurate with its immense power.

Against that, however, there is one aspect of racism that I have not seen mentioned in any conference programme, but which, to my mind, is the most perilous one. Because, undefined by class or gender and largely without planned intent, it enters, as of adolescence, almost by some kind of insidious osmosis, the minds or spirits of much of mankind. This is what I would call 'inner racism'. I do not mean *innate* racism. Babies, we know, are not born with it; toddlers have no sense of it; children below the age of 8 or even 10 appear immune to it. Yet, as of that age, or just beyond it, playgrounds echo with the invectives expressing it; only a little later violent streetfights grow out of it; social and political life is permeated by it, and finally people, young and old, see their lives ruined and indeed some die by it.

But there are exceptions, from which we can take heart and learn. As I was first working on this lecture, I went to a theatre in London, which was showing a play acted by black actors about life years ago in the townships of South Africa. Sitting on cushions on the floor at the edge of the stage were three rows of young people, aged between, I would say, 18 and 25. And watching their rapt faces as the action unrolled before them, I realized that the 'inner racism' I was going to speak about was not in them; that somehow, by dint of background, or constant positive educational pressure, not only by schools but the media and all the arts—a kind of shield had been created in them against this invasion. This applies very strongly to the young German generations because of their emotional involvement through grandparents and great grandparents with events of appalling violence. I have observed this change in what one might call the German character time and again over the years, and have written about it in my most recent book *The German Trauma*.[7]

But these young generations are still a minority, the few, not the many, not us. In order to understand what provokes our reaction of rejection, dislike or even repugnance to another's colour, his religion, the shape of her face, or his manner of living or being, we have to first acknowledge its existence in us. We have consciously to recognize it and to realize its power of corruption. There are many examples, past and present, of the consequences of these feelings in us, on this and other continents. These individual reactions of inner racism which remain passive in most of us, can, when they become active in some, lead to men, women and children, marked as inferior outsiders, being harassed and hounded.

Isolated from the community, denied their civic liberties, deprived of their homes and possessions, they become emotionally, psychologically and physically diminished while we, the passively inner racist majority, stand by surprised, certain of personal blamelessness of violence, but incapable of resisting it.

Let me use history to illustrate my points. Anti-Semitism is now only one and perhaps potentially not the most dangerous of prejudices. But even though I feel, with many others now, that Hitler's murder of the Jews should now gradually be considered albeit the most dreadful part of the Third Reich, not the totality of its history, the fact is that nothing so tragically and clearly delineates the reality and the danger of inner racism as that most dreadful of genocides. The case of the attacks in the late 1980s on Kurt Waldheim, then President of Austria, for denying or lying about some of his wartime past, is perhaps the most familiar of recent times. My long conversations with Waldheim in 1988, while demonstrating his intellectual or imaginative limitations, and the danger these deficiencies represent, at the same time showed up the hysteria of the accusations.[8] There can be no doubt that he was elected, not because he was politically able, or even particularly popular, but because the accusations against him (some of them, it turned out, quite wrong) came mostly from American Jews. The Austrians were not going to be dictated to, either by Jews or America. But in fact it would become, both for Waldheim himself within the limitations of his capacities and for Austria, a stage in maturing. Eleven years later, as a result of the Haider affair, this would express itself differently, more creatively and more positively for their future.

'You ask me whether I feel bitter', Waldheim said.

One young student asked me recently why I didn't just take off my uniform, throw away my weapons. He is right, it is a fundamental question. Of course, I could have. Perhaps I should have—it is true of course. I could have resisted, deserted, and I didn't.

That was what he said now, I said, but did he actually consider such a choice?

One did think about it, of course but . . . You see, my father and my brother were both active anti-Nazis—my father lost his teaching job, was imprisoned, beaten up . . . I think it was because my family was so endangered that I felt army life was safer than being a civilian. It is true, I wanted to survive.

Did he know any Jews? I asked.

Oh yes, I'm in touch now with three of my Jewish school friends: one in America, one here, and then of course Lord Weidenfeld—my old friend Georg—he was kind enough to give me an affidavit.

If that was a sad term for a head of state to use, he didn't notice.

Had he known about Hitler's feelings about Jews? Had he read *Mein Kampf*? He smiled: it is extraordinary in Germany and Austria how many people smile when asked this question. The old condescension toward 'Corporal Hitler, the house-painter' still survives.

'Perhaps I should have read it', he said. 'I might have understood more: people say that everything was in there . . .'. 'Of course', he said, 'one knew about concentration camps, where they sent many non-Jews too. Of course one realized that Jews were disappearing in Austria: one thought they were interned.' Women, children? I asked, but he bypassed the question. 'Can you imagine what this is doing to my family? My 11-year old grandson comes home and asks, "Is it true that grandfather is a war criminal?" Good God, knowledge, after all, is not guilt.' But wasn't what he had been saying precisely that he knew nothing? 'I never *saw* anything.'

'But you guessed, and thought?' I asked.

Of course one *thought*. But in law there is a big difference between knowing and doing. Anyway, what could one have done? Nothing. Even if I had given my life, it wouldn't have helped.

I said that I recognized that it was too much to ask of people to be heroes and that I wasn't at all sure I could have been. But was there no moral responsibility apart from practicality? 'In that case, where does guilt lie?', I asked.

'Not in mere knowledge', he said. 'Only in not doing anything, if one was in a position *to* do something. I am religious. I pray. I often prayed that these horrors of war should stop.'

But didn't he feel it facile, not worthy of him, just to do away with the horrors by justifying them with war, to *use* war for justification?

'But it *was* war', he said despairingly. 'Greece, Yugoslavia, Russian savage war. But Pearl Harbor too; Hiroshima, and later, what about Vietnam, and now the West Bank—in all these places the innocent died and die, women and children by the hundreds of thousands: who spoke for them, who protested there?'

'How about horrors then which had nothing whatever to do with war?', I said. 'Can you apply the same standard to Pearl Harbor, for instance, and Treblinka? What about Treblinka?'

Treblinka is something entirely different. You are right: it had nothing to do with war. It was a political act. It was an abomination. It was a crime. But you see, I knew nothing about these terrible

**247**

places until after the war: how could a normal person imagine that anything like this *could* be done?[9]

Well, at the very least, we will never be able to say that again, will we? We all know now what can be done. I have read Michael Ignatieff's thoughts on human rights, sovereignty and intervention.[10] I suspect he is as worried as I am at the thought of any justification for intervention by force. It is the insoluble conundrum: how to stop violence without using force; how to create limitations to force once it takes over. Waldheim, as you can see, with all his prejudices, his inner racism intact—as he is probably too old to change—is nevertheless finally able to say, 'Even if I did know, what could I do?' What he could neither recognize as applying to himself as a young man, nor bring himself to say or *know* how to say—for it would have required an intellectual and moral step beyond his capacity—is that individual men change when they use legitimized force. That is the problem; we see it in armies, both during a war and in occupation; we see it in police forces, in prison guards, and indeed in those who command them, whether in the field, the streets, the prisons or indeed in government.

My interviews with Albert Speer and with Franz Stangl, the Commandant of Treblinka, further illustrate my points of inner racism, and the corruption it can cause. One such illustration is the answer given to me by Stangl who, probably no more anti-Semitic than most Austrian provincials at the time, became entirely conditioned to violence and disastrously corrupted by it.[11] Toward the end of our long conversation in Düsseldorf prison in 1971, I asked whether it would be true to say that he got used to the liquidations. 'To tell the truth', he said slowly, 'one did become used to it.' 'Would it be true to say that you finally felt they weren't really human beings?', I asked. He answered:

When I was on a trip once years later in Brazil my train stopped next to a slaughter house. The cattle in the pens trotted up to the fence and stared at the steaming, hissing train. They were very close to my window, one crowding the other, looking at me through that fence. I thought then, 'Look at this; this reminds me of Poland; that's just how the people looked, trustingly, before they went into the tins . . .'.

'You said "tins"', I interrupted. 'What do you mean?' But he went on without hearing, or answering me. 'I couldn't eat tinned meat after that . . .'. 'So you didn't feel they were human beings?' I asked again. 'Cargo', he said tonelessly. 'They were cargo.'[12]

Eleven years later, in 1982, I began the research for my book on Albert Speer, whom I had known well for the last four years of his life, and his daughter Hilde gave me the letters he had written to her from Spandau prison. Irrespective of whether one likes or believes Speer, something he said in a long agonized letter to his 16-year-old daughter, who had asked to him explain to her how he could have remained part of a system that was so evil, is as telling of passive inner racism as anything we might find:

There can be no excuse; there is no justification, and in that sense I am convinced of my own guilt. To reassure you, however: of the dreadful things [the gas chambers] I knew nothing . . . [And] as far as practising anti-Semitism . . . my conscience is entirely clear.

And then, to young Hilde's horror, he ended,

I really have no aversion to them, or rather no more than the slight discomfort all of us sometimes feel when in contact with them.[13]

That 'slight discomfort'—a discomfiting awareness of difference—is what many if not most of us, black, brown,

yellow, white, Muslims, Hindus, Jews, Christians, have probably, *do* probably, if only fleetingly feel in our bones at one
time or another about one or other of our fellow-men. We
think of ourselves as good people, innocent of prejudice. But
perhaps—as Albert Speer would only do toward the end of
his life—we need to remember that this innocence is only as
real as our capacity to maintain denial. When we admit to
inner racism, as we must, then we must fight it, or there is no
more innocence and we lay ourselves open to corruption.

# Introduction to Susan Sontag

*Hermione Lee*

I am proud and delighted to be introducing Susan Sontag's Amnesty lecture, since for me, as for many women of my generation and younger, she has been for many years an intellectual heroine and example, for her brilliance, her ardour, her intellectual courage, her toughness and her voracious energies. Novelist, critic and historian, champion of human rights, commentator and interpreter on an astounding range of cultural issues, from politics and illness to photography, opera, film, drama and painting, there seems to be nothing she hasn't read, nothing she wouldn't be able to write about, and nothing she can't do.

This exciting and eclectic range of work can't be easily generalized about, because it is always moving on and developing, so that we should now describe first and foremost as a novelist a writer who 40 years ago would have been defined as an essayist. But there are two features which do repeatedly strike me. One is the wisdom of the world traveller, the person who exists edge-on to her own country and is not narrowly defined by it. She is a European intellectual in America, a global observer of nations and countries and people. This sense of her goes back to her passionate opposition to American foreign policy in the 1960s and 1970s, and continues in her more recent writing on, and practical involvement with, the situation in the Balkans. She lived in Sarajevo from 1993–96 and in her 1999 essay on the Balkans as the 'other' Europe, called 'Why Are We in Kosovo?' she wrote, 'It is easy to turn your eyes from what is happening if it is not happening to you. Or if you have not put yourself where it is happening.'

The other thing I notice about her work is her passionate interest in self-transformation. The characters in her last two novels, *The Volcano Lover* (1992) and *In America* (2000), invite us to think about the power of the will and the possibilities of freedom and change; and her own writing is constantly challenging conventions, mental inertia and stasis. And the key to self-transformation is, in her view, looking outwards at the business of the world, not looking inwards. It's what her most recent fictional heroine, the actress Maryna, calls the 'exit from the self'. 'Happiness' (she thinks), 'depended on not being trapped in your individual existence, a container with your name on it. You have to forget yourself, your container. You have to attach yourself to what takes you outside yourself, what stretches the world.' In her Amnesty lecture, she talks to us about images of atrocity, and whether or not we are desensitized to them, whether or not their ubiquity devalues what they show us. So here, to stretch the world for us a little, is Susan Sontag.

# War and Photography

## Susan Sontag

I am honoured to have been invited to give a lecture in this distinguished series, and pleased to have the opportunity to express my solidarity with the work of Amnesty International: drawing attention to, with the aim of inspiring action against, violations of human rights wherever these are taking place.

Oxford is far from the killing fields and the refugee camps. We are not the unjustly jailed.

Since those with the means to curb injustice are rarely those enduring it, how then do the privileged—such as the membership of Amnesty International, and the larger constituency reached by its appeals and those of other humanitarian organizations—learn about these crimes? Monitoring, reporting on, and campaigning on behalf of individuals and causes is first of all a pedagogic task. In identifying sites of distress and making that distress vivid to us, photographic images have come to play a decisive role. I should like to examine the role of photographs in identifying subjects of concern and mobilizing the practical will to do something about what arouses indignation.

The iconography of suffering has a long pedigree. The suffering most often deemed worthy of representation is that understood to be the product of wrath, divine or human. (Suffering induced by natural causes, such as illness or childbirth, is scantily represented in the history of art.) The statue group of the writhing Laocoön and his sons, the innumerable representations in painting and statuary of the Passion of Christ, and the vast visual catalogue of the fiendish martyrdoms of the Christian saints—these are surely intended to move and excite. But the images do not, principally, *protest* against these horrors.

The practice of representing atrocious suffering as something to be deplored, and if possible stopped, enters the history of images fairly recently, and the sufferings depicted are those endured by a civilian population at the hands of a victorious army on the rampage.

The project begins in the era of hand-made images, and its most celebrated practitioners are Jacques Callot and Francisco Goya. Since 1839, when cameras were invented, the suffering caused by war has become a widely disseminated, canonical subject.

A photograph is like a quotation, or a maxim or a proverb. Easy to retain. All of us mentally stock hundreds of photographs, subject to instant recall. Cite the most famous photograph taken during the Spanish Civil War, the Republican soldier 'shot' by Robert Capa's camera just as he was shot by a bullet, and I wager that virtually everyone who has heard of that war can summon the grainy black-and-white figure collapsing on the slope, his right arm flung backward as he loses his grip on his rifle, at the very moment of death.

Photographs identify events. Photographs confer importance on events and make them memorable. We may understand through narrative, but we remember through photographs, as David Rieff has written, apropos of Ron Haviv's pictures of Serb-perpetrated atrocities and devastation in Bosnia between 1992 and 1995.

In the first important wars to be photographed, the

Crimean War and the American Civil War, indeed through the First World War, photographs played only a small role in whatever awareness the public had of the cost of combat. Our knowledge of the human catastrophe of the 1914–18 European war, for example, owes far more to the testimony of journalists and the drawings of war artists than to the photographs that were taken at the front and published. The published photographs, in so far as they conveyed something of the terrors and devastation being endured, were mostly in the epic or panoramic mode, and mostly depictions of an aftermath: the corpse-strewn or lunar landscapes left by trench warfare; the gutted French villages that the war had passed through.

Regular 'coverage' of a war, on the front lines, had to wait for the Spanish Civil War, the first war to be extensively surveyed by the camera with an eye to the immediate publication of images—in this instance, in the daily and weekly press in Britain and France. And new kinds of photographs were taken. In the intervening two decades, equipment had become more portable; pictures could be taken in the thick of battle; civilian victims and exhausted begrimed soldiers could be studied close up. The photographs of the Spanish Civil War set the standards for the photojournalists of all subsequent wars, most notably the wars in Vietnam and the Balkan wars of the 1990s.

Mathew Brady, Alexander Gardner and Timothy O'Sullivan did not have to think of themselves as expressing an opinion about the war with their wide-angle photographs of dead soldiers lying on American Civil War battlefields, any more than such a thought would have occurred to the great photographers of the Second World War, such as Margaret Bourke-White. But in recent years the most ambitious photographers who bring us news of war and other human-made devastations think of themselves as witnesses and accusers: Don McCullin, Sebastião Salgado, Gilles Peress. James Nachtwey, whose work has recently been collected in a book called *Inferno*, has been described as a war photographer who is an anti-war photographer.

Photojournalism, which some of its practitioners call 'concerned photography' or 'the photography of conscience', has become a principal vehicle of the protest against war. Even absent such a message, since photographs are 'mass images'— reproducible images designed for the widest possible circulation—our understanding of war is now chiefly a product of the impact of images made with cameras.

Photographic images have become essential. To make a crisis take up residence in the consciousness of those who follow the 'news' requires a non-stop photographic account, diffused through television and video streaming. Something is not 'real'—to those who are not experiencing it, but following it, consuming it, as 'news'—until it is photographed.

Take the most neglected theatre of horrors, postcolonial Africa. Our knowledge—our sense—of the catastrophes taking place there is largely pointed, and framed, by appalling images we carry in our heads, starting with photographs taken during the famine in Biafra to, in the mid-1990s, the photographic documentation of the genocide of the Rwandan Tutsis and, most recently, photographs of the limbless victims, children and adults, of a programme of terror inflicted upon thousands by the 'RUF', the rebel forces in Sierra Leone. The cruelties and loss of life in the conflicts in Angola, lacking extensive photographic evidence (though we have every other kind of evidence), have hardly registered on mainstream consciousness.

★

Photographs both create and secure the significance of what is photographed. That is why everyone is eager to photograph what is important or cherished.

Often something looks, or is felt to look, 'better' in a photograph. Indeed, it is one of the functions of photography to improve the way things appear as we normally take them in. (Hence, we're always disappointed by a photograph that is not flattering; that is, that doesn't show us looking more attractive than we actually are.) A photograph is a way of showing something at its 'best'. After the tour of the new house, its proud owners might show the visitors an album of photographs of it, and surely more than one mother has exclaimed to someone admiring her baby in the pram, 'You should see her photographs!'

Beautification is a primary purpose of photography. So, for didactic purposes, is uglification: showing something at its worst. If beautifying bleaches out moral response, showing what is hard to look at invites an active judgement. Shock may be the point of the photograph. For photographs to accuse, they must shock.

Recently, the public health authorities in Canada, where it has been estimated that smoking kills 45,000 people a year, decided to supplement the warning printed on every pack of cigarettes with a photograph—a photograph of cancerous lungs, or a stroke-clotted brain, or a damaged heart, or a bloody mouth in acute periodontal distress. A pack with a warning about the deleterious effects of smoking accompanied by such a picture would be *sixty* times more likely to inspire smokers to quit, public research had calculated (how?), than a pack with only the verbal warning.

Assume it's true. But for how long will it stay true? Right now, the smokers of Canada are recoiling in disgust, if they do examine these photographs. If similar pictures are still on the cigarette packs five years from now, will they still be upset?

Photographs build our sense of the present. And photographs construct—and revise—our sense of the past.

An example: a trove of photographs of black victims of lynching in small towns in the United States between the 1890s and the 1930s, which provided a shattering, revelatory experience for the tens of thousands of people who saw them exhibited in New York in 2000. The lynching pictures tell us about human wickedness. About inhumanity. They also instruct us, specifically, about the extent of the evil unleashed by racism. Intrinsic to the perpetration of this evil is the desire to photograph it: pictures were taken as 'souvenirs', and more than a few show grinning spectators, good church-going citizens as most of them had to be, posing for a camera beneath the charred, mutilated bodies.

Now the display of these horrendous pictures makes us spectators, too. What is the point of exhibiting them? To awaken indignation? To make us feel 'bad'; that is, to appal and sadden? Is looking at such pictures really 'necessary', given that these horrors are in a past remote enough to be beyond punishment?

The eminent American historian of African slavery and its aftermath, Leon Litwack, wrote in an essay accompanying the book of these photographs entitled *Beyond Sanctuary*:

The need for this grisly photographic display may be disputed as catering to voyeuristic appetites and perpetuating images of black victimization. This is not an easy history to assimilate. It's far easier to view what is depicted on these pages as so depraved and barbaric as to be beyond the realm of reason. The photographs stretch our credulity, even numb our minds to the full extent of the horror, but they must be examined if we are to understand how normal men and women could live with, participate in, and defend such atrocities, even reinterpret them so they would not see themselves or be perceived as less than civilized. This was not the outburst of crazed men or uncontrolled barbarians but the triumph of a belief system that defined one people as less human than another.[1]

Litwack's view is that there is an obligation to examine these pictures—not to mourn (one could never mourn enough), but to understand.

Still, questions remain about our capacity actually to assimilate (as opposed to think about) these horrors. Not all reactions to the pictures may be under the supervision of reason and conscience. There is always the suspicion that the representation of these mutilated bodies may arouse a prurient interest as well. Following a similar thought, Roy Porter and others have speculated, with respect to centuries of paintings of the gruesome executions of the early Christian saints, that there had to have been an exploitative or sensationalist aspect to the intense absorption of so many artists in the torments of flesh.

The cruelties depicted in Goya's *The Disasters of War* are meant to awaken, shock, rend, and the expressive comments on what is depicted—the captions, as it were—are no less partisan. We expect a photograph's caption to supply only neutral-sounding information: date, place, names.

Ordinary language fixes the difference between handmade images like Goya's and photographs by the conventions that artists 'make' drawings and paintings while photographers 'take' photographs. The difference holds only up to a point.

True, the hand-made image is openly a construction—that is a report, filtered through the artist's mind and hand—of what may or may not have been witnessed, while a photographic image *entails* witnessing, because the photograph is itself a light-trace of an actual event. But the photographic image, while a trace, can't be a transparency of something that did really happen. It is always the image that someone else chose; to photograph is to frame, and to frame is to exclude. For a long time, the fact that the images were produced by a machine obscured the many senses in which photographs are as much 'made' by the person operating the camera as drawings and paintings are 'made' by an artist.

Further, it has always been possible—from the beginning, long before the era of digital manipulation—for a photograph to misrepresent what it shows. A painting or drawing is judged a fake when it has been discovered to be not by the artist to whom it had been attributed. A photograph is judged a fake when it turns out to deceive the viewer about the scene it purports to record.

If nothing like the atrocities perpetrated by the soldiers in Goya's images had taken place during the French invasion of Spain, we would think the images a fraud. But the fact that what happened didn't happen exactly in this way, with someone who looked exactly like this, against exactly that background, doesn't disqualify the picture. The image is a report. It says: things *like* this happened.

In contrast, a photograph claims to present—to represent—exactly. What you see—rather, what you think you see—is actually what was there: say, somebody being shot. A photograph makes a claim of witnessing. It says: 'it's true' (it's a record, a trace), and, therefore, has the status of evidence. So any clues that suggest manipulation would discredit or disqualify the photograph. The persistent suspicion that Robert Capa's 'Death of a Republican Soldier' was staged, continues to haunt discussions of war photography.

Goya's images cannot count as evidence; no hand-made image can. Of course it was this soldiery, the Napoleonic soldiery in Spain, which committed these atrocities, but the images also propose a more general denunciation: of the horrors of all war and of the human talent for wickedness. And even photographic evidence of the apportioning of guilt in a particular conflict eventually become general denunciations of human cruelty, human savagery as such.

There is an illusion that you 'know' something through a photograph of a zone of monstrous suffering, beside the fact that there is pain and human cruelty; know something about what went on; know something about victims and murderers, right and wrong.

Consider the most famous image to come out of the Vietnam War: a child doused in napalm, naked, arms upraised, shrieking with pain, running down the road . . . toward us. That image, by Huynh Cong Ut, crystallized the revulsion against the war. Or consider Eugene Smith's pictures of the victims of mercury poisoning by the Chisso Chemical Company in Minimata, Japan. Or let me conjure up for you one of the most unforgettable images of the war in Bosnia, a photograph of which the distinguished *New York Times* foreign correspondent John Kifner wrote:

The image is stark, one of the most enduring of the Balkan wars: a Serb militiaman casually kicking a dying Muslim woman in the head. It tells you everything you need to know.[2]

But, of course, it doesn't tell us everything you need to know.

From the photographer, Ron Haviv, we know the photograph was taken in the town of Bijelina in April 1992, which was the first month of the Serb rampage through Bosnia. It shows us from behind a uniformed Serb soldier (there's no reason to think he's a militiaman), an elegant youthful figure, sunglasses perched on top of his head, a cigarette held between the second and third fingers of his raised left hand, downward pointing rifle gripped in his right hand, right leg raised, about to kick a woman lying between two other bodies on the sidewalk. The photograph doesn't tell us whether she is dying or already dead. It certainly doesn't tell us she is a Muslim, though likely that would be the label applied to her.

Far from the photograph telling us everything we need to know, it tells us very little. Since we know that the Serbs were the aggressors and the Bosnians were the victims, we read that knowledge into the picture. But one could as well say that all the photograph tells us, all it 'knows', so to speak, is that war is hell, and that handsome graceful young men are capable of kicking older overweight women in the head while they're lying face down on sidewalks.

There are two widespread views—one could call them *idées reçues,* in the Flaubertian sense—on the impact of photography. Since I find these ideas formulated in my own essays on photography—the earliest of which was written nearly 30 years ago—I feel an irresistible temptation to quarrel with them.

The first idea is that public attention is steered by the attentions of 'the media', which means, most decisively, images. When there are photographs, a war becomes 'real'. Thus, the protest against the Vietnam War was mobilized by images such as the photograph by Huynh Cong Ut. The feeling that something had to be done about the war in Bosnia was built from the attentions of journalists—'the CNN effect' it was sometimes called—which brought images of besieged Sarajevo into hundreds of millions of living rooms night after night for the almost three years of the siege.

The second idea—which may seem the converse of what I've just described: the determining influence of photographs in shaping what catastrophes and crises we pay attention to, what we care about, and ultimately what evaluations we place on these conflicts—is that in a world hypersaturated by images, those that should matter to us have a diminishing effect. We become inured. In the end, such images make us more callous, a little less able to feel and respond as we should.

From the earliest of the six essays, this one written in 1972, which make up the book I published in 1977 called *On Photography*:

Images transfix. Images anaesthetize. An event known through photographs certainly becomes more real than it would have been if one had never seen the photographs—think of the Vietnam War. (For a counter-example, think of the Gulag Archipelago, of which we have no photographs.) But after repeated exposure to images, it also becomes less real.

The same holds for evil as for photography. The shock of photographed atrocities wears off with repeated viewings ... The vast photographic catalogue of misery and injustice throughout the world has given everyone a certain familiarity with atrocity, making the horrible seem more ordinary—making it appear familiar, remote ('it's only a photograph'), inevitable. At the time of the first photographs of the Nazi camps, there was nothing banal about these images. After thirty years, a saturation point may have been reached. In the last decades, 'concerned' photography has done at least as much to deaden conscience as to arouse it.[3]

Well . . . No.

In another variant of the argument of the uselessness of images for moral mobilization—an argument which I did not make in *On Photography*—our relation to these images is compromised by the fact that they are, in a certain sense, pornographic. The slowing down of highway traffic going past a horrific car crash is not mere curiosity. It is a wish to see something gruesome. The attraction to such sights is genuine, deep, and often a source of mental conflict.

Indeed, the very first acknowledgement (as far as I am aware) of the attraction of mutilated bodies occurs in a description of mental conflict. I am speaking of an astonishing passage in *The Republic*, where Plato evokes a concrete situation in which our 'desires' might force us to go against our 'reason', which would then lead us to revile ourselves and become indignant with a part of our nature. It occurs while Plato is developing his tripartite theory of mental functioning, consisting of reason, anger or indignation, and appetite or desire—which anticipates the Freudian scheme of superego, ego and id (with the difference that Plato puts reason on top and conscience, represented by indignation, in the middle). In the course of this argument, he has Socrates relate to Glaucon the following story to illustrate how we may yield, reluctantly, to repulsive attractions:

The story is, that Leontius, the son of Aglaion, coming up one day from the Piraeus, under the north wall on the outside, observed some dead bodies lying on the ground at the place of execution. He felt a desire to see them, and also a dread and abhorrence of them; for a time he struggled and covered his eyes, but at length the desire got the better of him; and forcing them open, he ran up to the dead bodies, crying, 'There you are, curse you, feast yourselves on this lovely sight'.[4]

Eschewing the more obvious example of inappropriate sexual passion or some other encumbering bodily appetites, Plato takes for granted that we also have an appetite—repulsive but authentic—to feast on sights of degradation and suffering and mutilation.

Surely the undertow of this despised impulse must be taken into account when discussing the effect of images of suffering and atrocity.

In *On Photography*, I wrote:

Protected middle-class inhabitants of the more affluent corners of the world—those regions where most photographs are taken and consumed—learn about the world's horrors mainly through the camera; photographs can and do distress. But the aestheticizing tendency of photography is such that the medium which conveys distress ends by neutralizing it. Cameras miniaturize experience, transform history into spectacle. As much as they create sympathy, photographs cut sympathy, distance the emotions. Photography's realism creates a confusion about the real which is (in the long run) analgesic morally as well as (both in the long and in the short run) sensorially stimulating . . .[5]

Is this true? I certainly thought it was when I wrote it, in the early 1970s. But I'm not so certain now—in part because, since writing these words, I've spent some time in the company of journalists in the middle of a much-photographed war. (My three years living part-time in Sarajevo during the siege have surely influenced these considerations.) What, I now ask myself, is the evidence that photographs have less and less impact, that our culture of spectacle neutralizes the moral impact of photographs of real horrors, that we are simply creating a culture of callousness?

It is true that there is an increasing level of violence and sadism in the acceptable images of mass culture: films, TV, video games. Imagery that would have been unbearable, unwatchable 40 years ago is watched without flinching by teenagers in rich countries. Indeed, violence is entertaining rather than shocking to many people in most modern cultures. But this does not mean that the images earmarked as 'real' are watched with the same detachment.

Let me offer some rather general theses. What makes a life or a society 'modern' is, above all else, its saturation by 'information'—a central category of contemporary life. And the critique of modernity is essentially a description of the inexorably dehumanizing or alienating consequences of the ever accelerating production (that is, overproduction) of information, whether of the abstract and statistical, or of the assaultive and pointlessly overstimulating.

The argument that modern life consists of a diet of horrors to which we gradually become habituated is as old as the critique of modernity, which is well over 150 years old. (Almost the same age as cameras.) Here is Baudelaire writing in the 1860s in his journal:

It is impossible to glance through any newspaper, no matter what the day, the month or the year, without finding on every line the most frightful traces of human perversity . . . Every newspaper, from the first line to the last, is nothing but a tissue of horrors. War, crimes, thefts, lecheries, tortures, the evil deeds of princes, of nations, of private individuals; an orgy of universal atrocity.

And it is with this loathsome appetizer that civilized man daily washes down his morning repast . . .[6]

That newspapers didn't carry photographs then doesn't make Baudelaire's accusatory description of the bourgeois sitting down with his morning newspaper to breakfast on a cavalcade of the world's horrors, before going off to the temple of commerce for the day's money-making, any different from the contemporary critique of breakfasting with the TV as well as the morning paper—our way of taking in a display of the world's horrors, to which we become ever more inured.

The two leading clichés of the discussion of images of atrocity are that they have little effect and that there is something innately cynical and corrupting about their diffusion.

Michael Ignatieff has written that 'war photography— thanks to television—has now become a nightly banality. We are flooded with images of atrocity.' This 'nightly barrage of images of atrocity' risks deadening our 'delicate human capacity to transmute aesthetic vision into moral insight'. It is hard to know what is being really asked for here. That images of carnage be rationed—say, to once a week—so that they have a chance of maintaining their power to shock? More generally, that we work toward what I called for in *On Photography*: an 'ecology of images'?

The complaint—I mean this criticism to apply to myself, in *On Photography*, as well as to Michael Ignatieff—seems rather crudely rhetorical. There isn't going to be an ecology of images. No Committee of Guardians is going to ration horror, so we can feel more horrified. And the horrors themselves are not going to abate either.

The view I proposed in *On Photography*, which Michael Ignatieff has recently revisited—that reality, or rather our capacity to respond with emotional freshness and ethical pertinence to reality, is being sapped by the profusion of vulgar and appalling images—is the conservative critique of the omnipresence of such images.

I call this critique conservative because it takes for granted the existence of 'reality' and our ability to respond to it. In the radical version of the argument, there is no reality to defend. The vast maw of modernity has chewed up reality and spat the whole mess out as images. According to a highly influential analysis of modernity, ours is a 'society of spectacle'. Something has to be turned into a spectacle to be real—that is, interesting to us. People themselves become images: celebrities. There are only media representations: reality is obsolete.

Fancy rhetoric, this. And very persuasive to many, because one of the characteristics of modernity is that people like to feel that they are ahead of their own experience. The view is associated in particular with the writings of the late Guy Debord and of Jean Baudrillard, but not only these writers. It seems to be something of a French speciality.

In Sarajevo in the summer of 1993 I attended a noon press conference given by André Glucksmann, who had flown from Paris that morning on a French military plane to declare his support for the besieged city. What he told the assembled youthful members of the local press corps, a few curious foreign journalists, and myself tagging along—we were about twenty in all, huddling in a sandbagged room used for such events at the PTT—was that this was the first war that was entirely *médiatique*. That meant, he explained to his bemused auditors, that it would be won or lost not by anything taking place in Sarajevo or elsewhere in Bosnia but by what happened in the foreign media. Indeed, he said, war was now essentially a media event. For those of us living in Sarajevo, it was hard to think of the war as entirely *médiatique*. Perhaps

André Glucksmann, well intentioned as he was, didn't altogether believe his own rhetoric, since he left for Paris by the same military plane at the end of the afternoon. Even he must have realized there was something extra-*médiatique* about shells and bullets. Reports of the death of reality—like the death of the author, the death of the novel—seem to be rather exaggerated.

It may even be that exactly the opposite is true: that images have never been so powerful. Starting with the formation of Médécins sans Frontières, which was created in response to the Biafran famine, the rise of humanitarian organizations (NGOs) is directly related to a shift in both elite and public opinion, in the mobilization of which a principal instrument has been painful-to-look-at photographs. Sometimes even governments consider themselves obliged to make at least a token response to the events named by widely disseminated horrific photographs. And occasionally a change of public stance on the part of someone politically prominent can be keyed to the impact of a photograph. For example, the senior Senator from California, Diane Feinstein, said that she changed her vote about the proposed NATO action in 1995 after seeing a photograph of a refugee from Srebrenica who, after having been gang-raped by Serb soldiers, had hanged herself in the woods outside Tuzla.

But this does not dispel the suspicion that surrounds the taking of these images from two extremes of the spectrum: cynics who have never been near a war, and the people who are enduring the miseries being photographed.

The feeling persists that the creation of such images satisfies a vulgar or low appetite; that it is commercial ghoulishness. In Sarajevo in the years of siege, it was not uncommon to hear somebody yelling at the photojournalists, easily recognizable

by the equipment hanging round their necks: 'Are you waiting for a shell to go off so you can photograph some corpses?'
Never mind that the photographer on the street in the middle
of a bombardment or a burst of sniper fire, was running just as
much risk of being killed as the civilians she or he was tracking. And, as I can testify, the journalists were not neutral.
Indeed, they were, almost to a man and woman, passionately
pro-Bosnian. Further, the Sarajevans themselves knew how
much the continued survival of the city owed to the advocacy
of the foreign journalists who stayed on to cover the story.
Nevertheless, the foreign journalists, but more particularly
the war photographers, were derided and mocked. Ordinary
Sarajevans called them 'angels of death'. And the truth was,
the photographer might have been lurking about waiting for
such a photograph.

In 1994, at the height of the bombardment, one of the best
journalists to cover the siege, the BBC's Alan Little, wrote
about a small child grievously wounded by shrapnel; this ran
on the front page of daily papers throughout the world, illus-
trated by a colour photograph of 'Little Irma', as she'd been
nicknamed. As a result, the then Prime Minister, John Major,
felt obliged to send a British military plane to Sarajevo to
evacuate the hopelessly brain-injured child and bring her to
die in a hospital in England.

Citizens of modernity, consumers of events as spectacle, are
schooled to be cynical about 'the sincere'. Thus, deriding the
efforts of those who seek to bear witness as the 'tourism of
misery' is a recurrent cliché in the discussion of 'concerned'
photography. It seems as if some people will do anything to
prevent themselves from being moved. How much easier it is
to establish one's position of superiority, risking nothing.

What is true, however, is that there are too many things to which we are invited to pay attention, and it is quite understandable that we turn away from images that simply make us feel bad.

A woman in Sarajevo whom I met not long after I arrived in the city the first time in April 1993 (a year after the siege began), told me:

In 1991 I sat in my nice apartment here in peaceful Sarajevo, watching footage on Bosnian TV of what the Serbs were doing in Croatia, just a couple of hundred miles away. I remember when the evening news showed images of the destruction of Vukovar; I thought to myself, 'Oh, how terrible', and switched the channel. How can I be shocked when people in France or Italy or Germany see the massacres of civilians taking place here in Sarajevo on their evening news and say, 'Oh, how terrible', and switch to another channel? It's normal. It's human.

Parked in front of our TV screens and computers, we can switch on to images and brief reports of disasters happening everywhere in the world. We have gone far beyond the bourgeois breakfasting with his newspaper. New technologies give us a non-stop feed: as many images of disaster and atrocity as we can make time to look at.

In fact, we're being invited to respond to everything, and we're not hard-wired to do this. It's normal that most people not directly affected by the sufferings of those far away will want to avert their eyes.

But it's not true, I think, that because of the surfeit of images we're responding to less. (Less compared to when? When was the baseline for optimum responsiveness?) We're probably responding to more.

The arousal of conscience is not generally regarded as an end in itself. It is understood as a prelude, the necessary prelude, to embarking on some course of action. An image seems an appeal to do something, not just to feel disturbed. Indignant. The image says: Stop this. Intervene, take action. And, in an important sense, this is the correct response. For it says that these situations are human-made and not inevitable. The kinds of images I am referring to ought not to be objects of contemplation, like the Passion of Christ.

To designate a hell is not, of course, to tell us anything about how to extract people from that hell, how to moderate hell's flames. Still, I would like to suggest that it is a good in itself to acknowledge, to have enlarged, one's sense of how much suffering there is in the world we share with others. And that someone who is perennially surprised that depravity exists, who continues to experience disillusionment (even incredulity) when confronted with evidence of what humans are capable of inflicting in the way of gruesome, hands-on cruelties upon other humans, has not reached moral or psychological adulthood.

No one after a certain age has the right to this kind of innocence, of superficiality, to this degree of ignorance, of amnesia.

We now have a vast repository of images that make it harder to maintain this kind of moral defectiveness. Let the atrocious images haunt us. Even if they are only tokens, and cannot possibly encompass most of the reality to which they refer, they still perform a vital function. The images say: keep these events in your memory.

The fact that we are not totally transformed, that we can turn away, turn the page, switch the channel, does not impugn the ethical value of the image-aggression. (It is not a defect that we do not suffer *enough* when we see these painful images.) Neither is the fact that a photograph can't repair our ignorance about the history and causes of the suffering it picks out and frames. To see something in the form of an image is an invitation to observe, to learn, to attend to. Photographs can't do the moral or the intellectual work for us. But they can start us on our way.

# Introduction to Eva Hoffman

*Roy Foster*

With her classic study *Lost in Translation* (1989), Eva Hoffman established her mastery as an analyst of recovered memory and deferred emotion—and also of the way that what we leave behind us follows us around. Her subsequent books dealt with interactions between past and present in Eastern Europe, and demonstrated her Geiger-counter sensitivity to rifts within societies, the stratagems by which they are circumvented, and the ways that they are projected into the future. These preoccupations are clear in her Amnesty lecture, which explores the transmission of remembered wrongs into the future. In dealing with the 'return of the repressed past' she avoids, on the one hand, the danger of simply applying the language of individual psychotherapy to the complex question of social consciousness; and, on the other, the equally simplistic assumption that rectification is ever possible for horrific injustices against the dead. The word she prefers to stress is 'recognition', which recurs throughout this thought-provoking meditation.

At best, the process can produce a symbolic justice; but it requires something more than symbolism. Hoffman calls in addition for a 'recognition of what actually happened'. Despite the Rankean echo, she does not assume that an unproblematic actuality can ever be recaptured; equivocation and ambiguity hang around evidence as well as memory. She is tough-minded about the way vague memories of a distant past allow both blame and appropriation to become self-interested—a psychological process she explored unforgettably in *Shtetl: the History of a Small Town and an Extinguished World* (1997), where she excavated the memory of a shared life between Gentile and Jew in pre-Holocaust Poland. In that book, the perspective stretched back to medieval Europe; in the lecture here, she is dealing with the particular horrors of the century just gone by. The traumas of the Holocaust, or Cambodia, or Bosnia, or South Africa are still in living memory—and, perhaps more significantly, some of the perpetrators as well as the surviving victims can still be reached. But attempts to recognize the truth, and come to terms with the past, remain problematic. For all the impressive work of the South African Truth and Reconciliation Commission, its decision to subdivide evidence into kinds of truth raises a new set of evidential problems: Albie Sachs's metaphor, 'a theatre of the real', quoted by Hoffman, suggests levels of self-presentation and even role-playing which may impose their own distortions.

But distortion, as Hoffman accepts, is part of the picture. Traumatic memory distorts even time itself. Whether or not any kind of closure is possible with the actual participants, the appropriations by second-generation inheritors may open up new agendas altogether. Here is where a clear-sighted recognition becomes more important than ever. The understanding of ambivalence does not mean ethical blurring; nor does a recognition of the pressures brought by inherited social attitudes, fears and insecurities. We are, perhaps, readier to examine such assumptions now than even 50-odd years ago—as may be indicated by Richard Overy's riveting volume *Interrogations: the Nazi Elite in Allied Hands, 1945* (2001). Overy's analysis of the strategies of denial and limits of responsibility which emerge from the questioning of Nazi officials has enduring relevance, but the implications embedded in the questioners' techniques are also arresting. 'If the interrogation transcripts reveal anything', he concludes, 'it is the unwritten assumption on the part of the interrogators that anti-Semitic sentiment is a sufficient explanation for racial murder' (p. 197).

Overy's subsequent analysis of moral brutalization and degeneration is too weighty to paraphrase here, but the issue is relevant to Hoffman's lecture—since she too is preoccupied with 'recognizing' what makes a perpetrator as well as a victim, and more specifically what marks the generations that follow them. Her belief that the cultures of separation impose a 'distance' that can have continuing reverberations, moral as well as social, might be applied to many conflicts that continue in today's world. Northern Ireland comes to mind as well as Eastern Europe. Intimate enmities can be sustained in circumstances where the processes of everyday life are sealed off from each other, fuelling the fear and ignorance that is a precondition of projection and dehumanization. She offers a very suggestive speculation why the extent of inherited trauma seems to be markedly less in Russian victims of oppression: attributing it to a sense of solidarity, a common experience, a historical continuance in one familiar place. Perhaps, it might be added, the agents of injustice and oppression in Russia also seemed abstracted, established, institutionalized. Holocausts, by contrast, can descend in a furious burst on the heads of those who have been—like the inhabitants of the shtetl at Bransk—involved for generations in the negotiations of everyday life with neighbours who are different but not, apparently, hostile.

Thus if Eva Hoffman concludes by arguing for multiculturalism, by a stringent redefinition she recaptures it from the tired-sounding shibboleth it has become. In her definition, a multicultural approach involves examination of 'the common history of antagonistic groups' in a longer historical perspective than the immediate memory of trauma, and for a critique of the dubious and propagandistic exploitation of supposedly 'collective' memory. It is, therefore, the kind of 'recognition' that can be projected into the past as well as the future. This lecture, like her remarkable books, demonstrates the subtle and exacting intelligence necessary for the task.

# The Balm of Recognition: Rectifying Wrongs through the Generations

## Eva Hoffman

Questions of human rights and wrongs are enormous, and central to our world. It is difficult to know how to speak about them in the abstract in terms that are sufficient to the occasion. It is even more difficult, of course, to intervene in specific wrongs, and try to prevent abuses of rights in ways that are both ethical and effective—which is why the work of organizations like Amnesty International is so important and deserves our great respect.

But my subject has to do not so much with prevention or intervention, but with the aftermath of wrongs that have already been committed—of large-scale violence and atrocity. This may seem an admission of pessimism, for it would of course be best if we could eradicate the root causes of conflict in advance, or at least see it coming and nip it in the bud. But so far, we have not been able to do so, and as long as the recurrence of collective violence remains a fact, we have to deal with its consequences. I do not mean to start from the point of resignation. Thinking about the aftermath of large-scale wrongs does call for considerable moral realism and tolerance for ambivalence; for once they have been done, they cannot be undone—the world cannot be entirely righted. At the same time, I think that especially in the last few decades, we've become more and more aware that how we deal with the legacy of violence—how we react to its immediate impact, how we try to rectify its damage, how we process it in individual and social memory—matters. It matters for the present, and it may matter in ways that point towards some possibilities of prevention, or at least the containment of our worst impulses in the future.

I come to these questions not as a professional historian or a political philosopher, but as someone for whom questions of individual and historical memory have been of quite vital interest, both for personal and for broader reasons. I suppose my thoughts on this subject begin with my own experience of having grown up in Poland after the Second World War, in a country terribly ravaged by war, and as a daughter of Jewish parents who had endured and survived the Holocaust. My more sociological curiosity, so to speak, comes from travelling through several Eastern European countries shortly after the velvet revolutions of 1989, and observing various societies as they were trying to come to terms with a prolonged heritage of oppressive regimes. It also comes from thinking about the longer history, and the fiercely contested memories of the Polish–Jewish relationship. I am speaking, then, from a particular site, and with the consciousness that my reflections can only be provisional and tentative; or rather, that I can at best pose some questions. What are the reverberations of violence and atrocity in society and the psyche? After great and systematic wrongs, what rectification can be found in action—or relief in memory? And how should we think about terrible events as they recede into the further past and become the object of collective remembrance, and of history?

In this essay, I am most concerned with the kinds of violence that involve attacks of the powerful on the powerless, rather than contests between armed antagonists; and I am most interested in the internalized effects of violence, and especially with second-generation memory. However, since I think that questions of society and the psyche are inseparable in these matters, I want to frame my discussion with some admittedly rudimentary reflections on the public and political responses to widespread wrongs.

At all these stages and levels, we need to give full weight to the grief and anguish of coming to terms with terrible histories. I want to propose the broad notion of recognition, (which is increasingly understood as a crucial aspect of social relations), as the reparative element which can lead to some kind of acceptance and reconciliation. Once wrongs are done, they cannot be undone. But I believe that recognition of what actually happened—of the victims' experience and the perpetrators' responsibility, and ultimately of the broader structures of cause and effect, can provide at least a symbolic redress which can allow some healing to take place, and individual societies to move on.

Systematic violence—especially what Primo Levi called unnecessary violence—that is, the violence that does not serve the ends of battle or victory but is meant to humiliate and brutalize the victim, is the ultimate form of mis-recognition, or deliberate non-recognition. It has been suggested, in a certain vein of contemporary thought, that such entirely gratuitous violence—torture, rape, other forms of sadism—is an attempt to wipe out the narrative of the other, the victim's story of him or herself. I'm not sure that narrative is the central issue, but certainly, deliberate cruelty is an attempt to discount, negate, ultimately destroy the identity—the subjectivity—of its target. On the collective level, an attack on another group—and I am thinking particularly of aggression justified on religious or ethnic grounds—is a denial of that group's identity, cultural ethos, historical version of itself.

Whether such violence comes from the outside, from another country, or whether it is perpetrated by governments on their citizens, or by neighbour on neighbour, its damage to the moral sense—the moral world—of the victims is profound. The first need of the victims then is for justice and the restoration of a basic moral order. Our desire for justice is powerful; it is what some philosophers call a moral emotion. In the first instance, the desire can include the impulse of raw retribution or retaliation; landscapes after battle are usually strewn with partisan vengeance and personal vendettas—as we see even in Kosovo today. And it is partly to contain those impulses that the first and most urgent need in societies that have been subjected to or riven by violence is to restore a shared moral order by recognizing the wrongs that have been committed, and to invert the perverse order of atrocity—its principled injustice, one might say—by establishing the very principles and norms of justice. Whatever the specific criteria of judgement or punishment, the first task is to name wrongs *as* wrongs, and to bring some of those responsible to account.

While this may seem both obvious and obviously desirable, we know from lengthening experience that it is in practice extremely complex. Especially in countries in which abuses have been internal—in the transitions from repressive regimes in Argentina or Chile, or in the former Yugoslavia or Rwanda—the attempt to name deeds and names is almost always accompanied by equally forceful attempts to suppress the truth. Political pressures and continuing social rifts mean that legal procedures set up to discover wrongdoing—or even to define it—are rarely impartial. Even in the best-intentioned attempts to deal with large-scale crimes fairly, pragmatic limitations of massive legal procedures mean that some of the less guilty are tried, and some of the more guilty go free.

At the same time, I think we have also come to understand that suppression of painful facts is rarely effective; that the disappeared never really disappear, but live on in the memory—the moral conscience—of others; that wrongs which are not acknowledged do not dissolve into ether, but continue to live an underground existence in the societies where they took place. Certainly, one of the striking things about travelling through Eastern Europe shortly after the velvet revolutions of 1989 was to see the palpable return of the repressed past. After more than 40 years of communist censorship, the injustices of the intervening decades resurfaced into public consciousness, sometimes with a fierce bitterness; at the same time, long-suppressed phenomena, such as ethnic prejudices or anti-Semitism, erupted in disturbing and unprocessed forms. The process of reckoning with the past has taken different forms in each country, as each has tried to balance the passions of the past with the interests of the present. But in each society, the reckoning has been necessary for the transition from a repressive past to a more open present to take place.

Seamus Heaney, in a clearly pessimistic moment, said that it sometimes seems we can learn as much from history as from a visit to an abbatoir.[1] But sometimes—by small increments and in exceptional situations—I think we do learn. One example of this can be seen in that daring and innovative experiment in confronting the heritage of systematic wrong—South Africa's Truth and Reconciliation Commission. The circumstances in which the Commission was set up condensed a lot of the problems involved in dealing with legacies of injustices elsewhere, and the Commission, I think, learned a lot from the mistakes that were made in these earlier situations. The abuses of apartheid had a long history, of which only the latest period could be directly addressed. They were committed under the aegis of a political system that made extreme violations of human rights legal, and in which large numbers of people were implicated. Moreover, there were practical problems of costs which made judicial prosecutions on the requisite scale untenable, and in any case, such prosecutions were excluded by a deal struck by Mandela with the outgoing De Klerk government—a deal which offered amnesty to its leading officials. So the Commission was a strategic and a political compromise.

And yet, what is so interesting and even inspiring in what the Truth and Reconciliation Commission did was the attempt to give expression to both the political and the individual processes of recognition. The Commission provided a forum on which perpetrator and victim could confront each other and tell the truth freely. The victim could confront the perpetrator directly with the facts of what took place, but also with a fuller narrative of what it felt like to have loved ones tortured or murdered with impunity; or what it was like to be tortured oneself. The perpetrator was given a chance to tell the truth without fear of punishment, and the opportunity, when faced with an actual person whom he has grievously harmed, to experience something like remorse—although remorse was not necessary for amnesty. The Commission came in for a lot of criticism. Given the extent of the atrocities committed in South Africa and the viciousness of the principles underlying apartheid, the very idea of forfeit and amnesty was thought by some commentators to be unacceptable and even harmful. They felt that the spectacle of legal impunity for the culprits would only increase the sense of grievance among people who already had many reasons to feel aggrieved. And it didn't help that known apartheid criminals sometimes lied about their role in the previous regime, or used disclosure opportunistically in exchange for amnesty.

As I thought about what had gone on in South Africa, I too sometimes felt that the qualities of soul required to restrain the impulse of retributive justice came close to saintliness. And yet, from the accounts I have read, the Commission, in its actual workings, seems to have had a powerful reparative dimension. I recently listened to Albie Sachs, a man who had been a freedom fighter under apartheid and who lost his arm when an assassination attempt was made on him by the South African security forces. Sachs, who is now a Justice in South Africa's constitutional court, said that the Commission was an arena on which pragmatism and idealism met. He described it as a kind of theatre, in which the drama of the movement from knowledge to acknowledgement could be enacted.

Indeed, some of the accounts from the proceedings of the Commission read like most charged drama. But this is theatre that comes very close to reality—or rather, it is a theatre of the real. I quote just one arbitrary fragment from such an exchange, between a man who had been tortured and his torturer. The victim, in the course of torture, had had his head repeatedly forced inside a wet bag, so for much of the time he could not breathe and had not known what was going on. Here is the exchange:

MR JACOBS [the man who had been tortured]: Let's just go to the shock treatment. Why was that necessary, given that you were saying that the bag and all of that, I mean why would that make a difference?

MR BENZIEN [the torturer]: I was using any means at my disposal to get you to tell us where your friend or compatriot was hiding.

MR JACOBS: Now, the question is then anything to get me to talk, is that what you are saying, anything?

MR BENZIEN: Anything short of killing you, yes.

MR JACOBS: So, when I was—after a few times what had happened, you would undress me, tie my blue belt around my feet, throw me on the ground, put the handcuffs which was this round, I think it was the handcuffs with the cloth over my arm to prevent me from having, because of the struggle you will do that and that will happen quite a few times. But at some point, I think it is about the fourth time, when I thought I am dying, you woke me up and you said, Peter, I will take you to the verge of death as many times as I want to. But here you are going to talk and if it means that, then you will die, that is okay. Do you remember that?

MR BENZIEN: I concede I may have said that, Sir.

MR JACOBS: I want you to know, I want you to tell me, because this is important for me. The Truth Commission can amnesty, but this is important for me, did you say that?

MR BENZIEN: Yes, I did say that.[2]

It is hard to know, of course, what transpires subjectively for the two people involved in such an exchange. But it seems that the urge to know exactly what was done to you is powerful—maybe it is a kind of undoing of the powerlessness felt in the initial situation. And perhaps forcing your abuser to confront your own humanity and forcing him to understand—admit—confirm—the reality of his deeds, is as close to moral catharsis (or closure, as we say nowadays) as we can come. Perhaps also such direct confrontation forces the perpetrator to recognize himself, so to speak—to know that he inflicted hurt on an actual person, and that his actions—his intentions—were heinous. Perhaps, in the best-case scenario, this can lead to a small transformation in the soul. Benzien came close, although in a very minimal kind of way, to giving a kind of apology and saying that he wondered what enabled him to do what he had done.

In thinking about ethical justice, we veer between the notions of forgiveness and retribution. Neither seems viable on a large scale. It seems to me that the limits of tolerance and forgiveness are also imposed by a kind of recognition—the recognition of the perpetrator's agency, and the awful but human reality of the deeds he committed. But large-scale retribution is untenable as well—if only because it leads to widespread bitterness and the next cycle of vengeance. Public justice can only be partial and imperfect—a kind of metonymy for the ideal of justice. Perhaps the symbolic justice of recognition is the best we can achieve. For the victim, such recognition is needed for the restoration of basic moral coherence. For the society as a whole, the public disclosure and acknowledgement of what happened is a way of placing a metaphoric marker between the past and present.

Albie Sachs talked about meeting his would-be assassin, a man named Henry, when the latter appeared on his doorstep one day, wanting to talk. They did talk; and at the end, Albie was able to shake Henry's hand. But Sachs vigorously denied that what he felt—or even wanted to feel—was forgiveness. No, he said; it was not about that. What he wanted was to be able to live side by side with Henry in the same country, and within the same moral order. The handshake was a symbolic gesture signifying that intention. However, symbolic gestures—symbolic drama—can have great force. Apparently, when Sachs asked one of Henry's friends how the encounter had affected him, the friend said that Henry went home and cried for a week.

Public recognition then, has important moral and psychological repercussions; but there is a certain level of grief and loss that it cannot address. In the world of subjectivity, symbolic markers are less easy to install, and long after public and legal forums have done their work, the inward injuries caused by abusive violence continue to live their underground life. Such injuries can be both persistent and deeply hidden. Hard though it is now to believe, it came as a surprise to psychiatrists interviewing Holocaust survivors in the 1950s, to find that many of their interviewees were deeply disturbed by their experiences, and that the impact of these experiences did not wear off instantly once they were over.

These days, we have become much more aware of the psychological impact of traumatic experience in theory—though it is still sometimes hard to discern it in particular persons. In the last two decades in particular, we have had a growing literature of testimony, much of it written by survivors of the Holocaust, but also emerging from other dark events. Another valuable body of writing has come from the work of psychotherapy and psychoanalysis—situations that afford a unique combination of close intimacy and rigorous observation. It is clearly impossible to summarize this literature or the masses of detailed case-material; but one of the main insights into traumatic memory that has emerged from such studies is that it is also a kind of recognition—*of* memory and *through* memory—that is needed to address the most private damage incurred in the wake of historical calamity. In order partially to dissolve the compressed power of terrible experiences, it seems the sufferer needs neither to remember them obsessively, nor to forget prematurely—but to remember fully in order to separate the past from the present.

It is a characteristic of trauma—this recurs again and again in testimonies—that it arrests time, fixes it in the moment of threat or pain; the lasting potency of traumatic memories derives from their persistent, all-too-vivid presentness. In waking memory, or in dreams, the moment of horror keeps overwhelming the actual experiences of the present. The lost family may become more important, more compelling, than the family belonging to the new life. The fear felt so legitimately during the time of atrocity may affect and infect all mundane interactions of ordinary time. The images of humiliation and physical pain repeating in the mind may drown out perceptions of the more benign reality of the peacetime world. The guilt for having failed to save close ones may erupt suddenly in ways that seem perplexing or unwarranted.

Let me cite one example of the disturbing specifics: Dinora Pines, a psychoanalyst who has written movingly about working with Holocaust survivors and their children, tells the story of a woman who had spent her adolescence in Auschwitz, and who experienced extreme states of psychic death there.[3] Her subsequent development was contorted by one particular moment—a glimpse of a handsome man who was called Dr Mengele, and who seemed to 'prefer' her mother and sister to herself in choosing them for what later turned out to be his grotesque medical experiments. In her therapeutic work, this woman reverted to the states of psychic death she'd experienced earlier; but also, she had to contend with and confront surges of sadistic and cruel feelings—a kind of vengeful eroticism directed via others at the awful figure of Dr Mengele. It was only many years after emerging from Auschwitz and excavating her experiences in all their troubling and terrible details that she was able to mourn her family, which had been murdered there. It was only then that she was able to make some separation between the past and the present, to distinguish the affective texture of her current life from the unbearable fears that were so warranted in the murderous universe of concentration camps.

I recount such painful details not in order to engage in a kind of psychic sensationalism, but to indicate the convoluted and wrenching ways in which trauma is inscribed on the psyche; and to suggest the measure of difficulty involved in unearthing and acknowledging these deepest effects of collective violence. At the same time, it seems that the concept of trauma—and certainly the forms of its expression—may not be universal. Many Russians, who have gone through so many horrors of their own history, protest vehemently at the very idea of deep psychic damage. At the other end of the spectrum, I once read an account of over 100 Cambodian women living in America, who had become psychosomatically blind after having lived through the horrors of the Khmer Rouge invasion—horrors which I think were truly holocaustal. Clearly, there was something culturally determined, or at least informed, about the symptom of psychosomatic blindness, about extreme pain taking this particular form. I think we don't know enough about the cultural elements of this problem; and it is also possible that—as was true for many Holocaust survivors—traumatic memories may do their work even if they are not articulated, or understood within specifically Western therapeutic categories.

But while trauma may be a culturally informed concept, suffering is surely the transcultural bottom line—and clearly, given the extent of losses suffered by many victims of violence, the work of memory and of mourning is a daunting task. But for many, what converts the unbearable experience into a bearable one seems to be a full recognition of one's experience by oneself and by others—the affective justice of having one's story truly and deeply understood. And, aside from the intimate understanding afforded by therapy or private relationships, I think that here too, the quality of public or cultural acknowledgement matters. I wonder if one reason why the Russian participants in so much terror did not feel themselves to be deeply injured by it was because the hardship was so widely shared and understood. And I wonder if the specific quality of radical despair felt by so many Holocaust survivors came from the fact that they emigrated to places where their experiences seemed beyond the pale of imagining or understanding, and where their accounts were often met with incredulity and averted eyes. Even in their own countries, Holocaust survivors were victims of a separate war—an atrocity that was not easily fitted into common frameworks of understanding, and for a long time was surrounded by silence and denial. I wonder—though now I'm purely conjecturing in an area where perhaps one shouldn't do so—whether those Cambodian women went blind in part because they felt their terrifying experiences were not seen by those around them. As I was thinking about this, I read of a man testifying to the Truth and Reconciliation Commission in South Africa who had been literally blinded in the course of apartheid but who, after finishing his testimony, said, 'I want to thank the Commission, because I now feel after telling my story that I have regained my vision.'

Nevertheless—although sensitivity and solidarity are incumbent upon us—I do not think we should reify survivors into figures of woe, or cult figures of wisdom, as has sometimes happened with Holocaust survivors recently. People who have lived through terrible experiences exist in more than one dimension and should not have their lives or identities reduced to the category of survivors.

But what of the second generation—the generation that comes after disaster? How are experiences of historical catastrophe transmitted to its literal and figurative inheritors— what I'd like to call the post-generation as a whole? How should we remember experiences that are close to us, but which are not really ours—or rather, how should we think about them? Such questions may seem more diffuse or soft than addressing the immediate and direct impact of violence; but problems of second-generation memory are to my mind important for several reasons. The post-generation is a kind of hinge between the past and the future, and much depends on how it turns from one to the other. It is the generation that inherits the experience of violence as still living memory; and which moulds and converts this remembrance into some form of collective memory or historical knowledge. It is in this crucial interval that the past can be frozen into fixed mythology, or comprehended in its historical complexity; and in which the cycles of revenge can be perpetuated or interrupted. The moment of transmission is worth dwelling on, because it is a moment of real danger; but also of genuine possibility and hope.

In talking about the transmission of difficult memories, I want to start with the inward experience, and move outwards—because that is the direction in which, for the children of violence, the experience travels. In contrast to the adult participants in a historical disaster, who confront catastrophe with their emotions and ideas already formed, and usually with some understanding of the event's social and political dimensions, the next generation—or those who were small children when it happened—first receive their knowledge of extreme events in childish ways, and with childish instruments of perception.

Some months ago, I listened to a South African woman who had witnessed what she thought was a massacre on her street when she was a small child. In her memory, there were many people shot dead that day; the street on which she lived ran with blood. It was only much later, when she researched this event as a scholar, that she found out that only one person had been killed in that incident. This is not to say that the killing of one person is not terrible enough, or that there were not massacres in South Africa in which many more people perished, but only to point out—as this young scholar herself did—that awful events register as even more utterly horrific in the childish mind.

I think the same is true of events that have not been directly seen, but only conveyed in the family, or through the atmosphere and images of post-violent landscapes. In the literature by and about children of Holocaust survivors, there are many testimonies to the dark incoherence of that first, received knowledge. In the family transmission of such knowledge, the stories recounted by survivors are often fragmented; the moments remembered are usually those of utmost tension or danger, of fear and threat by the enemy. It often takes the children in such families a long time to put together a chronological sequence, a coherent narrative, from the intensely charged fragments and phrases in which memories of trauma erupt. And in the intimate setting of the family, painful experience is expressed in less verbal, sometimes quite unconscious ways as well—through actions, moods, silences and withdrawals; through the eloquent language of the body.

In a way, what is conveyed through such messages is a universe of terrifying irrationality, or enormous, impersonal forces. In a context far removed from the Holocaust, Sudhir Kakar, an Indian psychoanalyst, has analysed the social and psychological structure of the communal riots in India in a book called *The Colors of Violence*.[4] This is how Kakar comments on the family stories he'd heard as a child, of the sweeping riots accompanying the Indian partition:

It is only now that I can reflect more composedly, even tranquilly, to give a psychological gloss to the stories of the riots. At the time I heard them, their fearful images coursed unimpeded through my mind which reverberated wildly with their narrators' flushes of emotion. There was a frantic tone to the stories, an underlying hysteria I felt as a child but could only name as an adult. After all, my uncles, aunts and cousins had not yet recovered from the trauma of what had befallen them.[5]

So I do not want to underestimate the force of the traumatic inheritance, or the depth of its intergenerational passage. In some children of survivors, the incorporation of memories—or a kind of unconscious identification with them—takes the form of a ghostly re-enactment of tragic events and lives. The literature on the subject gives many accounts of this: stories in which survivors' children take on the persona of a relative who perished; or express their elders' unspoken—but unconsciously conveyed—fears in odd rituals and symptoms. I think, for example, of people who in elaborate ways repeat the situation of hiding which their parents lived through; or of Anne Karpf, who in her important book, *The War After*,[6] tells of her extreme difficulty in separating from her parents—a theme familiar to many with similar backgrounds—because of a deeply internalized duty to protect them.

What often makes this identification so strong is that it contains a kind of moral element—a deep imperative to honour the experience of parental suffering by remaining psychically faithful to it. But this is honouring by a kind of haunting. Here too, from the therapeutic point of view, it seems that if the haunting is to cease, the spectres have to be imagined fully. In her moving book, *Memorial Candles*,[7] Dina Wardi, an Israeli psychotherapist who conducted group therapy with children of survivors, tells how difficult it was for her patients to know what really happened to their parents and other relatives. She also relates how necessary it was to pin down the received memories, in all their disturbing details, and with all the troubling attendant feelings—shame for the parents' humiliation, perhaps, or anger at their tactics of survival; the desire to avenge the wrongs done to them, or, on the contrary, to punish them for their subjection. It was only when the transmitted memories were brought into the light of day that their hold lifted. The confirmation of experiences which had been so unspoken and shadowy by sympathetic others was also important to this. It was only through a kind of shared internal recognition that a distinction between the past and the present could be made, and the past could be viewed, or felt, from a certain distance, as existing in a different time-realm.

Separating the past from the present—understanding the past *as* the past—is always an achievement. In the generation of survivors, the realities troubling memory are sometimes too weighty to be put completely in the past; one lifetime may not be enough to forgive and forget. But for the second generation, for the post-generation as a whole, I believe that separation is its task, even its obligation. Wrestling with shadows can be psychologically more disorientating than wrestling with realities; but unlike realities, shadows can be dispelled.

This is vital, because if the haunting is not ended, if the separation is not achieved, the danger is that the transmitted

THE BALM OF RECOGNITION

memories are converted into dogmatic conviction of adult thought and can lead to a retributive repetition of the past. The historical experience of one generation is received as childhood mythology in the next. In the post-generation, the mythology can come to include a world divided into two opposing forces: the force of evil and of idealized victimhood, of persecutor and persecuted. I turn again to Sudhir Kakar:

It is sobering to think of hundreds of thousands of children over many parts of the subcontinent, Hindu and Muslim, who have listened to stories from their parents and other family elders . . . on the fierceness of an implacable enemy. This is a primary channel through which historical enmity is transmitted from one generation to the next, as the child, ignoring the surface interpretations and rationalizations, hears the note of helpless fury and impotence in the accounts of beloved adults and fantasizes scenarios of revenge against those who have humiliated family and kin.[8]

One can sadly imagine the same kind of passage of bitter enmity to the children of Bosnia and Serbia today; to the young Hutus and Tutsis growing up after the terrifying massacres in Rwanda. How we intervene at that stage, what we teach children and young people growing up in landscapes ravaged by violence, can clearly have considerable repercussions for the future. I don't know who it was that said that history is a race between education and catastrophe. But this is at no time more true than in the interval of the second generation. So therefore, how we publicly think about memory—how we transmit memories and histories in public forums and discussion—also matters.

And so I want to comment just briefly on the current rhetoric—the politics—of memory in our own culture. In recent years, perhaps especially in America, there has been a rising fascination with the subject of collective memory in general, and traumatic memory in particular. In this cultural preoccupation, memory almost always stands for victimological memory, embraced by particular groups, and foregrounding the darkest episodes of various pasts: for the Nanking Massacre, or the Irish Famine, and above all, for the Holocaust.

I do not want to underestimate the need to mourn people who fell victim to such events, or to honour ancestral narratives. These events need to be commemorated, processed by their inheritors, historically acknowledged. And yet there is something that troubles me about the current discourse of memory. For one thing, the injunctions to remember, if reiterated too often, can become formulaic—an injunction precisely not to think or grapple with the past. Moreover, the uses of collective memory to bolster a group's identity; or a fixed identification with parental victimhood, seem sometimes to verge on a kind of appropriation, or even bad faith. The transmitted memories bear a great weight on the minds of the second generation but they are not ours. Moreover—and this is a delicate point—there is no reason for the inheritors of the victims to derive a kind of referred sense of rightness—which can so easily change to righteousness—from putatively belonging to the right side of history. There is no more reason for this than for collectively blaming the children of the aggressors for the sins of their parents. Both positions are tempting, and to some extent emotionally understandable. And both are strenuously to be avoided.

It seems to me that on both sides of a terrible past, the second generation needs not only to remember but to remember rigorously—to examine its past thoughtfully and critically. Clearly, if the inheritors of the perpetrators' history fail to do so, the violence can be simply perpetuated and re-peated; aggressive regimes can last a long time and reproduce themselves very successfully. But what we see just as often is the marshalling of victimological, defensive memory for the purposes of aggression. In the recent Yugoslav wars, for example, the Serbian propaganda machine repeatedly invoked memories of Serbian martyrdom at Muslim hands to justify its acts of aggression, and stoke warriors' mettle.

So if the logic of the feud—of deed and counter-deed, violence and revenge—is to be interrupted, then I believe the second generation on both sides needs to move away from the logic of identification with an ancestral past, to the logic of broader understanding—and the kind of dialogue that can lead to a recognition rather than mis-recognition of the other. There is one empirical factor which is in no way fortunate, but which—if one is to judge by the German–Jewish example—makes the task of dialogue easier in the post-generation: that in this generation, the damage that was so unequally distributed in the first generation is to some extent equalized. In the first generation it seems to be one of the inward injustices that follow overt injustice that it is the victims who, in addition to the sufferings they have undergone, are left carrying the great-est burdens of trauma and even guilt. The perpetrators, as far as can be discerned—and the problem is that we know much less about this side of the story—seem to suffer such consequences much less. There are of course exceptions. However, from accounts of Nazi perpetrators, or indeed from the testimony of some of the leading culprits in South Africa, it seems that such figures, while undoubtedly regretting the loss of their power and living with the fear of retribution, very often continue to uphold the rightness of their conviction, and a strong inner justification for what they have done.

Why this is so is a mystery that has been insufficiently examined. For one thing, we don't have enough psychological observations of such figures. Tyrants and torturers go into therapy much less frequently than their subjects and victims, and don't often leave soul-searching testimonies. The torturer Benzien expressed embarrassment at only one point in the proceedings, when it was revealed that he had consulted a psychiatrist. We do know that people recruited to commit heinous acts in a systematic way receive a kind of education in sadism—a training in the cauterization of feeling via a gradual habituation to brutality, and an extreme contempt for the objects of their assaults. This is a training in the utter distancing from the other—in what Zygmunt Bauman, in a brilliant book *Modernity and the Holocaust* called 'the production of distance'.[9] And perhaps this cauterization of the capacity for compassion and empathy persists as a cauterization of conscience and an imperviousness to guilt.

We don't know enough about the inner dynamics through which this happens—about the defensive strategies through which a sense of inadequacy, say, is transformed into a sense of grandiosity and power, or the way in which normal ambivalence and confusion are simplified into the rigidity of belief. Freud made, I think, still apposite observations about the mechanisms of yielding one's superego to a leader or a belief. I was thinking about this recently when I read about one of the defectors from Bin Laden's terrorist operation, who kept saying that the reason he could engage in terrorist actions was because he believed implicitly in Bin Laden's interpretation of Islam, and his moral code of vengeance and martyrdom. In other words, he wasn't just obeying orders, he was transferring to his leader the capacity to think and form beliefs.

But in the generations after the cessation of violence, the

story is very different. While the perpetrators themselves often seem not to suffer deep qualms about what they have done, their children are often as burdened by the weight of their legacy as the children of the victims. Again, I speak from the most studied example of Nazi Germany.

Here too, there is a growing literature on this subject, and both first-person accounts and psychoanalytic case-studies show that the vicissitudes of psychic distress for the heirs of perpetrators are as complex as for the post-generation on the other side. It seems that in many postwar German families there was secrecy and silence, which created a confusing gap between what the children knew consciously and sensed unconsciously. Often the parents were perceived as chilly and unable to admit the sins of the past; the gradual discovery of their role in the war provoked in the children great rage and a kind of transferred guilt. Just recently, I read a case of a woman who, as a child, divined from fragments of overheard conversation or by other semi-conscious means, that her parents were involved in the euthanasia programme in Nazi Germany. It was discovered, through an excavation of her memories, that she was afraid that she might herself be killed in such a way if she were in any way imperfect or flawed. Later, she transposed such early feelings into a full identification with the victim—as did many others in her generation of Germans.

In a sense, the process of coming to terms with their inherited past is harder for the children of perpetrators than for those of the victims—for in their case, the simple need to love the parents, or at least accept them, pulls so strongly against the moral imperative to condemn what they did. On the other hand, it is easier for the aggressors' children to detach themselves from a historical identification with the past—for the moral imperative is to condemn that past; while for the post-generation on the victims' side, the imperative may seem to remain attached. The Austrian journalist Peter Sichrovsky, in a book of interviews with children of leading Nazis, notes that the detachment from the past was enabled by the painful—but ultimately fruitful—contradiction between what he calls a 'fascist family structure', an ethos of patriarchal severity and authoritarianism, and the democratic values which the children absorbed in school and public life.[10]

That the legacy of awful histories is transmitted to the children on either side is not fair; but in the post-generation, it sometimes instigates the possibility of dialogue or even mutual sympathy, where no such sympathy can really be expected in the immediate aftermath of atrocity. Actual face-to-face dialogue can be a very real antidote to the perception of the other as a collective enemy and I think should be attempted wherever possible. It has certainly helped in German–Jewish relations since the war, and it is beginning to thaw the very vexed relationship between Poles and Jews, where the dialogue was delayed by decades of communist repression.

But the very possibility of dialogue not only facilitates—it also implies—the kind of understanding I think we need to attain in the second generation, and the kinds of questions we need to ask about the past. For the fact of generational change—and the possibility of transforming relations between groups—suggests what by now we well know that no group is intrinsically aggressive or intrinsically innocent; and that no conflict between collectivities is intrinsically determined. And so we need to ask what motives and circumstances lead, say, to the eruptions of Hindu–Muslim riots, or phases of anti-Semitism in the long Polish–Jewish coexistence; and what factors promote harmony, or at least benign indifference.

Of course, the causes of violence are usually over-determined, and conflicts are propelled by a plethora of factors—power politics, conflicts over territory, economic misery and competition. But especially in conflicts in which the main stakes are racial or ethnic or religious identity—of which we see so many today—the psycho-social dynamics of antagonism and contempt, of projection and creation of a hostile other, need also to be understood. Sudhir Kakar observes that the Hindu–Muslim riots are ignited by specific incidents and quarrels—but that they are underwritten by a permanent perception of difference between the two groups. This perception of difference is based on a projection of certain undesirable qualities on to others—the idea, for example, that they have bad morals or unclean habits, or suspect sexual customs. Most of the time, such perceptions exist in a kind of latent quiescence; but for the duration of the violence, the participants on both sides become inspired by a fanatical hatred, and become convinced that their neighbours with whom they otherwise live in a state of benign indifference if not perfect understanding, have become the absolute enemy—a hostile, threatening other. This echoes my own sense of the patterns of conflict and co-existence in the long Polish–Jewish history: the episodes of active hostility and anti-Semitic violence were ignited by specific and sometimes material conflicts; but they were made possible by the permanent condition of cultural and spiritual separateness in which the two groups lived.

The production of distance leads to the creation of an alien Other, which is so often a precondition for violence; and violence leads to the production of great distance. If there is a way to cut into the vicious circle, it is in the intervals in which the difficult emotions are still alive, but can be contemplated in relative tranquillity. In that interval, we need to think about the kinds of social and political structures that promote solidarity and militate against the vision of others as radically Other. In my study of Polish–Jewish history, I thought there was a failure on both sides to establish such structures— common education, common language, common civic forums—and that this had a great bearing on Polish behaviour towards Jews during the Holocaust.[11] And it seems to me that in the second, or post-generation, we need to look beyond the fixed moment of trauma to those longer historical patterns, to supplement partisan memory with a more complex and encompassing view of history—a view that might examine the common history of the antagonistic groups and that might, among other things, enable us to question and criticize dubious and propagandistic uses of collective memory. Again, I am not advocating a dispassionate forgiveness of past wrongs, but the kind of reflection that strives not to reproduce—by repetition or inversion—their legacy.

I think one of the most hopeful projects I've heard about is a proposal, connected with the work of the Bosnian Truth Commission, to bring leading Bosnian, Croat and Serbian historians together to write a common history of the war. I was also interested to read a proposal for a conference in Rwanda which is going to bring together survivors—and children of survivors—of other atrocities and genocides. I don't know whether the children of the perpetrators are included in this—but I think it would be useful if they were. It is an unhappy fact that we have had enough atrocities within living memory to be able to hold a comparative conference on them. And yet, I think it is hopeful if we can try to learn something from the terrible, turbulent history of the last few decades—if we can recognize the tragic experiences of others, and recognize ourselves in their experience. We cannot undo the past, or cure it, but we can perhaps—by small increments, and with sufficient awareness—derive from it the kind of insight that can be potentially reparative, and that can begin to transform the potent forces of destruction into the energy of a more constructive vision.

# Endnotes

*Notes to Chapter 1*

1. *Le Monde*, 22 September 1999.
2. *Le Monde*, 14 September 1999.
3. Vaclav Havel, 'Kosovo and the End of the Nation-State', *The New York Review of Books*, XLVI (10), 10 June 1999.
4. I have studied this question in *The Conquest of America* (New York: Harper & Row, 1984; Norman: University of Oklahoma Press, 1999).
5. See, for further examples, my book *On Human Diversity* (Cambridge, MA: Harvard University Press, 1993), p. 259.
6. Margarete Buber-Neumann, *La révolution mondiale* (Paris: Casterman, 1971), p. 24.
7. Ibid., p. 394.
8. Cited in *Le Monde*, 13 May 1999.
9. Ibid.
10. On this subject, see Kishore Mahbubani, *Can Asians Think?* (Singapore: Time Books International, 1998).
11. Charles Péguy, *L'Argent suite*, *Cahiers de la quinzaine*, sér. 14, cah. 9 (Paris, 1913), p. 143.
12. Organization of African Unity, *The Preventable Genocide: International Panel of Eminent Personalities to Investigate the 1994 Genocide in Rwanda and Surrounding Events*, July 2000.
13. See Philip Gourevitch, *We Wish to Inform You that Tomorrow We Will Be Killed With Our Families: Stories from Rwanda* (New York: Farrar, Strauss & Giroux, 1998).
14. *Le Monde*, 8 November 2000.
15. Charles Péguy, *L'Argent suite*, p. 149.
16. Montesquieu, *De l'Esprit des lois*, XXVI, 22.

17. Condorcet, Marie-Jean-Antoine-Nicolas de Caritat, marquis de, *Observations de Condorcet sur XXIXe livre de l'Esprit des lois*, in *Oeuvres*, vol. I (Paris: Didot, 1847), p. 378.

18. Condorcet, *Esquisse d'un tableau historique des progrès de l'esprit humain* (Paris: Editions sociales, 1971), p. 248.

19. Montaigne, *Essais*, I. 20.

*Notes to Chapter 3*

1. Numbers, 31, v. 1–18, King James Version.

2. See, for example, Deuteronomy 3:1–7, 7:1–26, 20:13–17; I Samuel 15:3; Joshua 8:26–28; Ezekiel 9:5.

3. Thucydides, *History of the Peloponnesian War*, Book V.

4. Lawrence Keeley, *War before Civilization* (New York: Oxford University Press, 1996). See especially chapter 6.

5. Richard Wrangham and Dale Peterson, *Demonic Males: Apes and the Origins of Human Violence* (Boston: Houghton Mifflin, 1996), pp. 5–21; see also Jane Goodall, *The Chimpanzees of Gombe: Patterns of Behavior* (Cambridge, MA: Belknap Press of Harvard University Press, 1986).

6. Robert Trivers, 'The Evolution of Reciprocal Altruism', *Quarterly Review of Biology*, 46 (1972), pp. 35–7; Robert Axelrod, *The Evolution of Cooperation* (New York: Basic Books, 1984) and *The Complexity of Cooperation: Agent-Based Models of Competition and Collaboration* (Princeton, NJ: Princeton University Press, 1997).

7. Timothy Garton Ash, *History of the Present: Essays, Sketches and Dispatches from Europe in the 1990s* (London: Allen Lane, 1999), p. 368.

8. *Charter of the International Military Tribunal*, Article 6. The proceedings of the International Military Tribunal at Nuremberg are reported in the first 22 volumes of *Trials of the War Criminals before the International Military Tribunal* (Nuremberg, 1947–49).

The Charter is available on the internet at *http://www.yale.edu/lawweb/avalon/imt/proc/imtconst.htm*.

9. See the opinion of Lord Browne-Wilkinson, in *Regina v. Bow Street Metropolitan Stipendiary Magistrate and Others, ex parte Pinochet Ugarte*, judgement of 24 March 1999, (2000) 1 AC 147 (Pinochet No. 3). This document is available on the internet at *http://www.parliament.the-stationery-office.co.uk/pa/ld199899/ldjudgmt/jd990324/pino1.htm* and following pages.

10. Amnesty International, *The Pinochet Case—Universal Jurisdiction and the Absence of Immunity for Crimes Against Humanity*. Report EUR 45/01/99, January 1999, United Kingdom. This document is available on the internet at *http://www.amnesty.org/ailib/aipub/1999/EUR/44500199.htm*.

11. *Attorney General of Israel v. Eichmann*, 36 Intl. L. Rep. 5 (Israel, Dist. Ct. Jerusalem 1961); Supreme Court of Israel (1962) 136 I.L.R. 277.

12. See the discussion by Lord Millett in *Regina v. Bow Street Metropolitan Stipendiary Magistrate and Others, ex parte Pinochet Ugarte*, cited in note 9 above.

13. See the discussion by Lord Phillips in *Regina v. Bow Street Metropolitan Stipendiary Magistrate and Others, ex parte Pinochet Ugarte*, cited in note 9 above.

14. *Statement by NATO Secretary-General Lord Robertson, on actions by SFOR to detain persons indicted for war crimes*, NATO Press Release, 3 April 2000, *http://www.nato.int/docu/pr/2000/p00-036e.htm*.

15. Rome Statute of the International Criminal Court of 17 July 1998, UN Doc. A/CONF.183/9, reprinted in 37 ILM 998 (1998). For up to date information on the progress towards ratification, see *http://www.un.org/law/icc*.

16. Immanuel Kant, *Perpetual Peace: A Philosophic Sketch* (1795), second supplement.

17. John Stuart Mill, 'A Few Words on Non-Intervention', in John Stuart Mill, *Essays on Politics and Culture*, ed. Gertrude

Himmelfarb (New York: Anchor Books, 1963), p. 377 (first published in *Fraser's Magazine*, December 1859). For further discussion, see Michael Doyle, 'The New Interventionism', *Metaphilosophy* 32/1–2 (January 2001), pp. 212–35.

18. Lassa Oppenheim, *International Law*, Vol. 1 (London: Longman, 1948), p. 279.

19. Michael Walzer, *Just and Unjust Wars* (Harmondsworth: Penguin, 1980), p. 107.

20. Some of the criticism can be found in the lectures by Michael Ignatieff and Tzvetan Todorov in this volume.

21. Michael Walzer, 'The Argument about Humanitarian Intervention', unpublished typescript, p. 1. I am grateful to Michael Walzer for making this work-in-progress available to me.

22. Michael Walzer, 'The Politics of Rescue', *Dissent*, Winter 1995, p. 36 and 'The Argument about Humanitarian Intervention', p. 2.

23. Michael Walzer, *Just and Unjust Wars*, pp. 53–4, 86, 89.

24. Walzer, 'Politics of Rescue', p. 36.

25. Kofi Annan, 'Two Concepts of Sovereignty', *The Economist*, 18 September 1999.

26. *Convention on the Prevention and Punishment of the Crime of Genocide*, adopted and proclaimed by the UN General Assembly, Resolution 260A(III), 9 December 1948.

27. UN Press Release SG/SM/7136, GA/9596: Speech of Secretary-General to the General Assembly of the United Nations, 20 September 1999.

28. Brad Roth, *Governmental Illegitimacy in International Law* (Oxford: Clarendon Press, 1999), p. 324.

29. General Assembly Resolution 2625 (XXV), Annex, 25 UN GAOR, Supp. (no. 28), UN Dec A/5217 (1970), at 121, also cited in Roth, *Government Illegitimacy*, pp. 161–2.

30. Security Council Resolution 688 (5 April 1991). I owe this and the following two examples to Gregory Fox, 'The Right to Political Participation in International Law', in Cecelia Lynch

and Michael Loriaux (eds.), *Law and Moral Action in World Politics* (Minneapolis: University of Minnesota Press, 1999), p. 91. Security Council Resolutions may be found on the internet at *http://srcho.un.org/Docs/scres*.

31. Security Council Resolution 794 (3 December 1992).

32. Security Council Resolution 841 (16 June 1993).

33. The thesis goes back to Kant's *Perpetual Peace*, section II, and is also associated with Joseph Schumpeter. See Michael Doyle, 'Liberal Institutions and International Ethics', in Kenneth Kipnis and Diana Meyers (eds.), *Political Realism and International Morality* (Boulder, CO: Westview, 1987), pp. 185–211; first published as 'Liberalism and World Politics', *American Political Science Review*, 80(4) (1986), pp. 1152–69.

34. Rome Statute of the International Criminal Court, Article 7.

35. Lassa Oppenheim, *International Law*, vol. I (London: Longman, 1905), p. 403, cited by Fox, 'The Right to Political Participation in International Law', p. 83.

36. Roth, *Governmental Illegitimacy*, pp. 162–3.

37. Thomas Jefferson to Gouverneur Morris, 7 November 1792, *Works* (4th edn), vol. III, p. 489, cited in Roth, *Governmental Illegitimacy*, p. 321.

38. Of course, not all regimes that are not democracies can be characterized as gangs of thugs. For more on this see section 'Objections' below. The preceding paragraph has been influenced by Fox, 'The Right to Political Participation in International Law'. See also Thomas M. Franck, 'The Emerging Right to Democratic Governance', *American Journal of International Law*, vol. 86 (1992), pp. 46–91. For criticism and further references, see Roth, *Governmental Illegitimacy*, pp. 323ff.

39. United Nations General Assembly, Millennium Declaration, A/RES/55/2, 8 September 2000, Articles 24 and 25. This document is available on the internet at *http://www.un.org/documents/ga/res/55/a55r002.pdf*.

40. See Thomas Pogge, 'Achieving Democracy', *Ethics and International Affairs* 15:1 (2001), pp. 3–23.

41. *Final Warsaw Declaration: Towards a Community of Democracies*, 27 June 2000, circulated by the United Nations and Secretariat as General Assembly Document A/55/328, and available on the internet at *http://www.democracyconference.org/declaration.html*.

42. Anthony DePalma, 'Talks Tie Trade in the Americas to Democracy', *New York Times*, 23 April 2001.

43. Reciprocity, at least, seems to be common to ethical systems everywhere. See Alvin Gouldner, 'The Norm of Reciprocity', *American Sociological Review*, 25:2 (1960), p. 171, and the references given in note 6, above.

44. For further discussion of the basis of ethics see my *Practical Ethics* (2nd edition, Cambridge: Cambridge University Press, 1993), chapter 1; R. M. Hare, *Moral Thinking* (Oxford: Oxford University Press, 1981).

45. This objection was pressed by John Broome when I gave this lecture in Oxford. My response partially reflects some comments made by Nir Eyal, who was also present on that occasion.

46. Speech to SS leaders in Posen, 4 October 1943, cited in Karl Dietrich Bracher, *The German Dictatorship* (New York: Praeger Publishers, 1971), p. 423.

47. The preceding paragraph owes much to Leif Wenar's thoughtful comments.

48. Mill, 'A Few Words on Non-Intervention', p. 381. The passage is discussed in Doyle, 'The New Interventionism'.

49. See Michael Ignatieff's contribution to this volume.

50. Doyle, 'New Interventionism', p. 220. See this paper generally for a discussion, with many contemporary illustrations, of some of the consequentialist aspects of humanitarian intervention.

51. Tzvetan Todorov, this volume.

52. Michael Ignatieff, this volume.

53. See Samuel Huntington, *The Clash of Civilizations and the Remaking of World Order* (New York: Simon & Schuster, 1996).

54. I thank Aaron Jackson for researching these figures, which were accurate as of 2000.

55. Quoted from Erskine Childers, 'Empowering the people in their United Nations', a speech given at a symposium on 'The United Nations at Fifty: Creating a More Democratic and Effective UN', Hesburgh Centre for International Studies, University of Notre Dame, 2 December 1994, *http://www.globalpolicy.org/resource/pubs/childer1.htm*.

56. Well, maybe not so basic—if the United States were to apply for admission to the European Union, its application would be rejected because the EU considers the death penalty to be a violation of human rights.

57. I thank John Broome, Paula Casal, Michael Doyle, Nir Eyal, Bob Herbst, Nick Owen, Leif Wenar, and all those who offered helpful comments when I presented earlier versions of this lecture at Oxford University, at the Center for Human Values, Princeton University, and at the Graduate Center of the City University of New York.

*Notes to Chapter 4*

1. The proceedings of the International Military Tribunal at Nuremberg are reported in the first 22 volumes of *Trials of the War Criminals before the International Military Tribunal* (Nuremberg, 1947–49).

2. For accounts of the Nuremberg Trials, see Telford Taylor, *The Anatomy of the Nuremberg Trial. A Personal Memoir* (New York: Knopf, 1992); Bradley Smith, *Reaching Judgment at Nuremberg: The Untold Story* (New York: Basic Books, 1976); and Joseph Persico, *Nuremberg: Infamy on Trial* (New York: Viking, 1994).

3. The judgement of the Tokyo War Crimes Trial is reprinted in part in Richard Falk, Gabriel Kolko and Robert Jay Lifton (eds.), *Crimes of War: A Legal, Political Documentary, and*

*Psychological Inquiry into the Responsibility of Leaders, Citizens, and Soldiers for Criminal Acts in Wars* (New York: Random House, 1971), p. 113.

4. The European Court of Justice (ECJ) was set up in 1952 as an institution of the European Community in order to ensure the consistent and effective application of Community law throughout what is now the European Union. While not specifically tasked with the protection of human rights of the citizens of the Union against its member states, the creation of the court demonstrates a willingness of the member states of the European Union to submit themselves to the authority of an external judicial body.

5. The European Court of Human Rights protects the rights and freedoms guaranteed by the European Convention on Human Rights (ECHR), which was drawn up within the Council of Europe and opened for signature on 4 November 1950, and which today boasts a virtually complete membership amongst the countries of Europe. The most important task of the Court is to deal with complaints about human rights violations brought by member states' citizens who have exhausted all domestic remedies.

6. Article 56 in conjunction with Article 55 (c) of the Charter of the United Nations, signed on 26 June 1945 and entered into force on 24 October 1945, United Nations Conference on International Organization Documents, vol. XV (1945), p. 335.

7. Adopted and proclaimed by General Assembly resolution 217 A (III) of 10 December 1948.

8. United Nations, Treaty Series, vol. 993, p. 3.

9. United Nations, Treaty Series, vol. 999, p. 171.

10. *Bleier v. Uruguay*, Comm. no. R.7/30, 37 UN GAOR Supp. (no. 40), Annex X, UN Doc. A/37/40 (1982); *Quinteros v. Uruguay*, Comm. no. 107/1981, 38 UN GAOR Supp. (no. 40), Annex XXII, UN Doc. A/38/40 (1983); *Baboeram v. Suriname*, Comm.

nos. 146/1983 and 148–54/1983, 40 UN GAOR Supp. (no. 40), Annex X, UN Doc. A/40/40 (1985).

11. International Tribunal for the Prosecution of Persons Responsible for Serious Violations of International Humanitarian Law Committed in the Territory of the Former Yugoslavia since 1991 (ICTY), Statute, UN Doc. S/25704, annex (1993), reprinted in 33 ILM 1192 (1993).

12. International Criminal Tribunal for the Prosecution of Persons Responsible for Genocide and Other Serious Violations of International Humanitarian Law Committed in the Territory of Rwanda and Rwandan Citizens Responsible for Genocide and Other such Violations Committed in the Territory of Neighbouring States, between 1 January 1994 and 31 December 1994 (ICTR), Statute, SC Res. 995, annex, UN SCOR, 49th Sess., UN Doc. S/INF/50 (1994), reprinted in 33 ILM 1602 (1994).

13. At the time of writing, the ICTR has concluded the trials of nine individuals, one of whom was acquitted, while the others were convicted and sentenced, mostly to life imprisonment. In three of these cases, appeals are still pending. The ICTY has publicly indicted 111 persons altogether, against eight of whom indictments have later been withdrawn, and handed down 14 judgements on the merits. These judgements concern ten different event clusters and deal with altogether 46 accused.

14. Richard Goldstone, *For Humanity: Reflections of a War Crimes Investigator* (New Haven: Yale University Press, 2000), p. 123.

15. The trial of Jean Kambanda, the former Prime Minister of Rwanda, began on 1 May 1998 and ended on 4 September 1998 with Kambanda's conviction on charges of genocide and crimes against humanity. Kambanda, who had pleaded guilty as charged, was sentenced to life imprisonment. His appeal was dismissed on 19 October 2000, and he is since 9 December 2001 serving his sentence in a prison in Mali.

16. Following his electoral defeat in September 2000, Milosevic was originally arrested in Serbia on charges unrelated to crimes against humanity. Following an offer of a multi-billion-dollar loan to the new Serbian government made conditional upon Milosevic's surrender to the ICTY, he was extradited to stand trial in The Hague on charges of genocide, crimes against humanity and war crimes. He first appeared in Court on 3 July 2001, taking a defiant attitude towards the legitimacy of the tribunal. At the time of writing, his trial is still in progress. The indictments against Milosevic consist of the following: (IT-01–51) 'Bosnia and Herzegovina', initial indictment on charges of genocide, crimes against humanity, grave breaches of the Geneva Conventions and violations of the laws and customs of war; (IT-01–50) 'Croatia', initial indictment of 8 October 2001 on charges of crimes against humanity, grave breaches of the Geneva Conventions and violations of the laws and customs of war; and (IT-99–36) 'Kosovo', initial and amended indictments on charges of crimes against humanity and violations of the laws and customs of war.

17. All 56 ICTR detainees were arrested in third countries. Only 15 of them were arrested in the immediate aftermath of the genocide in 1995–96, and 12 were arrested as late as 2001.

18. Ian Black, 'Milosevic indicted for Croatia', *Guardian*, 29 September 2001.

19. Goldstone, *For Humanity*, pp. 82–8 and 104.

20. Ibid., p. 116.

21. Ibid., p. 128.

22. Ibid., pp. 109–12.

23. Art. 126, Rome Statute of the International Criminal Court of 17 July 1998, UN Doc. A/CONF.183/9, reprinted in 37 ILM 998 (1998), hereafter referred to as 'ICC Statute'.

24. The UK legislation consists of the *International Criminal Court Act* (2001).

25. Art. 7, ICC Statute.

26. Art. 6, ICC Statute.

27. Art. 8, ICC Statute.

28. See Art. 12, ICC Statute.

29. Iran, however, signed the treaty on 31 December 2000.

30. This view is shared by Charney, 'Progress in International Criminal Law?', (1999) 93 *AJIL* 452, 456, n. 29.

31. Art. 11, ICC Statute.

32. Art. 17, para. 1 lit (a) and (b) ICC Statute.

33. Preamble, para. 10, ICC Statute.

34. In order to avoid abuse, the ICC will be competent to declare a case admissible if proceedings in the state which exercises its jurisdiction over the matter are marred by that state's unwillingness or inability 'genuinely to carry out the investigation' (see Art. 17, para. 1 lit (a) and (b) ICC Statute).

35. See Art. 28, ICC Statute on the responsibility of commanders and other superiors.

36. See Art. 25, ICC Statute on individual criminal responsibility.

37. Art. 17, para. 1, ICC Statute.

38. The principle of universal jurisdiction over war crimes was accepted as early as 1949 in the four Geneva Conventions on the laws of war. See Art. 49 of the *Geneva Convention for the Amelioration of the Condition of the Wounded and Sick in Armed Forces in the Field* (1949); Art. 50 of the *Geneva Convention for the Amelioration of the Condition of the Wounded, Sick and Shipwrecked Members of the Armed Forces at Sea* (1949); Art. 129 of the *Geneva Convention Relative to the Treatment of Prisoners of War* (1949); and Art. 146 of the *Geneva Convention Relative to the Protection of Civilian Persons in Time of War* (1949).

39. These activities resulted in two judgements by the House of Lords concerning the validity of the provisional arrest warrants which had been issued by London magistrates. See *Regina v. Bow Street Metropolitan Stipendiary Magistrate and Others, ex parte Pinochet Ugarte*, judgement of 25 November 1998, (2000) 1 AC 61 (Pinochet No. 1) and *Regina v. Bow Street Metropolitan*

*Stipendiary Magistrate and Others, ex parte Pinochet Ugarte,* judgement of 24 March 1999, (2000) 1 AC 147 (Pinochet No. 3).

40. The then Home Secretary, Jack Straw, provided full reasons for his decision in a written answer of 2 March 2000 and in a parliamentary statement given the same day. *Hansard (Parliamentary Debates)* 2 March 2000, vol. 345, cols. 357W–371W and 571–5.

41. The Convention was opened for signature on 10 December 1984, 1465 UNTS 85.

42. Art. 5, Torture Convention.

43. Compare Art. 7, para. 1, Torture Convention.

44. Sec. 20 of the State Immunity Act 1978 read in conjunction with sec. 2 of the Diplomatic Privileges Act 1964 and Art. 39 para. 2 of the Vienna Convention on Diplomatic Relations 1961.

45. See case notes by Fox (1999) 48 *ICLQ,* 207–16 (on Pinochet No. 1), (1999) 48 *ICLQ,* 687–702 (on Pinochet No. 3) and by Chinkin (1999) 93, *AJII,* 703–11.

46. *Al-Adsani v. Government of Kuwait* (1996) 107 ILR 536 (CA).

47. See the provisions of the *State Immunity Act* 1978.

48. *Al-Adsani v. The United Kingdom* (Application no. 35763/97), judgement of 21 November 2001.

49. Ibid., §§ 39, 40.

50. Ibid., §§ 55, 56. The ruling on Art. 6 was agreed by the narrowest possible majority of the Court: nine in favour, eight against. The President of the Court was among the minority.

51. Priscilla B. Hayner, *Unspeakable Truths. Confronting State Terror and Atrocities* (New York and London: Routledge, 2001).

52. Muvunyi is now in the custody of the ICTR and awaiting trial (Case No. ICTR-2000–55–1).

*Notes to Chapter 5*

1. George Shelton incidentally provides a gloss on the native English-speaker's take on the word 'wrong' in *Morality and Sovereignty in the Philosophy of Hobbes* (New York: St Martin's, 1992), pp. 128–9. See also D. D. Raphael, 'Hobbes on Justice', in G. A. J. Rodgers and Alan Ryan (eds.), *Perspectives on Thomas Hobbes* (Oxford: Clarendon, 1988), pp. 164–5. Alex Callinicos gives other examples of Social Darwinism in *Social Theory: A Historical Introduction* (Oxford: Blackwell, 1999).

2. Spivak, *A Critique of Postcolonial Reason: Toward a History of the Vanishing Present* (Cambridge, MA: Harvard University Press, 1999), p. 217, n. 33. This is a much-revised version of earlier work. The initial thinking and writing of the piece took place in 1982–83. In other words, I have been thinking of the access to the European Enlightenment through colonization as an enablement for some 20 years. I am so often stereotyped as a rejecter of the Enlightenment that I feel obliged to make this clear at the outset. But I thought of this particular method of access to the Enlightenment as a violation as well. In 1992, I presented 'Thinking Academic Freedom in Gendered Postcoloniality' in Cape Town, where I laid out the idea of ab-using the Enlightenment, in ways similar to, but not identical with, the present argument. That essay has been reprinted in Joan Vicent, *The Anthropology of Politics* (Oxford: Blackwell, 2002). The editor describes it as 'prescient' about South Africa, because presented as early as 1992. She describes the piece as the 'sting in the tail of her collection', because Spivak, contrary to her stereotype, recommends using the Enlightenment from below. This, then, was a decade ago. Indeed, this is one of the reasons why I hang in with Derrida, because here is one critic of ethnocentrism (*Of Grammatology*, tr. Spivak, Baltimore: Johns Hopkins University Press, 1976, p. 3) who continues, as I remarked in 'Responsibility', to indicate the danger and bad

faith in a wholesale rejection of the Enlightenment (Spivak, 'Responsibility', *boundary 2* 31 (3), Fall 1994, pp. 38–46). My double-edged attitude to the European Enlightenment is thus not a sudden change of heart.

3. Mel James, 'Country Mechanisms of the United Nations Commission on Human Rights', in Yael Danieli, Elsa Stamatopoulou and Clarence J. Dias (eds.), *The Universal Declaration of Human Rights: Fifty Years and Beyond* (Amityville, NY: Baywood Publishing, Inc., 1999), pp. 76–7.

4. Cited in Thomas Paine, *Rights of Man* (Indianapolis: Hackett, 1992), p. 79.

5. The identity of the nation and the state is generally associated with the Peace of Westphalia (1648), often thought of as one of the inaugurations of the Enlightenment. See, for example, R. Paul Churchill, 'Hobbes and the Assumption of Power', in Peter Caws (ed.), *The Causes of Quarrel: Essays on Peace, War, and Thomas Hobbes* (Boston: Beacon Press, 1988), p. 17.

6. Thomas Risse, Stephen C. Roppe and Kathryn Sikkink (eds.), *The Power of Human Rights: International Norms and Domestic Change* (New York: Cambridge University Press, 1999).

7. I have written about this class in Spivak, *A Critique*, p. 392. They are not only involved in righting wrongs, of course. The head of the Space Vehicle Directorate's innovative concepts group, behind George W. Bush's new space war initiative, is a model minority diasporic; hardly righting wrongs!

8. I am not tendentious in being critical of this. Ian Martin, Secretary-General of Amnesty International from 1986 to 1992, is similarly critical. See Ian Martin, 'Closer to the Victim: United Nations Human Rights Field Operations', in Danieli *et al.*, *Universal Declaration*, p. 92.

9. Risse *et al.*, *Power*, p. 170. The next quoted passage is from p. 167.

10. Edward W. Said, *Reflections on Exile and Other Essays* (Cambridge, MA: Harvard University Press, 2000), p. xi. It is interesting that Mary Shelley calls imperial Rome 'capital of the world,

the crown of man's achievements' (*The Last Man*, London: Pickering, 1996, p. 356). I am grateful to Lecia Rosenthal for this reference.

11. Lee Kuan Yew, *From Third World to First: the Singapore Story, 1965–2000* (New York: Harper, 2000); the sentiment about detention is to be found on p. 488. Rorty, 'Human Rights, Rationality, and Sentimentality', in Stephen Shute and Susan Hurley (eds.), *On Human Rights* (New York: Basic Books, 1993), p. 127. Meanwhile, general pieces like Asbjørn Eide, 'Historical Significance of the Universal Declaration', *International Social Science Journal* 50 (4) (Dec. 1998), pp. 475–96, share neither Rorty's wit nor the realism of the rest.

12. I think there is something like a relationship between these and the 'tutored preferences' discussed in Philip Kitcher, *Science, Truth, and Democracy* (New York: Oxford University Press, 2001), pp. 118–19 and *passim*. Professor Kitcher is speaking of an ideal community of taxpaying citizens and he is concerned about 'well-ordered science', whereas I shall be speaking of students in general, including the rural poor in the global South. Even with these differences, I would argue that 'transmitting information' (p. 118) would not necessarily lead to a tutoring of preferences. This is part of a more general interrogation of 'consciousness raising' as a basis for social change.

13. I had not read Dewey when I began my work with the children of the rural poor. In order to write this piece I took a quick look, too quick, I fear. I am certainly with Dewey in his emphasis on intelligent habit formation and his contempt for rote learning. It must, however, be said that Dewey's work operates on the assumption that the educator is of the same 'culture' and society/class as the person to be educated; my idea of cultural suturing, to be developed later in the essay, does not reside within those assumptions. Dewey has a holistic and unitary view of the inside of the child which I find difficult to

accept. I am grateful to Benjamin Conisbee Baer for research assistance in my quick preliminary foray into Dewey.

14. I am so often asked to distinguish my position from Martha Nussbaum's that I feel compelled to write this note, somewhat unwillingly. In spite of her valiant efforts, Martha Nussbaum's work seems to me to remain on the metropolitan side of the undergirding discontinuity of which I speak in my text. Her informants, even when seemingly subaltern, are mediated by the domestic 'below', the descendants of the colonial subject, the morally outraged top-drawer activist. Although she certainly wants to understand the situation of poor women, her real project is to advance the best possible theory for that undertaking, on the way to public interest intervention, by the international 'above', who is represented by the 'us' in the following typical quote: 'understood at its best, the paternalism argument is not an argument against cross-cultural universals. For it is all about respect for the dignity of persons as choosers. This respect requires us to defend universally a wide range of liberties' (*Women and Human Development: the Capabilities Approach* [WHD], Cambridge: Cambridge University Press, 2000, pp. 59–60).

It is not a coincidence that Nussbaum became aware of poor women by way of a stint at the educational wing of the UN (*Poetic Justice: the Literary Imagination and Public Life* [PJ], Boston: Beacon Press, 1995, pp. xv–xvi and p. 123, n. 4). She went to India 'to learn as much as [she] could about women's development projects', and worked through interpreters in order to find both a philosophical justification for universalism and to draw conclusions about the pros and cons of public interest litigation. (Her book ends with three legal case studies.) The 'cases' are exceptional subalterns prepared by SEWA—one of the most spectacular social experiments in the Third World. I have mentioned elsewhere that this organization is the invariable example cited when micro-credit lenders are questioned

about their lack of social involvement (Spivak, 'Claiming Transformations: Travel Notes with Pictures', in Sara Ahmed *et al.*
(eds.), *Transformations: Thinking Through Feminism*, London:
Routledge, 2000, pp. 119–30).

If Nussbaum's informants are urban radical leaders of the
rural, her sources of inspiration—Gandhi, Nehru, Tagore—
belong to national liberationist leadership from the progressive
bourgeoisie. (She has an epigraph about women from Iswarchandra Vidyasagar [WHD, p. 242], whose activist intervention in
rural education I cite later in this essay. His intervention on
behalf of women engaged caste-Hindus, since widow remar-
riage was not unknown among the so-called tribals and lower
castes. My great-great-grandfather Biharilal Bhaduri was an
associate of Vidyasagar's and arranged a second marriage for his
daughter Barahini, widowed in childhood. The repercussions of
this bold step have been felt in my family. The point I'm trying
to make is that, whereas Vidyasagar's literacy activism, aware of
the detail of rural education, applies to the subaltern classes
even today, his feminist activism applied to the metropolitan
middle class, to which I belong.)

Nussbaum certainly believes in the 'value' of 'education' and
'literacy', but these are contentless words for her. She also
believes in the virtues of the literary imagination, but her idea
of it is a sympathetic identification, a bringing of the other into
the self (PJ, pp. 31, 34, 38), a guarantee that literature 'makes us
acknowledge the equal humanity of members of social classes
other than our own'. This is rather far from the dangerous self-
renouncing 'delusion', a risky othering of the self, that has to be
toned down for the reader's benefit, which remains my Words-
worthian model (William Wordsworth, *Lyrical Ballads and Other
Poems*, Ithaca, NY: Cornell University Press, 1992, pp. 751, 755).
It is not without significance that her models are social-realist
novels and Walt Whitman read as expository prose. Wordsworth's project was pedagogic—to change public taste (ibid.,

pp. 742–5). There is not a word about pedagogy in Nussbaum's text. Like many academic liberals, she imagines that everyone feels the same complicated pleasures from a Dickens text. As a teacher of reading, my entire effort is to train students away from the sort of characterological plot summary approach that she uses. In the brief compass of a note I am obliged to refer the reader to my reading of Woolf in 'Deconstruction and Cultural Studies: Arguments for A Deconstructive Cultural Studies', in Nicholas Royle (ed.), *Deconstructions* (Oxford: Blackwell, 2000), pp. 14–43, Jamaica Kincaid in 'Thinking Cultural Questions in "Pure" Literary Terms', in Paul Gilroy *et al.* (eds.), *Without Guarantees: In Honor of Stuart Hall* (London: Verso, 2000), pp. 335–57, and Maryse Condé in 'The Staging of Time in Maryse Condé's *Heremakhonon*' (forthcoming in *Cultural Studies*) for accounts of such teaching. The only rhetorical reading Nussbaum performs is of Judge Posner's opinion on *Mary Carr v. GM* (PJ, pp. 104–11). (The piece in Royle will also give a sense of my activist reading of the *poiesis/istoria* argument in Aristotle.)

I have remarked that, in the context of 'Indian women', 'education' is a contentless good for Nussbaum. In the context of her own world, the 'moral education' offered by literature is simply there (PJ, p. 84). For me the task of teaching in the two worlds is related but different; in each case interruptive, supplementary. In the disenfranchised world there is a call to suspend all the fine analytic machinery that gives Nussbaum the confidence to 'claim that the standard of judgment constructed in [her] conception of "poetic justice" passes . . . [the] tests' of Whitman's 'general call for the poet-judge' (PJ, p. 120) and so on. To attend to the unleashing of the ethical gives no guarantee that it will produce a 'good' result—just that it will bring in a relation, perhaps. As the literary Melville and the literary Faulkner knew, the relationship between the hunter and the prey steps into the relational domain we will call 'ethical'.

The dominant appropriation of the necessary and impossible aporia between the political and ethical into the convenience of a bridge named race-class-gender-sensitivity is what we must constantly keep at bay, even as we cross and recross.

Although Nussbaum knows the limitations of behaviourism (WHD, pp. 119–35), it is clear from her discussion of central capabilities and, especially, the value of religion—'something having to do with ideals and aspirations' (WHD, p. 198)—that she knows *about* cultural difference but cannot imagine it. Her model of the human mind is wedded to the autonomous subject, a gift of the European Enlightenment broadly understood. The emotions are named. They are yoked to belief and thus led to reason. This trajectory produces Adam Smith's idea of the 'literary judge'. For better or for worse, my view of the mind is forever marked by the commonsense plausibility of Freud's 'stricture' of repression—the mind feeling an unpleasure as pleasure to protect itself. Therefore my notion of political agency rests on a restricted and accountable model of the person that bears a discontinuous and fractured relationship with the subject. The most difficult part of the pedagogic effort outlined later in my essay may be precisely this: that in opening myself to be 'othered' by the subaltern, it is this broader, more mysterious arena of the subject that the self hopes to enter; and then, through the task of teaching, rehearse the aporia between subjectship and the more tractable field of agency. For us, 'politics' can never claim to 'speak with a full and fully human voice' (PJ, p. 72). Nussbaum's work is thus premised on the asymmetry in the title of this lecture series. My modest efforts are a hands-on undertaking, with the subaltern, to undo this asymmetry, some day. Without this effortful task of 'doing' in the mode of 'to come', rather than only 'thinking' in the mode of 'my way is the best', there is indeed a scary superficial similarity (PJ, pp. 76, 86, 89–90) between the two of us, enough to mislead people. I admire her scholarship and her intelligence but I can learn little from her. My teacher is the subaltern.

15. Anthony de Reuck comments on the discontinuity between subaltern and elite (using a 'periphery/centre' vocabulary) as 'styles of perceptual incoherence ... on the threshold of a cultural anthropology of philosophical controversy' and veers away from it: 'that, as they say, is another story!' ('Culture in Conflict', in Caws, *Causes*, pp. 59–63). My essay lays out the practical politics of that other story, if you like. The superiority of Northern epistemes, however, remains an implicit presupposition. Jonathan Glover analyses the possibility of the Nazi mindset in numbing detail and discusses Rwanda with no reference to a mental theatre at all (*Humanity: A Moral History of the Twentieth Century*, London: Jonathan Cape, 1999). Risse, Roppe and Sikkink vary their definition of the domestic as 'below' by considering freedom of expression only in the case of Eastern Europe and not in the cases of Kenya, Uganda, South Africa, Tunisia, Morocco, Indonesia, Philippines, Chile and Guatemala. The luxury of an expressive or contaminable mind is implicitly not granted to the subaltern of the global South.

16. This forgetfulness is the condition and effect of the simple value-judgement that rights-thinking is superior—'fitter'. Social psychology is now producing abundant retroactive 'proof' that each separate 'developing' culture is 'collective', whereas 'America' (synecdochically the US) and 'Europe' (synecdochically Northwestern Europe and Scandinavia) is 'individualistic'. This 'collectivism' is a trivialization of the thinking of responsibility I shall discuss below. 'Multiculturalism' (synecdochically 'global' if we remember the important role of upward mobility among diasporics and the economically restructured New World) is now factored into this authoritative and scientific division, although all comparisons relating to actually 'developing' countries are resolutely bilateral between one nation/state/culture and the (Euro) US. The sampling

techniques of such work are pathetic in their suggestive nudging of the informant groups to produce the required 'evidence' (Susan M. Ervin-Tripp *et al.*, *A Field Manual for Cross-Cultural Study of the Acquisition of Communicative Competence*, Second Draft—July 1967, Berkeley: University of California Press, 1967; Geert H. Hofstede, *Cultures and Organizations: Software of the Mind*, New York: McGraw-Hill, 1991; Saburo Iwawaki *et al.* (eds.), Innovations in Cross-Cultural Psychology, Amsterdam: Swets & Zeitlinger, 1992; Gail McKoon and Roger Ratcliff, 'The Minimalist Hypothesis: Directions for Research', in Charles A. Weaver *et al.* (eds.), *Discourse Comprehension: Essays in Honor of Walter Kintsch*, Hillsdale, NJ: L. Erlbaum, 1995, pp. 97–116; Paul DiMaggio, 'Culture and Cognition', in *Annual Review of Sociology* 23, 1997, pp. 263–87; Huong Nguyen, Lawrence Messé and Gary Stollak, 'Toward a More Complex Understanding of Acculturation and Adjustment: Cultural Involvements and Psychosocial Functioning in Vietnamese Youth', *Journal of Cross-Cultural Psychology* 30 (1), January 1999, pp. 5–31; Arie W. Kruglanski and Donna M. Webster, 'Motivated Closing of the Mind: "Seizing" and "Freezing"', in E. Tory Higgins and Arie W. Kruglanski (eds.), *Motivational Science: Social and Personality Perspectives*, Philadelphia: Psychology Press, 2000, pp. 354–75; Hong Ying-yi *et al.*, 'Multicultural Minds: A Dynamic Constructivist Approach to Culture and Cognition', *American Psychologist* 55, July 2000, pp. 709–20). The sophistication of the vocabulary and the poverty of the conclusions rest on an uncritical idea of the human mind. We cannot ask social psychology to become qualitative cognitive psychology or philosophical ontology. Yet these sorts of academic subdisciplinary endeavour, especially when confidently offered up by female diasporics (my last terrifying encounter with this type of scholarship came from a young, intelligent, innocent, confident, power-dressed Hong Kong Chinese woman trained in California), directly or indirectly sustain the asymmetrical division between human rights and human wrongs that inform our title. The division that we are speaking of is a class division dissimulated as a cultural division in order to recode the unequal distribution of agency. It is in that context that I am suggesting that the begging of the question of human nature/freedom, much discussed when the question of human rights was confined to Europe, has been withheld from a seemingly culturally divided terrain not only by dominant political theorizing and policy-making, but also by disciplinary tendencies. Alex Callinicos, whom no one would associate with deconstruction, places the nature/polity hesitation as the conflict at the very heart of the European Enlightenment, arguing its saliency for today on those grounds (*Social Theory*, pp. 25, 26, 29, 31, 37, 67, 83, 178, 179 and *passim*).

17. Thomas Paine, *Rights of Man; Common Sense* (New York: Knopf, 1994), p. 38.

18. Derrida, 'Force of Law', in Gil Anidjar, tr. *Acts of Religion* (New York: Routledge, 2002), pp. 228–98. Benjamin's essay is included in *Reflections: Essays, Aphorisms, Autobiographical Writings*, tr. Edmund Jephcott (New York: Harcourt Brace, 1978), pp. 277–300. Derrida shows how Benjamin attempts to solve the problem both on the 'universal' register (the new state) and the 'singular' register (his own signature). In terms of the text's relationship to the subsequent development of a full-fledged Nazism, Derrida offers an alternative reading. Most readings (including Derrida's) miss Benjamin's conviction that 'the educative power' is a 'form of appearance [*Erscheinungsform*] of what Benjamin calls "divine power", because it breaks the crime/expiation chain that the law deals with. And yet the educative does not depend upon miracles for its definition' (Walter Benjamin, 'The Critique of Violence', in Edmund Jephcott, tr. *Reflections: Essays, Aphorisms, Autobiographical Writings*, New York: Schocken, 1986, p. 297; I am reading *entsünden* as breaking with the unavoidable link between guilt

and expiation—*Schuld* and *Sühne*—rather than as 'expiate', as in the English text, a translation that renders Benjamin's argument absurd. I thank Andreas Huyssen for corroborating my reading. The reader will see the connection between the guilt-and-shame of Human Rights enforcement, and our hope in the displacing power of education.)

19. George Shelton, *Morality and Sovereignty*, pp. 86–7, 175.

20. Ernst Bloch, *Natural Law and Human Dignity*, tr. Dennis J. Schmidt (Cambridge, MA: MIT Press, 1986), p. 263.

21. Michel Foucault, 'The Masked Philosopher', in *Politics, Philosophy, Culture: Interviews and Other Writings 1977–1984*, tr. Alan Sheridan (New York: Routledge, 1988), pp. 323–30; Derrida, 'My Chances/*Mes Chances*: A Rendezvous with Some Epicurean Stereophonies', in Joseph H. Smith and William Kerrigan (eds.), *Taking Chances: Derrida, Psychoanalysis, and Literature* (Baltimore: Johns Hopkins University Press, 1984), pp. 1–32. For the Nietzschean moment, see Derrida, *Politics of Friendship*, tr. George Collins (New York: Verso, 1997), pp. 79–80. It is of course silly to call Zeno and Epicurus 'colonial subjects', or Aristotle—who never became an Athenian citizen—a 'resident alien'. The point I am trying to make is that the removal of the Austro-Asiatic Aboriginals from the Indo-European colonizing loop—the narrative behind Indian constitutional policy—was active when Epicurus the Athenian from Samos, hugging the coast of Turkey, whose parents emigrated from Athens as colonists, and Zeno the Phoenician from Syrian Cyprus—both places the object of constant imperial grab-shifts—came to Athens to be educated and subsequently to found their philosophies. As I shall go on to elaborate, these Indian Aboriginals are among the disenfranchised groups whose contemporary educational situation seems crucial to the general argument of this essay. I discuss the resultant process of atrophy and dysfunction at greater length below.

22. Gregory Elliott puts together two distanced assertions by Louis

Althusser to sharpen the latter's sense of Machiavelli's uncanny engagement with this problematic: 'Machiavelli's "endeavour to think the conditions of possibility of an impossible task, to think the unthinkable" induces "a strange *vacillation* in the traditional philosophical status of [his] theoretical propositions: as if they were undermined by another instance than the one that produces them—the instance of political practice"' (G. Elliott, 'Introduction', in Louis Althusser, *Machiavelli and Us*, tr. Elliott, London: Verso, 1999, p. xviii). On pp. 123–6 of this text Althusser attempts to fix Machiavelli's place upon this chain of displacements. See also Adam D. Danel, *A Case for Freedom: Machiavellian Humanism* (New York: University Press of America, 1997). For the Hobbes–Bramhill debate, see Vere Chappell (ed.), *Hobbes and Bramhill on Liberty and Necessity* (Cambridge: Cambridge University Press, 1999). David Gauthier provides an interesting way of linking Hobbes and Paine (Gauthier, 'Hobbes's Social Contract', in Rodgers and Ryan, *Perspectives*, pp. 126–7, 148).

23. George Shelton, *Morality and Sovereignty*, pp. 20, 86–7, 175. 'Fiction' and 'reality' are Shelton's words. By indicating the slippage, Shelton makes room for my more radical position—that the fiction marks the begging of the question that produces the 'real'.

24. Patricia Springborg, 'Hobbes on Religion', in Tom Sorell (ed.), *The Cambridge Companion to Hobbes* (Cambridge: Cambridge University Press, 1996), pp. 354–60; see also Arrigo Pacchi, 'Hobbes and the Problem of God', in Rodgers and Ryan (eds.), *Perspectives*, pp. 182–7. Balibar suggests a double Hobbes: one in whose writings the violence of original sin was always ready to burst forth; and another who saw law immanent in natural self-interest and competition (private communication); a version, perhaps, of the discontinuity I am speaking of.

25. In his reading of Rousseau in *Of Grammatology* (tr. Spivak, Baltimore: Johns Hopkins University Press, 1976, pp. 95–316),

Derrida has indicated Rousseau's place on this chain. Locke's view of natural rights is another well-known concatenation on this chain (see John Locke, *Questions Concerning the Law of Nature*, tr. Diskin Clay, Ithaca, NY: Cornell University Press, 1990, for how Locke taught the issue; for a scholarly account, see A. John Simmons, *The Lockean Theory of Rights*, Princeton, NJ: Princeton University Press, 1992). Balibar suggests that, by 'privatizing nature on the one hand [as] he is also socializing it', Locke is able to reconcile natural society and artificial community ('"Possessive Individualism" Reversed: From Locke to Derrida', forthcoming in *Constellations*). For a contemporary discussion of the chain from at least Roman law, Richard Tuck, *Natural Rights Theories: Their Origin and Development* (Cambridge: Cambridge University Press, 1978) remains indispensable. This is of course a layperson's checklist, not a specialist bibliography.

26. I have no expertise in this area and write this note to provoke those who do. I am thinking of Bimal Krishna Matilal's attempts to connect with Oxford ordinary language philosophy when he was Spalding Professor there, his unpublished work on rational critique in the Indic tradition. I am thinking of Ayesha Jalal's work in progress on Iqbal. When one invokes Kautilya or the *A'in-I-Akbari*, or yet engages in sinocentric World Systems theory—as in the current different-yet-related work of André Gunder Frank, Immanuel Wallerstein and Giovanni Arrighi— one is either in the area of comparative specialisms or identitarian cultural conservatisms. These are the risks run by Walter Mignolo and Agustin Lao-Montes as well as by Gordon Brotherston in Americas studies, Paul Gilroy and Martin Bernal in Africana. I compose this inexpert footnote so that my practical-political concerns are not silenced by mere erudition.

27. Alan Gewirth, *Human Rights: Essays on Justification and Applications* (Chicago: Chicago University Press, 1982), p. 128.

28. I have argued this in *Imperatives to Reimagine the Planet* (Vienna: Passagen, 1999).

29. Gewirth, *Human Rights*, pp. 45, 132–3, 141.

30. Ibid., p. 140. What does the Golden Rule have to do with what I was saying in the preceding paragraph? For Gewirth, 'Human rights are . . . moral rights which all persons equally have simply because they are human' (p. 1). For him the Golden Rule is a 'common moral denominator' (p. 128), hence it is a grounding question. In the preceding paragraph I was suggesting that European political theory has stopped considering the relationship between grounding 'natural' questions and the establishment of civil polities. I am now suggesting that Gewirth is a philosopher who does worry about it, making the usual disciplinary arrangements. In my estimation, Rawls's separation of political and philosophical liberalism is a way of getting around the necessity for confronting the problem.

31. Derrida has discussed this with reference to Leibnitz in his 'The Principle of Reason: the University in the Eyes of its Pupils', *Diacritics* 13 (3) (Fall 1983), pp. 7–10.

32. Gewirth, *Human Rights*, p. 8; emphasis mine. Reason as 'white mythology' is the informing argument of Derrida, 'White Mythology: Metaphor in the Text of Philosophy', *Margins of Philosophy*, tr. Alan Bass (Chicago: University of Chicago Press, 1982), pp. 207–71. Ronald Dworkin describes the undecidable moment: 'the right to concern and respect is fundamental among rights in a different way, because it shows how the idea of a collective goal may itself be derived from that fundamental right. If so, then concern and respect is a right so fundamental that it is not captured by the general characterization of rights as trumps over collective goals, except as a limiting case, because it is the source both of the general authority of collective goals and of the special limitations on their authority that justify more particular rights. That promise of unity in political theory is indistinct in these essays, however. It must be defended, if

at all, elsewhere' (Ronald Dworkin, *Taking Rights Seriously*, Cambridge: Harvard Univ. Press, 1978, p. xv). I believe this indistinctness is generic and the 'elsewhere, if at all,' is an irreducible alibi. Later in the collection, Dworkin is able to dismiss the discontinuity between 'natural rights' and the 'best political program' because he is building an argument, not worrying about the justification for the foundation of states (pp. 176–7). To take his statement here as a final solution to the entire problem is to 'confuse the force of his [argument] for its range', a confusion he attributes to Gertrude Himmelfarb's reading of John Stuart Mill's *Of Liberty* (p. 261). Where I find Ronald Dworkin altogether inspiring is in his insistence on principle rather than policy in hard cases. The range of this insistence has an elasticity that can accommodate the force of my pleas to the dominant.

33. I use aporia to name a situation where there are two right ways that cancel each other and that we, by being agents, have already marked in one way, with a decision that makes us rather than we it. There are other, more philosophically complex ways of formalizing aporia.

34. For a more extensive definition, see Spivak, *A Critique*, pp. 269–274.

35. In the 1950s C. Wright Mills wrote his famous *Sociological Imagination* to suggest that sociology was the discipline of disciplines for the times. He claimed imagination totally for reason. The sociological imagination was a 'quality of mind that will help [us] to use information and to develop reason in order to achieve lucid summations of what is going on in the world and what may be happening within [ourselves].' (C. Wright Mills, *The Sociological Imagination*, New York: Oxford University Press, 1959, p. 5; the next quotation is from p. 17.) Within a hitherto humanistic culture, reason and imagination, analysis and synthesis, are ranked. That is how Shelley's *Defence of Poetry* starts, giving to imagination the primary place. Mills is writing a

defence of sociology, which he thinks will reconcile the inner life and external career of contemporary man. Nussbaum feminizes this model. For the humanities, the relationship between the two had been a site of conflict, a source of grounding paradoxes. Mills cannot find any comfort in such pursuits, because, in the 1950s, the quality of education in the humanities had become too ingrown, too formalist, too scientistic. It no longer nurtured the imagination, that in-built instrument of othering. Therefore Mills wrote, revealingly: 'It does not matter whether [the most important] qualities [of mind] *are* to be found [in literature]; what matters is that men do not often find them there', because, of course, they are no longer taught to read the world closely as they read closely.

36. 'The ability to make fine-grained predictions indicates that the task is unlikely to be error-tolerant' (Kitcher, *Science*, pp. 23–4). The effort I am speaking of must be error-tolerant, in teacher, trainer, trained and taught, since we are speaking of cultural shift, and thus a shift in the definition of error.

37. Think, for example, of the constructive undermining of triumphalist 'we must help because we are better' sentiments to the awareness at least that might help undo the difference between 'us helping' and 'them being helped', if the excellent teaching tool 'The Rohde to Srebernica: A Case Study of Human Rights Reporting', which 'documents US reporter David Rohde's journey through Bosnia' (*http://www.columbia.edu/itc/journalism/nelson/rohde*) were supplemented in the following way: in the long run, a literary-level entry into the nuance differences between Muslim and Serb Bosnian, and their relationship to the subaltern language Romani (which can also be accessed with deep focus), in order to tease out the compromised and disenfranchised elements of the local cultures before the most recent disasters, in their 'normality', atrophied by waves of imperialisms; This note properly belongs to p. 207, where I speak of learning subaltern languages,

and to p. 208, where I assure the reader that every human rights activist is not required to learn all languages at this depth. Here suffice it to notice that the difference between the existing teaching tool and its imagined supplementation is the difference between urgent decisions and long-term commitment. I refer the reader to the difference between 'doctors without frontiers' and primary healthcare workers with which I began. The analogy: short-term commitment to righting wrongs versus long-term involvement to learn from below the persistent undoing of the reproduction of class-apartheid and its attendant evils. The reason for avoiding this is its inconvenience, which is not a good reason when the goal is to establish the inalienable rights of all beings born human. For one case of the subalternization of the Romany, see Spivak, *A Critique*, pp. 406–9.

38. Spivak, *Imperatives*, p. 68. Marshall Sahlins lays out the general characteristics of these defects in his *Stone Age Economics* (New York: de Gruyter, 1972). Sahlins also points at the obvious absence of a 'public sphere' in such social formations. I am grateful to Henry Staten for bringing this book to my attention.

39. As I shall mention later in connection with Anthony Giddens's *Beyond Left and Right*, I am not extolling the virtues of poverty, not even the Christian virtues of poverty, as does Sahlins by association (*Stone Age*, pp. 32–3). I am only interested in bringing those virtues above, and concurrently instilling the principles of a public sphere below; teaching at both ends of the spectrum. For, from the point of view of the asymmetry of what I am calling class-apartheid in the global South, a responsibility-based disenfranchised neglected culture left to itself can only be described, in its current status within the modern nation-state, as 'a reversal of "possessive individualism"', the tragedy 'of "negative" individuality or individualism' (Etienne Balibar, ' "Possessive Individualism" Revisited').

40. Marx, 'Concerning Feuerbach', in *Early Writings*, tr. Rodney

Livingstone (New York: Vintage, 1975), p. 422; translation modified.

41. Marx, 'The Trinity Formula', *Capital: A Critique of Political Economy*, tr. David Fernbach (New York: Vintage, 1981), vol. 3, pp. 953–70.

42. I will be developing this concept-metaphor of suturing as a description of practice. To situate this within Marxist thought, see Callinicos's gloss on Marx's discussion of religion: 'Religious illusions . . . will survive any purely intellectual refutation so long as the social conditions which produced them continue to exist' (Callinicos, *Social Theory*, pp. 83–4). I would not, of course, accept the illusion/truth binary and would therefore activate and undo-reweave from within the imaginative resources of the earlier cultural formation—often called 'religious'—in order for any from-above change in social condition to last. This undo-reweave is 'suture', the model of pedagogy 'below'. What must be kept in mind is that the same applies to consciousness-raising style radical teaching 'above'. The problem with 'religious fundamentalism', the politicizing of elite religions, is not that they are religions, but that they are elite in leadership.

43. Interestingly enough, this very passage was used in a speech entitled 'Responsibility: the Price of Greatness' by Anthony F. Earley, Jr, Detroit Edison Chairman and Chief Executive Officer, at a conference on 'Business Ethics, Integrity and Values: A Global Perspective', held on 23 March 1999. Churchill's own speech, made at Harvard on Monday, 6 September 1943, was precisely about the United States as the saviour of the world: 'one cannot rise to be in many ways the leading community in the civilized world without being involved in its problems, without being convulsed by its agonies and inspired by its causes.' I am grateful to Lecia Rosenthal for bringing these connections to my attention. The point of my humble experiment is that the textural imperatives of such

responsibility, acknowledged in the national political and corporate sphere, the internalized reflex 'to save the environment', for example, do not follow automatically.

44. 'Muddying the Waters', *http://www.amnesty.it/ailib/aipub/1998/ IOR/14000298.htm*; emphasis mine.

45. For a discussion of the contradiction between individualism (rights) and communality (obligations) when they are seen in a linear way, see Tuck, *Natural Rights*, p. 82.

46. Emmanuel Levinas, *Totality and Infinity: An Essay on Exteriority*, tr. Alphonso Lingis (Pittsburgh: Duquesne University Press, 1969; first French edition 1961), pp. 255–66.

47. Derrida, *Monolingualism of the Other; or, the Prosthesis of Origin*, tr. Patrick Mensah (Stanford: Stanford University Press, 1998), pp. 70–2.

48. Indeed, that sentiment is implicit in the very last line of Spivak, *A Critique*: 'the scholarship on Derrida's ethical turn . . . when in the rare case it risks setting itself to work by breaking its frame, is still not identical with the setting to work of deconstruction outside the formalizing calculus specific to the academic institution' (p. 431). It must, however, be said that in European from-above discussions, it is the so-called poststructuralists who are insistent not only on questioning a blind faith in the rational abstractions of democracy, but also in recognizing that top-down human rights enforcement is not 'democratic' even by these terms. See, for example, the strong objections raised by Lyotard and Derrida after Claude Lefort's claim that '[a] politics of human rights and a democratic politics are thus two ways of responding to the same need' (Claude Lefort, 'Politics of Human Rights', *The Political Forms of Modern Society: Bureaucracy, Democracy, Totalitarianism*, tr. Alan Sheridan, Cambridge, MA: MIT Press, 1986, p. 272). The discussion is to be found in 'La question de la democratie' in Jacob Rogozinski et al. (eds), *Le Retrait du politique* (Paris: Galilée, 1983), pp. 71–88. I have recently read Derrida, 'Interpretations at War: Kant, the

Jew, the German', where Derrida traces the genealogy of the
Euro-US subject who dispenses human rights, with uncanny
clarity (in Anidjar, tr. *Acts of Religion*, pp. 135–88).

49. Anthony Giddens, *Beyond Left and Right: the Future of Radical
Politics* (Stanford: Stanford University Press, 1994). The passages
quoted are from pp. 165, 247, 184, 185, 190, 194. 'Third Way'
was, I believe, coined in a Fabian Society pamphlet (Tony Blair,
*New Politics for the New Century*, London: College Hill Press,
1998) confined to policies of a European Britain. (I am grateful
to Susan M. Brook for getting me this pamphlet.) It was used by
Bill Clinton in a round-table discussion sponsored by the
Democratic Leadership Council in Washington DC on 25
April 1999.

50. Giddens, *Beyond*, p. 197.

51. I have discussed the role of teaching in the formation of
collectivities in 'Schmitt and Post Stucturalism: A Response',
*Cardozo Law Review*, XXI (v–vi) (May 2000), pp. 1723–37.
Necessary but impossible tasks—like taking care of health
although it is impossible to be immortal; or continuing to listen,
read, write, talk and teach although it is impossible that everything be communicated—lead to renewed and persistent effort.
I use this formula because this is the only justification for
humanities pedagogy. This is distinct from the 'utopian mode',
which allows us to figure the impossible.

52. John Rawls, 'The Law of Peoples' in Shute and Hurley, *On
Human Rights*, p. 56. I have a pervasive objection to Rawls's
discipline-bound philosophical style of treating political problems but felt nervous about stating it. I feel some relief in George
Shelton, *Morality and Sovereignty*, p. 171, where the author
expresses similar objections. Callinicos describes such Rawlsian
requirements as 'wildly Utopian', offers an excuse, and then
goes on to say '[n]evertheless, some account is required of
the relationship between abstract norms and the historical
conditions of their realization' (*Social Theory*, pp. 313–14).

53. Marx, *Capital* 3, pp. 1015–16 puts it in a paragraph, in the mode of 'to come'.

54. I gave an account of this so-called 'post-state world' in *A Critique*, pp. 371–94.

55. Daniel M. Farrell, 'Hobbes and International Relations', in Caws, *Causes of Quarrel*, p. 77.

56. For an idea of the best in the cultural studies account of globalization, see *Public Culture* 12 (1) (Winter 2000).

57. I cite below the Kogut and Singh Index for Cultural Distance (1988), an important tool for management. It will give a sense of the distance between those whose wrongs are righted and the agents of corporate philanthropy, closely linked to human rights expenditure:

> We hypothesize that the more culturally distant the country of the investing firm from the United States, the more likely the choice to set up a joint venture. Using Hofstede's indices, a composite index was formed based on the deviation along each of the four cultural dimensions (i.e., power distance, uncertainty avoidance, masculinity / femininity, and individualism) of each country from the United States ranking. The deviations were corrected for differences in the variances of each dimension and then arithmetically averaged. Algebraically, we built the following index:
>
> $$CD_j = \sum_{i=1}^{4} \{(I_{ij} - I_{iu})^2 / V_i\} / 4,$$
>
> where $I_{ij}$ stands for the index for the $i$th cultural dimension and $j$th country, $V_i$ is the variance of the index of the $i$th dimension, $u$ indicates the United States, and $CD_j$ is cultural difference of the $j$th country from the United States. (Bruce Kogut and Harinder Singh, 'The Effect of National Culture on the Choice of Entry Mode', *Journal of International Business Studies* 19, 1988, p. 422.)

58. Pat Smith and Lynn Roney, *Wow the Dow! The Complete Guide to Teaching Your Kids How to Invest in the Stock Market* (New

York: Simon & Schuster, 2000), p. 18. Some other books are Robert T. Kiyosaki with Sharon L. Lechter, *Rich Dad, Poor Dad: What the Rich Teach Their Kids About Money—That the Poor and Middle Class Do Not!* (New York: Warner Books, 2000), Gail Karlitz *et al.*, *Growing Money: A Complete Investing Guide for Kids* (New York: Price Stern Sloan, 1999), and Diane Mayr, *The Everything Kids' Money Book: From Saving to Spending to Investing—Learn All About Money!* (Holbrook, MA: Adams Media Corp., 2000), Emmanuel Modu and Andrea Walker, *Teenvestor.Com: the Practical Investment Guide for Teens and Their Parents* (Newark: Gateway, 2000); Willard S. and William S. Stawski, *Kids, Parents and Money: Teaching Personal Finance from Piggy Bank to Prom* (New York: John Wiley, 2000); Janet Bamford, *Street Wise: A Guide for Teen Investors* (New York: Bloomberg, 2000). This information is taken from my 'Globalizing Globalization', forthcoming in *Rethinking Marxism*.

59. Here are passages from one of many undergraduate textbooks. This *is* standard cultural studies stuff, but the reminder remains necessary. The banality of these excerpts reminds us not to be absurdly out of touch when a Giddens counsels 'antiproductivism'.

> In a study, Campbell's Soup found that the men who are most likely to shop view themselves as liberated, considerate, achievement-oriented individuals. These are the types of males who do not feel the need to conform to a 'macho' image. As a result, a second change has occurred in male purchasing roles: Males are beginning to buy products that at one time might have been dismissed as too feminine—jewelry, skin care products, moisturizers, and cosmetics. In marketing these products, advertisers have had to depict males in a way that is very different from the traditional strong, masculine image of the Marlboro Cowboy or in the typical beer commercial. A new concept of masculinity has emerged—the sensitive male who is as vulnerable in many ways as his female counterpart. As a result, a growing number of advertisers have begun telling males that being sensitive and caring does not conflict with masculinity.

Psychoanalytic theory stresses the unconscious nature of consumer motives as determined in childhood by the conflicting demands of the id and the superego. Marketers have applied psychoanalytic theory by using depth and focus group interviews and projective techniques to uncover deep-seated purchasing motives. These applications are known as motivation research.

The broadest environmental factor affecting consumer behavior is *culture*, as reflected by the values and norms society emphasizes. Products and services such as Levi jeans, Coca-Cola, and McDonald's fast-food outlets have come to symbolize the individuality inherent in American values. This is one reason why East Germans quickly accepted Coke after the fall of the Berlin Wall (Henry Assael, *Consumer Behavior and Marketing Action*, Cincinnati, Ohio: South-Western College Publishing, 1995, pp. 386, 404, 451).

This is the dominant general global cultural formation, appropriating the emergent—feminism, psychoanalysis, cultural studies, now environmentalism—remember the humble experiment in the Columbia gym case study and take a look at Ruth La Ferla, 'Fashionistas, Ecofriendly and All-Natural' (*The New York Times*, 15 July 2001). The Derrida–Levinas line, if it were understood as a cultural formation rather than an ethical phenomenology, is an altogether minor enclave compared to this and will show up transmogrified on the dominant register any day now.

60. John P. Clark, *Going with the Cash Flow: Taoism and the New Managerial Wisdom* (Britannia.com) and Thomas V. Morris, *If Aristotle Ran General Motors: the New Soul of Business* (New York: Henry Holt & Co., 1997). Examples can be multiplied.

61. Paulo Freire, *Pedagogy of the Oppressed*, tr. Myra Bergman Ramos (New York: Continuum, 1981), pp. 29–31.

62. 'Our Voice', Bangkok NGO Declaration, *http://www.nativenet.uthsca.edu/archive/nl/9307*.

63. A word on the aboriginal–untouchable divide. I warn the reader, once again, that this is not the version of an academic

historian or anthropologist, but a summary of the narrative on which Indian constitutional sanctions are based. This narrative assumes that there were *adivasis* or 'original inhabitants' in what we now call 'India', when, in the second millennium BC, Indo-European speaking peoples began to 'colonize' that space. These are the 'Aboriginals' or 'tribals', and there are 67,758,380 of them according to the 1991 census. The constitution distinguishes between them and the Hindu untouchables. The constitution designates them as SCSTs (Scheduled Castes/ Scheduled Tribes). I have referred implicitly to this narrative in note 18. Because this distinction between 'colonizing Caucasians' (the Indo-European-speaking peoples) and the 'aboriginals' predates the colonial European models by so much, the latter cannot serve us as guides here. In the early days of the Indian case, there was bilingualism and other kinds of assimilation. Without venturing into contested academic territory, it can still be said that they are basically animist, and retain traces of their separate languages.

64. Between my talk in February and this revision, I have told this man, one of my chief allies in the education, land reclaim and ecological agriculture projects in the area, that I had spoken of the incident abroad. He told me that he had thought very carefully about the incident and it had been a learning experience for him (as indeed for me). One might remember that I have earned their trust by behaving quite differently from either caste-Hindus or NGO visitors in a sustained way over a number of years and that they are as desperate to find a better future for their children, without repercussions, as are migrants.

65. Because these small disenfranchised responsibility-based cultures have not been allowed entry into the progressive legitimation of the colony, they have remained 'economies organized by domestic groups and kinship relations' and yet been recoded as *voting* citizens of parliamentary democracies without imaginative access to a 'public sphere'. For them, without the

caring pedagogy that I shall be outlining, the 'distance between poles of reciprocity . . . has remained [an anachronistic] social distance', without imaginative access to the commonality of citizenship. The quoted phrases are from Sahlins, *Stone Age*, pp. 41, 191. If this seems too fast, blame the postcolonial state and please remember, first, that the model here is not Australia, Latin America, Africa; this is a 'precolonial settler colony'; and, second, that I am not there to study them but to learn from the children how to be their teacher. In the United States too, I can talk about teaching but cannot write for American Studies.

66. I believe because Marshall Sahlins intuits this that he defends Marcel Mauss's *Essay on the Gift* against disciplinary criticism of form and/or content although he recognizes that it 'is an idio-syncratic venture . . . unjustified moreover by any special study of the Maori or of the philosophers . . . invoked along the way.' Sahlins is writing about the economic calculus, but in his comments on Mauss, he touches on responsibility, only to transform it, via Mauss, into the principle of reason (Sahlins, *Stone Age*, pp. 149, 168–9, 175). As for himself, he ends his book in the mode of a supplemented capitalism 'to come': 'a primi-tive theory of exchange value is also necessary, and perhaps possible—without saying it yet exists' (p. 314). This is conson-ant with my sense that the ethical push for socialism must come from cultural formations defective for capitalism.

67. Justine Burley (ed.), *The Genetic Revolution and Human Rights* (Oxford: Oxford University Press, 1999).

68. I am no philosopher, but this is undoubtedly why the later Wittgenstein was interested in children's acquisition of lan-guage (Wittgenstein, *Philosophical Investigations*, tr. G. E. M. Anscombe (New York: Macmillan, 1972; first published 1953) §§1–32, pp. 200, 208). To mention the part of the mind that dreams would be to muddy the waters with arguments for and against Freud.

69. Luce Irigaray, 'The Fecundity of the Caress', in Richard A.

Cohen (ed.), *Face to Face with Levinas* (Albany: SUNY Press, 1986), pp. 231–56.

70. This case has been discussed in Spivak, 'The New Subaltern: a Silent Interview', in *Mapping Subaltern Studies and the Postcolonial*, ed. Vinayak Chaturvedi (London: Verso, 2000), pp. 335–6 and in Spivak, 'Discussion: an Afterword on the New Subaltern', in Partha Chatterjee and Pradeep Jeganathan (eds.), *Community, Gender and Violence: Subaltern Studies* XI (New York: Columbia University Press, 2000), pp. 324–40.

71. I say 'supposedly' because the Hindu population of India, somewhere between 700 million and 850 million (the 2001 census figures were not available), is of course not represented by the poor rural Hindus, although they themselves think of Hinduism generally as a unified set of codes. They are generally prejudiced against SCSTs in their rural poverty, but they are not therefore in the cultural dominant. This is why Raymond Williams, who introduced the powerful instrument of seeing a culture as a dance of archaic-residual-dominant-emergent, proposed it as a solution to the habit of seeing cultures as a 'system' rather than a process (Williams, *Marxism and Literature*, Oxford: Oxford University Press, 1977, pp. 121–7). It is interesting that the influential journal *Economic and Political Weekly* has this to say about '[g]rowing democracy': 'It requires sustained effort at institution building, transparency in government, effective governance and most importantly the rule of law' (36.23. 9–15 June 2001, p. 2011). Only benefit of the doubt would read the first item as proactive educational effort.

72. I hesitate to name these parties because part of my point is precisely that, when no real education is given, the ideational content of a party's platform does not coincide with the held opinions of the rural electorate, who do not hear these ideas except through the opaque high Bengali disquisitions at mass rallies. As it happens, the ruling party in this case is Communist Party of India (Marxist) (CPM) and the opposition parties

are Bharatiya Janata Party (BJP/Hindu nationalist) and Trinomul (Congress–CPM splinter). To consider this conflict in terms of communism and fundamentalism would be a complete mistake.

73. Marx, 'The Eighteenth Brumaire of Louis Bonaparte', in *Surveys from Exile*, tr. David Fernbach (New York: Vintage, 1973), p. 147; trans. modified.

74. Catharine A. MacKinnon, 'Crimes-War, Crimes-Peace', in Shute and Hurley (eds.), *Human Rights*, p. 84.

75. Carole Pateman, *The Sexual Contract* (Cambridge: Polity Press, 1988), p. x; the next passage quoted is on p. 60. I am not, of course, speaking of the provenance of social contract theories but rather of historical variations on something like actual social contracts.

76. Paine, *Rights*, p. 79.

77. William Sacksteder, 'Mutually Acceptable Glory', in Caws, *Causes*, p. 103.

78. For an uncritical summary of this cultural formation as universal history, see Ronald Reagan, 'Free Enterprise', Radio Essay (1979), retrieved from *The New York Times* archives on the worldwide web.

79. We should not forget that Kant fixed the subject of the Enlightenment as one who could write for posterity and the whole world *as a scholar* (Immanuel Kant, 'An Answer to the Question: What is Enlightenment?' in James Schmidt, ed. *What is Enlightenment? Eighteenth-Century Answers and Twentieth-Century Questions*, Berkeley: Univ. of California Press, 1996, pp. 60–61). As the reader will see, our effort is to suture a cultural inscription rather unlike Kant's into the thinking and practice of the public sphere and an education that will not preserve class apartheid. An unintended posterity, a world not imagined by him as participant in the cosmopolitical.

80. Thomas Babington Macaulay, 'Minute on Indian Education', in *Speeches by Lord Macaulay with his Minute on Indian Education*

(Oxford: Oxford University Press, 1935), p. 349. When Khushwant Singh, an Indian writer in English, opined last year that you could say 'blue sky' a million different ways in English, whereas in Hindi you could only say '*neela asman*', I realized the failure of Vidyasagar's experiment. The problem, then as now, is the one I have already indicated: one English, the superb and supple, technologically adroit language of the victor; the many languages of the vanquished; restricted permeability. Going down is easy; coming up is hard. The Ford Foundation can run a programme called 'Crossing Borders', but the literatures in the domestic languages are dying. And even this is a middle-class matter. Let us go back to the rural poor.

81. Iswarchandra Vidyasagar, *Barnaparichaya* (Calcutta: Benimadhab Sheel, n.d.).

82. Binaybhushan Ray, ' "Shikkhashar" theke "Barnaparichaya"— Shomajer Shange Shishu-Patthyer Paribartan', *Akadami Patrika* 6 (May, 1994), pp. 12–62 makes no mention of the experimental pedagogy of the text and the photocopies seem to have been obtained from the India Office Library in London.

83. For self-ethnography, see Rosalind Morris, *In the Place of Origins: Modernity and its Mediums in Northern Thailand* (Durham, NC: Duke University Press, 2000).

84. The message reads as follows: 'Sir, give us a tube well. We will drink water. Give it now. We are thirsty.'

. . . . . . . .

1. Abani Sabar 2. Kalomoni Sabar 3. Bharat Sabar 4. Shaymoli Sabar

[Serially ordered in Bengali alphabet]

. . . . . . . .

Sabar hamlet

vill:      P.O.: Police Station: Manbajar       District: Purulia

. . . . . . . .

[name of officer]    Kolkata

85. I have explained this phenomenon in 'Megacity', *Grey Room* I (Fall 2000), pp. 8–25.

86. W. E. B. DuBois, 'Of Mr. Booker T. Washington and Others', in *The Souls of Black Folk* (New York: Signet, 1995; first published 1903), pp. 78–95.

87. Jean Piaget, *The Moral Judgment of Children*, tr. Marjorie Gabain (New York: Free Press, 1965), p. 406. This difference between saying and doing is often honoured by the best sayers. Thus Sahlins distinguishes between 'a conventional metaphor of exposition' and 'a true history of experiment' (Sahlins, *Stone Age*, p. 192).

88. Isaiah Berlin, *The Hedgehog and the Fox: an Essay on Tolstoy's View of History* (New York: Simon & Schuster, 1986; first published 1953).

89. This point cannot be developed here. Please see Spivak, 'From Haverstock Hill Flat to US Classroom, What's Left of Theory?', in Judith Butler *et al.* (eds.), *What's Left of Theory? New Work on the Politics of Literary Theory* (New York: Routledge, 2000), pp. 1–40.

90. Please notice this earlier repetition of points made in the current essay. The piece itself was not about human rights and the humanities but about what I have learned from the oral formulaic as practised by the women in Manbhum:

> I'm a modernist literary scholar. Acknowledged research methods in my field would be to follow the life-detail of the author or authors beyond the definitive biography, follow through on pertinent items indicated in the correspondence and in interviews, check the relationship between the critical and creative materials, and of course, consult the critical tradition exhaustively. There is no requirement that the method of connecting these details go beyond the simplest cause–effect structure.
>
> No such research method has been followed in this afternoon's paper.
>
> My sources of speculation are some women in Manbhum and a

man from Birbhum. It occurs to me that an alternative research method could have been followed here. I could have consulted what anthropological and historical literature is available on the Kheriyas and the Dhekaros, the groups to which these people belong. With the latter, it is the very question of belonging that is being negotiated. There is nothing of that in this paper either.

To tell you the truth, the paper is hopelessly anecdotal. I have tried to encourage myself by saying that the anecdotes have something of the evidentiary contingence of the literary. Depth rather than breadth of evidence? Who knows? I place the facts in place of footnotes: I have been training teachers in Manbhum for the last ten years. My method is simple: to see how the students are learning and not learning, on the basis of these, to give simple practical instructions to the teacher . . .

Because I work hard to change this state of affairs, because I feed the children a hot meal a day, and because I live with them when I do this work, a certain acceptance has come from the men and women on the basis of which a mutual accountability has grown. My justification is this. The examples I offer may seem simple. But it has taken all this work to earn the right to be a person with whom these examples could be produced; and the right to claim a reading that's in the place of library work, detective work, fieldwork.

For the first few years, talk about this work in progress seemed forbidden, because it was too fragile. Now it seems not only possible, but called for, yet the risk of ridicule or worse, unexamined congratulations loom. Somewhat against my better judgment, then, I will add a word specifically about the work. In the field of subaltern education, the best talk statistics, money, school buildings, teachers, textbooks and supplies. These are fine things. I am focused elsewhere. In the field of training there are, first, some cases of altogether benevolent Eurocentric yet culturalist training. I hesitate to name names because these are, after all, good people. The training provided by the state is generally inferior and formulaic and usually does not trickle down to the level of which I am speaking. The training provided by activists is generally from above and emphasizes consciousness raising: rights, resistance, nationalism, identity spliced on to literacy and numeracy. My method is to learn from below how to fashion, together, a way of teaching that will put in place reflexes or habits of mind for which the shortcut name is 'democracy'. Since this is the largest sector of the future electorate, my belief is that without the habit of democracy, no reform will last. To make visible the lines of force here, I offer my first anecdote, by way of preamble. ('Travel and the Nation', Mary Keating Das Lecture, Columbia University, March 2000)

91. I am grateful to Henry Staten for the felicitous word 'civilizationism' (unpublished communication).

92. Marx, *Capital* 3, p. 959; trans. modified.

93. For an example of involving the children of exploitation in intense *matha khatano* on the other side, see John Tierney, 'Here Come the Alpha Pups', *New York Times Magazine* (5 August 2001), pp. 38–43.

94. Giddens, *Beyond*, pp. 93–4.

*Notes to Chapter 6*

1. *The Stockholm International Forum: Combating Intolerance*, 29–30 January 2001. Information about the International Forum may be found at *http://www.stockholmforum.gov.se*.

2. Gitta Sereny, *Cries Unheard: the Story of Mary Bell* (London: Macmillan, 1999).

3. Hans Magnus Enzensberger, 'The Great Migration', in *Civil War* (London: Granta Books, 1994), p. 108.

4. European Commission, Directorate General V (Employment, Industrial Relations and Social Affairs), Eurobarometer Report 47.1, *Racism and Xenophobia in Europe* (Brussels: European Commission, 1997).

5. Fergal Keane, 'The Conspiracy of Silence about Race in America', *The Independent*, 20 January 2001.

6. Gitta Sereny, *The Invisible Children: Child Prostitution in America, West Germany and Great Britain* (London: Pan, 1984).

7. Gitta Sereny, *The German Trauma: Experiences and Reflections, 1938–2000* (Harmondsworth: Penguin, 2001).

8. 'Kurt Waldheim's Mental Block', in *German Trauma*, pp. 247–61.

9. Ibid.

10. See the chapter by Michael Ignatieff in this volume.

11. Gitta Sereny, *Into That Darkness: from Mercy Killing to Mass Murder* (London: Pimlico, 1995).

12. Gitta Sereny, 'Colloquy with a Conscience', in *German Trauma*, pp. 87–134.

13. Gitta Sereny, *Albert Speer: His Battle with Truth* (London: Macmillan, 1996).

*Notes to Chapter 7*

1. James Allen *et al.*, *Without Sanctuary: Lynching Photography in America* (Santa Fe, NM: Twin Palms Publishers, 2000), pp. 33–4.

2. John Kifner, 'A Pictorial Guide to Hell', *The New York Times*, 24 January 2001.

3. Susan Sontag, *On Photography* (New York: Farrar, Straus & Giroux, 1977), p. 20.

4. Plato, *The Republic*, Book IV, tr. F. M. Cornford (New York: Oxford University Press, 1950), p. 137.

5. Susan Sontag, *On Photography*, pp. 109–10.

6. Charles Baudelaire, *Mon coeur mis à nu* [My Heart Laid Bare] in *The Intimate Journals of Charles Baudelaire*, tr. Christopher Isherwood (Boston: Beacon Press, 1957), pp. 52–3.

*Notes to Chapter 8*

1. Seamus Heaney, *Crediting Poetry*, Nobel Lecture, 7 December 1995, reprinted in his *Opened Ground: New Selected Poems 1966–1987* (London: Faber & Faber, 1998).

2. The transcripts of the hearings of the Truth and Reconciliation

Commission may be read at the Commission's website: *http://www.truth.org.za.*

3. Dinora Pines, 'Working with Women Survivors of the Holocaust: Affective Experiences in Transference and Counter-transference', *International Journal of Psycho-Analysis*, 67, Part 3 (1986), pp. 295–307.

4. Sudhir Kakar, *The Colors of Violence: Cultural Identities, Religion and Conflict* (Chicago: University of Chicago Press, 1996).

5. Ibid., p. 11.

6. Anne Karpf, *The War After: Living with the Holocaust* (London: Heinemann, 1996).

7. Dina Wardi, *Memorial Candles: Children of the Holocaust* (London: Routledge / Tavistock, 1992).

8. Kakar, *Colors of Violence*, p. 31.

9. Zygmunt Bauman, *Modernity and the Holocaust* (Cambridge: Polity Press, 1989).

10. Peter Sichrovsky, *Born Guilty: Children of Nazi Families* (London: I.B.Tauris, 1988).

11. Eva Hoffman, *Shtetl: The Life and Death of a Small Town and the World of Polish Jews* (London: Secker & Warburg, 1998).

# Index

Note: 'n.' after a page reference indicates the number of a note on that page.

Afghanistan 63, 70
aid packages 57
Al-Adsani, Suleiman 158
Albanians in Kosovo, Serb attacks on
    103
Albright, Madeleine 37
Allende regime, overthrow of 63
Althusser, Louis 326 n. 22
Amin, Idi 106
Amnesty International
    creation 54–5
    Pinochet extradition case 101, 138
    policy 143
anarchy 33–4, 65, 130
Angola 62, 87, 256
Annan, Kofi
    democracy and legitimacy 119
    immigration 241
    intervention, right of 28, 106–7, 108
    UN's authority 109–10, 111–12
Archilochus 218
Argentina 31, 160, 281
Aristide, Jean-Bertrand 113
Aristotle 326 n. 21
Armenian genocide 37, 99, 128
Arrighi, Giovanni 328 n. 26
assistance, duty of 3, 4, 46–8
Atahualpa, Emperor 41
Athenians 95–6
Australia 72, 234
Austria
    Haider 29, 238
    racism 237, 245

Balibar, Etienne 327 nn. 24–5

Banerjee (Vidyasagar), Iswarchandra
    209–12, 222, 225, 320 n. 14
Bangladesh 82–3, 84, 106
Baudelaire, Charles 266–7
Baudrillard, Jean 268
Bauman, Zygmunt 298
Belgium 237
Benjamin, Walter 175
Berlin, Isaiah 49, 218
Bernal, Martin 328 n. 26
Bert, Paul 31
Bevin, Ernest 134
Bharatiya Janata Party (BJP) 340 n. 72
Biafra 256, 269
Bible, genocide in the 93–4, 95–7
Bindman, Geoffrey 138–44
Bin Laden, Osama 298
BJP 340 n. 72
Blair, Tony 187
Bloch, Ernest 175–6
Bosnia 99
    democracy 128
    international law 103
    intervention 34, 74, 75, 86
    nation-building 84, 86
    neutrality, illusion of 68, 69–70
    photography 254, 261–2, 263, 268–71
    post-generation 295
    recognition of wrongs 302
Bourke-White, Margaret 255
Brady, Mathew 255
Bramhill, Bishop 176
Brotherston, Gordon 328 n. 26
Browne-Wilkinson, Lord 101
Buber-Neumann, Margarete 26–7

Burma 78
Bush, George W. 187, 317 n. 7

Callinicos, Alex 325 n. 16, 332 n. 42, 334
    n. 52
Callot, Jacques 254
Cambodian genocide 99, 128
    ethical relativism 125
    intervention, right of 44
    nation-building 84
    psychosomatic blindness 289, 290
    Vietnamese intervention 82–3, 86,
        106
Canada
    cigarette packets, photographs on
        257–8
    'human security' 72
    immigration 234
    International Criminal Court 156
Capa, Robert 254, 261
capitalism 55–6, 190
ceasefires 69, 79
Chechnya 34, 81
    Grozny 71, 76, 81
    non-intervention 76, 86–7, 131
Chile 63, 160, 281
    see also Pinochet, Auguste
chimpanzees, violence by 98
China
    education 178, 183–4
    International Criminal Court 151
    Tibet 34, 71, 83, 87, 131
    tyranny 65
    UN Security Council 81–3, 132
Chisso Chemical Company 262
Christianity 30, 32
Churchill, Winston 185
civil and natural rights 174–7, 191
Clinton, Bill 28, 37, 334 n. 49
Cold War
    human rights dilemmas 64–5
    sovereignty 52, 54, 55–6, 62
colonialism
    intervention, right of 30–1

legacy 62, 63, 169–70
    self-determination, right of 118–19
Columbus, Christopher 30
communism 31, 34, 62, 182–3
Communist Party of India (Marxist) 340
    n. 72
Community of Democracies 122
Condorcet, Marie-Jean-Antoine-
        Nicolas de Caritat, Marquis de
        41–2
Congo 62
consumerism 336–7 n. 59
Council of Europe 146
coups, military 77–8
Crimean War 255
Criminal Justice Act 1988 154
Croatia 69–70
Crow Creek, South Dakota 97–8
Crusades 30, 32
Cultural Distance, Index for 335 n. 57
Czechoslovakia 52

Dallaire, General Romeo 36, 38
Death Caravan 155
Debord, Guy 268
De Klerk, F. W. 283
democracy
    cultural imperialism, avoiding
        124–7
    genocide, protection against 127–8
    growing 340 n. 71
    interventions 129–31
    legitimacy 116–23
    peace 113–14
    sovereignty 60
    UN reform 135, 136
Denmark 237
Derrida, Jacques 175, 176, 186, 316 n. 2,
        327 n. 25
Development, Declaration of the Right
        To 193
Dewey, John 318–19 n. 13
Doyle, Michael 130
Drakulić, Slavenka 236–7

DuBois, W. E. B. 215

Earley, Anthony F. 332 n. 43
East Timor 89, 91, 99, 103
education 172–8
  and genocide 99, 100
  investment portfolios 192–3
  metropolitan 180–5
  subaltern 12–13, 188–9, 201, 208–27
Eichmann, Adolf 101–2
Eide, Asbjørn 318 n. 11
Elliott, Gregory 326 n. 22
Enlightenment 316–17 n. 2
Enzensberger, Hans Magnus 234, 241
Epicurus 176
eurocentrism of human rights 169–72
European Convention on Human
    Rights (ECHR) 158, 311 n. 5
European Court of Human Rights 147,
    158
European Court of Justice (ECJ) 146–7
European Union
  jurisdiction 146
  Kosovo, and right of intervention 45
  as model for UN reform 134–5
  and sovereignty 29
evolution 97

Faulkner, William 321 n. 14
Feinstein, Diane 269
Finland 237
First World War 255
Foucault, Michel 176
France
  colonialism 30–1, 32
  Declaration of the Rights of Man and
      of Citizens 170–1
  international solidarity 72
  racism 237
  republic, declaration of a 116
  Rwandan genocide 38
  UN Security Council 132
Frank, André Gunder 328 n. 26
Freire, Paulo 195–6

Freud, Sigmund 217, 298, 322 n. 14

Gardner, Alexander 255
Garton Ash, Timothy 99
gender oppression 196
Geneva Conventions 81–2, 314 n. 38
Geneva Conventions Act 1957 156
Genocide, Convention on the
      Prevention and Punishment of
      the Crime of 107
Germany
  education 99
  immigration 234–5
  nation-building 65–6
  neolithic grave at Talheim 97
  racism 237, 244
  Second World War 127–8, 299, 300
  see also Holocaust
Gewirth, Alan 178–80
Giddens, Anthony 187–8, 194, 336 n. 59
Gilroy, Paul 328 n. 26
globalization 43, 63, 159, 191–4
Glover, Jonathan 323 n. 15
Glucksmann, André 268–9
Goebbels, Joseph 128
Golden Rule 178, 179
Goldstone, Richard 148–9
Goodall, Jane 98
Goya, Francisco 20, 254, 259, 260, 261
Great Britain/United Kingdom
  colonialism 30
  immigration 234–5, 239
  International Criminal Court 145,
      150, 152, 156–7, 163
  internationalization of Northern
      Ireland issue 73–4
  international law 154, 156–9, 161–3
  Pinochet extradition case see
      Pinochet, Auguste, extradition
      case
  racism 237
  UN Security Council 132
Grenada, US intervention in 83
Grozny 71, 76, 81

Haider, Jörg 238
Hain, Peter 156–7
Haiti 76, 84, 86, 113
Havel, Vaclav 28, 30, 35, 46, 47
Haviv, Ron 20, 254, 262
Heaney, Seamus 282
Helsinki Final Act 55–6
Himmler, Heinrich 128
Hitler, Adolf 52, 53, 246
Hobbes, Thomas 175, 176–7, 185, 191
Hoffman, Eva 274–7
Holocaust 99
    Eichmann 101–2
    ethical relativism 125
    inner racism 245–8
    Nuremberg Tribunal 100–1, 146, 152
    post-generation 292
    recognition of wrongs 287, 288–9,
        290, 302
    return to Western imagination 53–4,
        55
Human Rights Watch 55
Hungary 43–4, 240
Hutus, see Rwandan genocide

ICC, see International Criminal Court
Iceland 134
Ignatieff, Michael 49–51, 267
immigration and racism 233–42, 243
India
    Bangladesh, intervention in 82–3, 84,
        106
    education 209–18, 222–6
    International Criminal Court 151
    Kashmir 34
    oppression 197–8
    partition riots 292–3
    police brutality of tribals 202–4
    UN General Assembly 134
Indonesia
    disintegration 63
    East Timor 84, 86, 99, 103
    International Criminal Court 151
information technology 191

Inter-American Development Bank 123
International Commission on
        Sovereignty and Intervention
        73
International Court of Justice (ICJ) 103
International Covenant on Civil and
        Political Rights (ICCPR)
        117–18, 147–8
International Covenant on Economic,
        Social and Cultural Rights
        (ICESCR) 147
International Criminal Court (ICC)
        9–11, 103, 150–3
    Great Britain 145, 150, 156–7, 163
    Rome Statute 107, 114–15
    sovereignty 161
    Truth and Reconciliation
        Commissions 160
internationalization of internal conflicts
        73–4
international law 9–11, 145–6
    development 100–3, 146–50
    Pinochet case 153–9
    truth, reconciliation and sovereignty
        159–63
    UN's authority 114
    see also International Court of Justice;
        International Criminal Court
International Law Commission 101,
        115
International Military Tribunal, see
        Nuremberg Tribunal
internet 243
intervention
    criteria for 104–8
    right of 3–4, 27, 28–9, 45–6
        assistance, duty of 46–8
        genocide 43–5
        national sovereignty 29–34
        pluralism 41–3
        universal justice 34–41
    see also sovereignty, and intervention
IRA 74
Iran 151, 314 n. 29

Iraq
  commercial blockade of 47
  International Criminal Court 151
  intervention, threshold conditions
      78
  Kurds 86, 112, 113
  tyranny 65
Irigaray, Luce 202
Irish Republican Army (IRA) 74
Islam and Muslims 30, 70, 126–7, 298
Israel 35, 53–4, 101–2, 186

Jalal, Ayesha 328 n. 26
Japan 66, 146, 262
Jefferson, Thomas 116
Jerusalem 30, 32
justice, see international law
'just war' theory 78–84

Kakar, Sudhir 292–3, 295, 301
Kambanda, Jean 149
Kant, Immanuel 104
Karadzic, Radovan 149
Karpf, Anne 293
Kashmir 34
Kazakh peasantry 43
Keane, Fergal 242
Keeley, Lawrence 97
Kennedy, Baroness 152
Khmer Rouge 88, 125, 128, 289
  see also Cambodian genocide
Kifner, John 261
Kitcher, Philip 318 n. 12
Klein, Melanie 217, 220
Kogut, Bruce 335 n. 57
Kosovo 99
  democracy 128
  international law 103
  intervention 86
    right of 28, 32, 34, 45
    threshold conditions 76
  'just war' theory 79, 80, 82
  nation-building 84, 85
  neutrality, illusion of 71

non-internationalization of problem
    by Serbs 74
  Rambouillet negotiations 79
  recognition of wrongs 281
  UN's authority 109
Kurds 35, 86, 112
Kuwait 126, 158

Lamont, Lord 160
language issues 208, 220
Lao-Montes, Agustin 328 n. 26
law, international, see international law
Lee, Kuan Yew 172, 181, 196
Lefort, Claude 333 n. 48
Leontius 264
Levi, Primo 280
Levinas, Emmanuel 186, 202
Libya 65, 151
Little, Alan 270
'Little Irma' 270
Litwack, Leon 258–9
loan packages 57
Locke, John 327 n. 25

Macaulay, Thomas Babington 209
McCullin, Don 256
Machiavelli, Niccolo 176, 185, 326
    n. 22
MacKinnon, Catharine A. 205
Madagascar 31
Major, John 270
Malagasy rebels 31
Mandela, Nelson 283
Martin, Ian 317 n. 8
Marx, Karl 176, 182–3, 223
masculinity, changing concepts of 336 n.
    59
Matilal, Bimal Krishna 328 n. 26
Mauss, Marcel 339 n. 66
Médécins sans Frontières 169–70, 269
media 105
  coverage 232–3
  democracy 127
  just war theory 82

media *cont.*
  self-censorship 243
  *see also* photography
Melians 95–6
Melville, Herman 321 n. 14
memory, current rhetoric of 295–7
Mengele, Dr 288
Merrill Lynch 192–3
Midianites 93–4, 95, 96–7
Mignolo, Walter 328 n. 26
military coups 77
Mill, John Stuart 104, 129–30
Mills, C. Wright 329–30 n. 25
Milosevic, Slobodan 45, 128, 149, 198
Mladic, Vlatka 149
Molotov, Vyacheslav Mikhailovich 31
Montaigne, Michel Eyquem de 44
Montesquieu, Charles Louis de
    Secondat, Baron de la Brède
    41–2
Morgan Stanley Dean Witter 192
Moses 93–4, 96–7
motivation research 337 n. 59
Murray, Charles 187
Muslims and Islam 30, 70, 126–7, 298
Muvunyi, Colonel 162
Myanmar 78

Nachtwey, James 256
nation-building 65–6, 84–6
NATO 33, 35, 109, 149
natural and civil rights 174–7, 191
neutrality in interventions 68–71
New Zealand 156
non-governmental organizations
    (NGOs)
  Bangkok Declaration 196
  education by 221
  rise 269
  Southern 171
  sovereignty 55, 56, 72
North Atlantic Treaty Organization
    (NATO) 33, 35, 109, 149
Northern Ireland issue 73–4

North Korea 65, 78
Nuremberg Tribunal 100–1, 146, 152
Nussbaum, Martha 319–23 n. 14

Oman 126
Oppenheim, David 92–3
Oppenheim, Lassa 104–5, 116
Organization for African Unity (OAU)
    36–7
Organization for Security and
    Cooperation in Europe (OSCE)
    45, 171
O'Sullivan, Timothy 255
Overy, Richard 275–6

Paine, Thomas 175
Pakistan 84
Palestinians 35
Panama, US intervention in 83
Pateman, Carole 206, 222
Péguy, Charles 34–5, 39
People's Republic of China, *see* China
Peress, Gilles 256
Persson, Goran 232, 240, 241
Philippines 172
Phillips, Lord 102
photography 19–20, 253–73
Piaget, Jean 217–18, 220
Pines, Dinora 288
Pinochet, Auguste
  extradition case 138, 153–6, 157, 160,
    162
    Torture Convention 101, 154–5
    universal jurisdiction 101, 102
  International Criminal Court 151
piracy 154
Plato 264–5
pluralism 41–3
Poland 31, 52
Popper, Karl 49
Porter, Ray 259
post-generation 290–300, 302
poverty
  disintegration of states 64

and genocide 1045
virtues of 187, 331 n. 39
Pressensé, Francis de 35

racism 16–19, 232–3
    immigration and European
        government 233–42
    inner 243–50
Rawls, John 189, 328–9 n. 30
recognition of wrongs 20–3, 278–303
    post-generation 290–300, 302
    South Africa's Truth and
        Reconciliation Commission
        282–6, 290
refugees 45, 233–42
religious issues
    Christianity 30, 32
    education 226–7
    elitism 332 n. 42
    Golden Rule 178
    intervention, right of 30
    Islam and Muslims 30, 70, 126–7, 298
    UN Security Council 133
Reuck, Anthony de 323 n. 15
Rieff, David 254
Rights of Man, Declaration of the 175,
        207
Risse, Thomas 171–2, 173, 323 n. 15
Rohde, David 330 n. 37
Rohrer, Anneliese 238
Roppe, Stephen C. 171–2, 173, 323 n. 15
Rorty, Richard 172, 174, 181
Roth, Brad 110, 116
Rousseau, Jean-Jacques 327 n. 25
Russia
    Afghanistan, intervention in 63
    Chechnya, see Chechnya
    Gulag 54
    imperialism 31
    international law 102
    Kosovo war 82
    non-intervention in Yugoslavia 36
    psychic damage, absence of 289, 290
    sovereignty 56–7

UN Security Council 83, 132
    see also Soviet Union
Rwandan genocide 99
    and democracy 128
    ethical relativism 125
    international law 148–50, 162
    intervention 92
        right of 36–7, 38, 44
        threshold conditions 75
    photography 256
    post-generation 295
    recognition of wrongs 281, 302
    UN's authority 109

Sachs, Albie 284, 286
Sahlins, Marshall 331 n. 38, 339 n. 66, 342
        n. 86
Said, Edward W. 172, 174, 181
Salgado, Sebastião 256
Saudi Arabia 126–7
Saussure, Ferdinand de 200
scientism 41
second-generation memory, see
        post-generation
Second World War
    Holocaust, see Holocaust
    inner racism 245–9
    international law 146
    photography 255
    Wallenberg, Raoul 240–1
Serbia/Serbs
    Bosnian war 69–70, 86
        democracy 128
        photography 254
        post-generation 295
        recognition of wrongs 302
    Kosovan war 71, 74
        democracy 128
        international law 102–3
        'just war' theory 79, 80, 82
        memory, rhetoric of 297
Sereny, Gitta 228–31
SEWA 319–20 n. 14
Shelley, Mary 317–18 n. 10

Shelton, George 175, 176–7, 316 n. 1,
    334 n. 52
Sichrovsky, Peter 300
Sierra Leone 62, 162, 256
Sikkink, Kathryn 171–2, 173, 323 n. 15
Singapore 172
Singer, Peter 89–91
Singh, Harinder 335 n. 57
Singh, Khushwant 341 n. 79
Slave Trade Act 1834 154
Smith, Adam 322 n. 14
Smith, Eugene 261
social psychology 323–4 n. 16
sociology 329–30 n. 35
Somalia 37, 63
    intervention 75, 76, 112–13
Sontag, Susan 251–2
South Africa
    Constitutional Court 148–9
    post-generation 291–2
    Truth and Reconciliation
        Commission 160, 282–6, 290
sovereignty, and intervention 4–6, 29–
        34, 86–7
    antagonistic history 52–60
    democracy and legitimacy 119, 121,
        129
    false debate 66–8
    fifth wave of state formation 60–6
    international law 159–63
    'just war' theory 78–84
    nation-building 84–6
    neutrality, illusion of 68–71
    protection, responsibility for 71–3
    threshold conditions 73–8
    UN's authority 109–10, 114–15
Soviet Union
    collapse 56, 57, 62
    Czechoslovakia, intervention in 83
    human rights concessions 55–6
    human rights dilemmas 64
    Hungary, intervention in 83
    intervention, right of 43–4
    Stalin 99, 128

UN Security Council 132
    see also Russia
Space Vehicle Directorate 317 n. 7
Spain
    Civil War 254, 255, 261
    Pinochet extradition case 101, 154–5,
        162
Speer, Albert 229, 248, 249–50
Spivak, Gayatri 164–7
Stalin, Joseph 99, 128
Stangl, Franz 228, 248–9
State Immunity Act 1978 159
Statue of Liberty 235
Stoics 176
Strasser, General 162
Straw, Jack 233, 315 n. 40
Sudan 37
Summit of the Americas (Quebec 2001)
        122–3
Suppression of Terrorism Act 1978
        154
Sweden 240–1

Taliban 70
Tanzania 82–3, 106
technology 82, 191
Thatcher, Lady 160
Third Way politics 187–8, 193
Thucydides 95–6
Tibet, Chinese occupation of 34, 71, 83
    non-intervention 87, 131
Tito, Marshal 60, 62
Todorov, Tzvetan 26–7
Tokyo War Crimes Trial 146
Torture Convention 101, 154–5
triage dilemmas 70–1
Trinomul 340 n. 72
Truth and Reconciliation Commissions
        159–60
    South Africa 160, 282–6, 290
Tuck, Richard 327–8 n. 25
Tukhachesvski, General 31
Turkey 35, 37, 99, 128
Tutsis, see Rwandan genocide

Uganda 82–3, 106
Ukrainian peasantry 43
UNESCO 221
Union of Soviet Socialist Republics, *see*
      Russia; Soviet Union
United Arab Emirates 126
United Kingdom, *see* Great Britain/
      United Kingdom
United Nations (UN)
   authority 109–16
   ballot box/peacekeeping mission
         choice 198
   Charter
      aim 106–7, 109–10
      authority of UN 109–16
      coercive integration 74, 77
      democracy and legitimacy 117,
         118–20
      international law 147, 153, 156
      sovereignty 52, 53, 76
   colonialism 170
   Convention on Refugees 233
   Declaration of Responsibilities
         185
   democracy 122, 123
   eurocentrism 171
   General Assembly 101, 120, 133–5
   Human Rights Commission 54
   International Criminal Court 103,
         150, 153
   international law 103, 147–9, 150,
         153
   intervention
      criteria for 105
      right of 34, 36–7, 44–5
      threshold conditions 74
   nation-building 84
   reform 7–9, 131–5, 136
   Security Council
      authority 112–13
      coercive intervention 74, 76
      international law 148
      just war theory 82–4
      membership 132–3

Torture Convention 101, 154–5
UNESCO 221
unexamined universalism 196–7
Universal Declaration of Human
      Rights 54
   cultural imperialism 124
   Declaration of Responsibilities 185
   democracy and legitimacy 117,
      119, 121
   international law 147
United States of America
   Afghanistan, intervention in 63
   anti-communist foreign policy 63
   capital punishment 59, 310 n. 56
   Civil War 255
   Crow Creek murders 97–8
   education 180–2, 183–5
   Grenada, intervention in 83
   immigration 234, 242
   International Criminal Court 152
   international law 149
   intervention, right of 35, 37, 45
   Jim Crow policy 54
   Northern Ireland 73–4
   Panama, intervention in 83
   photography 255, 258–9
   political reality 136
   presidential election (2000) 120–1
   slavery 258–9
   sovereignty 59
   UN Security Council 83, 132, 133
Universal Declaration of Human Rights
      54
   cultural imperialism 124
   Declaration of Responsibilities 185
   democracy and legitimacy 117, 119,
      121
   international law 147
universal jurisdiction, *see* international
      law
Ut, Huynh Cong 261, 262

Vidyasagar, Iswarchandra 209–12, 222,
      225, 320 n. 14

Vietnam
 Cambodian intervention 82–3, 106
 colonialism 31, 32
 War 132, 261, 262

Waldheim, Kurt 245–8
Wallenberg, Raoul 240–1
Wallerstein, Immanuel 328 n. 26
Walzer, Michael 105–6, 108
War Crimes Act 1991 154, 162
Wardi, Dina 294
Washington, Booker T. 215
Weidenfeld, Lord 246
Westphalia, Peace of (1648) 317 n. 5
Whitman, Walt 320 n. 14, 321 n. 14
Williams, Raymond 220, 340 n. 71
Wittgenstein, Ludwig 339 n. 68
Wordsworth, William 215, 320 n. 14

World Bank 123
World Trade Organization 123
World War I 255
World War II, see Second World War

xenophobia, see racism

Yugoslavia/former Yugoslavia
 democracy 60
 education 99
 international law 102, 148–9
 intervention, right of 35, 36
 recognition of wrongs 281
 state formation 62
 see also Bosnia; Croatia; Kosovo;
  Serbia/Serbs

Zeno 176

Lightning Source UK Ltd.
Milton Keynes UK
UKOW03f1446110714

234944UK00001B/4/P